Errors and expectations

Errors and expectations

A GUIDE FOR THE TEACHER
OF BASIC WRITING

MINA P. SHAUGHNESSY

City College of the City
University of New York

NEW YORK   OXFORD UNIVERSITY PRESS

Library of Congress Cataloging in Publication Data
Shaughnessy, Mina P.,
   Errors and expectations.
   Bibliography: p. 298–306   Includes index.
   1. English language—Rhetoric—Study and teaching. I. Title.
PE1404.S5   808'.042'0711   76-53701
ISBN 0-19-502394-3   ISBN 0-19-502507-5 pbk.

24 25 26 27 28 29
Printed in the United States of America
on acid-free paper

In Memory of My Mother
Ruby Johnson Pendo
1896 – 1975

Preface

I keep in my files a small folder of student papers that go back ten years in my teaching career. They are the first papers I ever read by severely unprepared freshman writers and I remember clearly the day I received them. The students who wrote the papers were then enrolled in the SEEK Program at City College, a program for poverty-area youth which preceded Open Admissions at City College and served in many ways as the model for the skills programs that were to be developed under that policy.

I remember sitting alone in the worn urban classroom where my students had just written their first essays and where I now began to read them, hoping to be able to assess quickly the sort of task that lay ahead of us that semester. But the writing was so stunningly unskilled that I could not begin to define the task nor even sort out the difficulties. I could only sit there, reading and re-reading the alien papers, wondering what had gone wrong and trying to understand what I at this eleventh hour of my students' academic lives could do about it.

Looking at these papers now, I have no difficulty assessing the work to be done nor believing that it *can* be done. Since that critical afternoon, I have seen many such students go through the long corridor of credits that begins with basic writing, and I have read and corrected and conferred over thousands of such papers. But at the time there were no precedents to raise my expectations, only those disturbing essays with their tangles of errors and puzzling incompetencies.

This book began that afternoon, although I did not start to write it until some years later. I have tried to make it the sort of book I could have used then. In writing it, I have assumed that we need not learn everything at our students' expense and that even among independent English teachers there are methods and insights to be shared, ways of reducing somewhat the costly lessons of experience.

I suspect I would not have undertaken to write this book, or certainly to finish it, had I not received generous assistance from the Carnegie Corporation of New York. I especially thank E. Alden Dunham for his advice and encouragement along the way. I thank also the basic writing teachers of the City College Department of English for the many ways in which they have enriched my understanding of our work. Where I have drawn specifically from reports or writing samples that were given to me by teachers, I have tried to note this.

There remain several individuals whose help I want especially to acknowledge. John Wright, my editor, has been an invaluable ally, first by respecting the purposes of this book and then by giving it the kind of wise and imaginative attention an author always hopes for. Stephanie Golden, through her craft and her grace, turned the editing of my manuscript into a stimulating exchange of the sort I would covet for students in their conferences with English teachers. Marilyn Rosenthal read the chapters on syntax and common errors from a linguist's perspective and was able not only to alert me to the different ways in which linguists and English teachers respond to student writing but to suggest changes in terminology and phrasing that would help clarify my own interpretations of error. Bridget Gellert Lyons and Robert Lyons read my manuscript with the care of friends and spotted some errors and inconsistencies that I had missed. More important, they encouraged me from the start to undertake this study. Janet Emig gave me valuable comments on the early chapters of the manuscript and, beyond that, shared generously with me her own insights into writing as a process and a subject of instruction.

Several people worked directly with me in gathering and analyzing student writing samples. Lou Karameros created order out of the thousands of essays that were my source of data on student writing problems. Dorethea McGill and Vera Daniel helped me with the searching and filing and copying that were so important a part of my task. I am much indebted to Erica Kenney for her year of patient and exacting assistance in classifying misspellings and faulty sentences and to Kathy Roe for her perceptive reports on the writing progress of basic writing students. Finally, I thank Marilyn Maiz for having been my companion in this effort from start to finish, for assembling thousands of essays, preparing some of the data from those essays for computer analysis, giving honest and informed criticism of each chapter, and preparing the final manuscript.

New York, N.Y.   M. P. S.
October 1976

Contents

Errors and expectations

1
Introduction

Background

Toward the end of the sixties and largely in response to the protests of that decade, many four-year colleges began admitting students who were not by traditional standards ready for college. The numbers of such students varied from college to college as did the commitment to the task of teaching them. In some, the numbers were token; in others, where comprehensive policies of admissions were adopted, the number threatened to "tip" freshman classes in favor of the less prepared students. For such colleges, this venture into mass education usually began abruptly, amidst the misgivings of administrators, who had to guess in the dark about the sorts of programs they ought to plan for the studdents they had never met, and the reluctancies of teachers, some of whom had already decided that the new students were ineducable.

It was in such an atmosphere that the boldest and earliest of these attempts to build a comprehensive system of higher education began: in the spring of 1970, the City University of New York adopted an admissions policy that guaranteed to every city resident with a high-school diploma a place in one of its eighteen tuition-free colleges (ten senior colleges and eight two-year colleges), thereby opening its doors not only to a larger population of students than it had ever had before (enrollment was to jump from 174,000 in 1969 to 266,000 in 1975) but to a wider range of students than any college had probably ever ad-

mitted or thought of admitting to its campus—academic winners and
losers from the best and worst high schools in the country, the children
of the lettered and the illiterate, the blue-collared, the white-collared,
and the unemployed, some who could barely afford the subway fare to
school and a few who came in the new cars their parents had given them
as a reward for staying in New York to go to college; in short, the sons
and daughters of New Yorkers, reflecting that city's intense, troubled
version of America.

One of the first tasks these students faced when they arrived at
college was to write a placement essay and take a reading test. Judged
by the results of these tests, the young men and women who were to
be known as open admissions students fell into one of three groups:
(1) those who met the traditional requirements for college work, who
appeared from their tests and their school performance to be competent
readers and writers with enough background in the subjects they would
be studying in college to be able to begin at the traditional starting
points; (2) those who had survived their secondary schooling but not
thrived on it, whose reading was seldom voluntary and whose writing
reflected a flat competence, by no means error-free but limited more
seriously by its utter predictability—its bare vocabulary, safe syntax,
and platitudinous tone, the writing of students who had learned to get
by but who seemed to have found no fun nor challenge in academic
tasks; (3) those who had been left so far behind the others in their
formal education that they appeared to have little chance of catching
up, students whose difficulties with the written language seemed of a
different order from those of the other groups, as if they had come, you
might say, from a different country, or at least through different
schools, where even very modest standards of high-school literacy had
not been met.

Of these groups, the first was clearly the group whom college teachers knew best. They were the students for whom college courses and
tests had been designed and about whom studies had been made. The
second group, however, was also known to them; its students resembled
the academic stragglers of another era, those who had tended to end up
in "bonehead English" perhaps but at least some of whom had been
known to take hold at a later point in their development and go on to
complete their academic work creditably. The third group contained the
true outsiders. Natives, for the most part, of New York, graduates of
the same public school system as the other students, they were none-

theless strangers in academia, unacquainted with the rules and rituals of college life, unprepared for the sorts of tasks their teachers were about to assign them. Most of them had grown up in one of New York's ethnic or racial enclaves. Many had spoken other languages or dialects at home and never successfully reconciled the worlds of home and school, a fact which by now had worked its way deep into their feelings about school and about themselves as students.

They were in college now for one reason: that their lives might be better than their parents', that the lives of their children might be better than theirs so far had been. Just how college was to accomplish these changes was not at all clear, but the faith that education was the one available route to change empowered large numbers of students who had already endured twelve years of compulsory schooling to *choose* to go to college when the doors of City University suddenly swung open.

Not surprisingly, the essays these students wrote during their first weeks of class stunned the teachers who read them. Nothing, it seemed, short of a miracle was going to turn such students into writers. Not uncommonly, teachers announced to their supervisors (or even their students) after only a week of class that everyone was probably going to fail. These were students, they insisted, whose problems at this stage were irremediable. To make matters worse, there were no studies nor guides, nor even suitable textbooks to turn to. Here were teachers trained to analyze the belletristic achievements of the centuries marooned in basic writing classrooms with adult student writers who appeared by college standards to be illiterate. Seldom had an educational venture begun so inauspiciously, the teachers unready in mind and heart to face their students, the students weighted by the disadvantages of poor training yet expected to "catch up" with the front-runners in a semester or two of low-intensity instruction.

Five years have passed since that first class of open admissions students entered City University. Some of those "ineducable" students have by now been graduated; some have dropped out; some have transferred to other types of programs after having found their vocational directions; and still others remain in college, delayed because of outside jobs that eat into their college time and because of the extra time they spent at the outset developing their skills as readers and writers. The teachers who five years ago questioned the educability of these students now know of their capabilities and have themselves undergone many shifts in attitude and methodology since their first encounters with the new students.

Despite such advances, the territory I am calling basic writing (and that others might call remedial or developmental writing) is still very much of a frontier, unmapped, except for a scattering of impressionistic articles and a few blazed trails that individual teachers propose through their texts. And like the settlers of other frontiers, the teachers who by choice or assignment are heading to this pedagogical West are certain to be carrying many things they will not be needing, that will clog their journey as they get further on. So too they will discover the need of other things they do not have and will need to fabricate by mother wit out of whatever is at hand.

This book is intended to be a guide for that kind of teacher, and it is certain to have the shortcomings of other frontier maps, with doubtless a few rivers in the wrong place and some trails that end nowhere. Still, it is also certain to prepare the inexperienced teacher for some of the difficulties he is likely to encounter and even provide him with a better inventory of necessary supplies than he is likely to draw up on his own.[1]

The book is mainly an attempt to be precise about the types of difficulties to be found in basic writing (BW) papers at the outset, and beyond that, to demonstrate how the sources of those difficulties can be explained without recourse to such pedagogically empty terms as "handicapped" or "disadvantaged." I have divided this territory of difficulty into familiar teaching categories, which serve as headings for the main sections of the book: Handwriting and Punctuation, Syntax, Common Errors, Spelling, Vocabulary, and Beyond the Sentence. In each of these sections, I have tried to do three things: first, to give examples of the range of problems that occur under each category of difficulty; second, to reason about the causes of these problems; and third, to suggest ways in which a teacher might approach them.

The examples have been drawn largely from placement essays, some 4,000 of them, that were written by incoming freshmen at City College of the City University of New York over the years 1970 through 1974. To the criticism that samples written under testing situations do not

---

1. After having tried various ways of circumventing the use of the masculine pronoun in situations where women teachers and students might easily outnumber men, I have settled for the convention, but I regret that the language resists my meaning in this important respect. When the reader sees *he*, I can only hope *she* will also be there.

represent the true competence of writers, I can only answer that where writers are as unskilled as the student writers we are considering, the conditions of writing seem to matter less than they do for more advanced writers. Thus the initial essays of this group proved to be highly accurate guides to placement. Indeed, it was not unusual to find students at this level doing better on their test essays than on outside assignments.

The reader will quickly—perhaps even impatiently—note that I have tended to use more examples of individual difficulties than he needs in order to identify the sort of problem I am discussing. I have done this in part to suggest that the problem I am naming occurs in a variety of contexts but also because I see a value to being immersed in examples. It deepens one's sense of pattern and thereby develops the ability to make swift assessments and classifications of writing difficulties. Should the reader feel no need for this immersion, however, he will be able to follow my line of analysis without heeding all the examples.

In reasoning about the causes of the various difficulties BW students have as writers, I have drawn from three resources: my students and the explanations they have given me, directly and indirectly, of their difficulties with written English; my colleagues, who have shared their insights with me over the years in many different settings, both formal and informal; and my own experience as someone who writes and therefore understands the pressures and peculiarities of that behavior.

From these resources, I have reached the persuasion that underlies this book—namely, that BW students write the way they do, not because they are slow or non-verbal, indifferent to or incapable of academic excellence, but because they are beginners and must, like all beginners, learn by making mistakes. These they make aplenty and for such a variety of reasons that the inexperienced teacher is almost certain to see nothing but a chaos of error when he first encounters their papers. Yet a closer look will reveal very little that is random or "illogical" in what they have written. And the keys to their development as writers often lie hidden in the very features of their writing that English teachers have been trained to brush aside with a marginal code letter or a scribbled injunction to "Proofread!" Such strategies ram at the doors of their incompetence while the keys that would open them lie in view. This is not to say that learning to write as a young adult does not involve hard work, for certainly it does, but only that the work must be informed by an understanding not only of what is missing or awry but of why this is so. In each chapter, I will therefore be trying to tease out the reasons that lie behind the problems I have illustrated.

My suggestions for helping students overcome these problems are of several sorts. Sometimes I offer actual lessons; sometimes I recommend a method or strategy, such as sentence-combining or free writing, that is already (or ought to be) part of a teacher's technology; and at others, I merely urge a fresh perspective on an old problem. The teacher therefore who is searching for a tightly and fully structured writing program will not find it here. This book is concerned with the orientations and perceptions of teachers in relation to a specific population of student writers. It assumes that programs are not the answers to the learning problems of students but that teachers are and that, indeed, good teachers create good programs, that the best programs are developed *in situ*, in response to the needs of individual student populations and as reflections of the particular histories and resources of individual colleges. Thus, while I have sketched out a course plan in my final chapter which arranges the pieces of my analysis into teaching order, I do not expect anyone to accept it as a prototype. It is, let us say, a tried way of beginning a writing apprenticeship.

The course plan also serves to suggest the proportion of time that would be given in class to the goal of achieving correct form. Without this indication, the reader is certain to conclude that the "basic" of basic writing is not how to write but how to be right, for five of the book's eight chapters are devoted to the errors students make. This attention to error is certain to raise questions—both pedagogical and political—in the minds of many teachers. Why, some will ask, do English teachers need to be told so much about errors? Isn't their concern with error already a kind of malignancy? Ought we not to dwell instead upon the options writers have rather than the constraints they must work under if they are to be read without prejudice?

There is a short answer to these questions—namely that the proportion of time I spend analyzing errors does not reflect the proportion of time a teacher should spend teaching students how to avoid them. But since teachers' preconceptions about errors are frequently at the center of their misconceptions about BW students, I have no choice but to dwell on errors. The long answer to these questions leads us into more controversial territory. Yet it is important, before this exploration of student writing begins, that I explain more fully why error figures so importantly in this book.

Some views on error

For the BW student, academic writing is a trap, not a way of saying something to someone. The spoken language, looping back and forth between speakers, offering chances for groping and backing up and even hiding, leaving room for the language of hands and faces, of pitch and pauses, is generous and inviting. Next to this rich orchestration, writing is but a line that moves haltingly across the page, exposing as it goes all that the writer doesn't know, then passing into the hands of a stranger who reads it with a lawyer's eyes, searching for flaws.

By the time he reaches college, the BW student both resents and resists his vulnerability as a writer. He is aware that he leaves a trail of errors behind him when he writes. He can usually think of little else while he is writing. But he doesn't know what to do about it. Writing puts him on a line, and he doesn't want to be there. For every three hundred words he writes, he is likely to use from ten to thirty forms that the academic reader regards as serious errors. Some writers, inhibited by their fear of error, produce but a few lines an hour or keep trying to begin, crossing out one try after another until the sentence is hopelessly tangled. The following passage illustrates the disintegration of one such writer:[2]

Start 1
> Seeing and hearing is something beautiful and strange to infant.

Start 2
> To a infant seeing and hearing is something beautiful and stronge to infl

Start 3
> I agree that seeing and hearing is something beautiful and stronge to a infants. A infants heres a strange sound such as work mother, he than acc

2. Unless otherwise indicated, the writers of sample passages are native to the United States, where they have had from twelve to thirteen years of public schooling, mostly in New York City. The topics of placement essays, from which many of the samples come, are given in the Appendix. In this essay, an initial class essay, the student was attempting to contrast the ways in which infants and adults see the world. Each of the "starts" in the present sample was crossed out in the original.

Start 4

> I agree that child is more sensitive to beauty, because its all so new to him and he apprec

Start 5

> The main point is that a child is more sensitive to beauty than there parents, because its the child a inftant can only express it feeling with reactions,

Start 6

> I agree a child is more senstive to seeing and hearing than his parent, because its also new to him and more appreciate. His

Start 7

> I agree that seeing and hearing have a different quality for infants than grownup, because when infants comes aware of a sound and can associate it with the object, he is indefeying and the parents acknowledge to to this

Start 8

> I agree and disagree that seeing and hearing have a different quality for infants than for grownups, because to see and hear for infants its all so new and mor appreciate, but I also feel that a child parent appreciate the sharing

Start 9

> I disagree I feel that it has the same quality to

Start 10

> I disagree I fell that seeig and hearing has the same quality to both infants and parents. Hearing and seeing is such a great quality to infants and parents, and they both appreciate, just because there aren't that many panters or musicians around dosen't mean that infants are more sensitive to beautiful that there parents.

So absolute is the importance of error in the minds of many writers that "good writing" to them means "correct writing," nothing more. "As long as I can remember," writes a student, "I wanted to be an English teacher. I know it is hard, keeping verbs in their right place, s's when they should be, etc., but one day I will make them part of me."

Much about the "remedial" situation encourages this obsession with error. First, there is the reality of academia, the fact that most college teachers have little tolerance for the kinds of errors BW students make, that they perceive certain types of errors as indicators of ineducability, and that they have the power of the F. Second there is the urgency of the students to meet their teachers' criteria, even to request more of the prescriptive teaching they have had before in the hope that this time it might "take." Third, there is the awareness of the teacher and administrator that remedial programs are likely to be evaluated (and budgeted) according to the speed with which they produce correct writers, correctness being a highly measurable feature of acceptable writing.

Teachers respond differently to these realities. Some rebel against the idea of error itself. All linguistic forms, they argue, are finally arbitrary. The spelling of a word, the inflectional systems that carry or reinforce certain kinds of information in sentences—these are merely conventions that differ from language to language and from dialect to dialect. And because the forms of language are arbitrary, the reasoning goes, they are not obligatory, not, at least, in those situations where variant forms can be understood by a reader or where the imposition of new forms undermines the writer's pride or confidence in his native language or vernacular.

Such a view excludes many forms from the province of "error." Certainly it leaves no room for those refinements of usage that have come to be associated with writing handbooks—who-whom and that-which distinctions, the possessive form with the genitive, the split infinitive, etc. Beyond this, it would exclude variant grammatical forms and syntactical patterns that originate in varieties of English that have long been spoken but only recently written, and then only in folk and imaginative literature. These forms would include double negatives, regularized irregular verbs (grow, growed, growed), zero inflections in redundant situations (e.g., the omission of the plural s in *ten jobs* because plurality is already indicated by the number), and various orthographic accommodations to vernacular forms.

When one considers the damage that has been done to students in the name of correct writing, this effort to redefine error so as to exclude most of the forms that give students trouble in school and to assert the legitimacy of other kinds of English is understandable. Doubtless it is part of a much vaster thrust within this society not only to reduce the penalties for being culturally different but to be enriched by that diversity.

Nonetheless, the teacher who faces a class of writers who have acquired but a rudimentary control of the skill discovers that the issue of error is much more complex and troubling than it seems in theory. He finds, for example, that the errors his students make cannot be neatly traced to one particular source, namely, the habitual preference of a vernacular form over a standard form. Instead he finds evidence of a number of interacting influences: the generally humiliating encounter with school language, which produces ambivalent feelings about mastery, persuading the child on the one hand that he cannot learn to read and write and on the other that he has to; the pleasures of peer and neighborhood talk, where language flows most naturally; the contagion of the media, those hours of TV and radio and movies and ads where standard forms blend with all that is alluring in the society.

The writing that emerges from these experiences bears traces of the different pressures and codes and confusions that have gone to make up "English" for the BW student. At times variant and standard forms mix, as if students had half-learned two inflectional systems; hypercorrections that belong to no system jut out in unexpected places; idiosyncratic schemes of punctuation and spelling substitute for systems that were never learned and possibly never taught; evasive circumlocutions, syntactical derailments, timid script, and near-guesses fog the meaning, if any remains after the student has thus spent himself on the sheer mechanics of getting something down on paper. One senses the struggle to fashion out of the fragments of past instruction a system that will relieve the writer of the task of deciding what to do in each instance where alternative forms or conventions stick in the mind. But the task seems too demanding and the rewards too stingy for someone who can step out of a classroom and in a moment be in the thick of conversation with friends.

Confusion, rather than conflict, seems to paralyze the writer at this level. Language learners at any level appear to seek out, either consciously or unconsciously, the underlying patterns that govern the language they are learning. They are pressed by their language-learning faculties to increase the degree of predictability and efficiency in their use of language. This is less a choice they make than an urge they have to move across the territory of language as if they had a map and not as if they were being forced to make their way across a mine field. What has been so damaging about the experience of BW students with written English is that it has been so confusing, and worse, that they have become resigned to this confusion, to not knowing, to the substitution of protective tactics or private systems or makeshift strategies for genuine mastery of written English in any form. Most damaging of all, they have lost confidence in the very faculties that serve all language learners: their ability to distinguish between essential and redundant features of a language left them logical but wrong; their ability to draw analogies between what they knew of language when they began school and what they had to learn produced mistakes; and such was the quality of their instruction that no one saw the intelligence of their mistakes or thought to harness that intelligence in the service of learning.

There is no easy or quick way to undo this damage. The absence of errors, it is true, does not count much toward good writing, yet the pile-up of errors that characterizes BW papers reflects more difficulty with written English than the term "error" is likely to imply. To try to persuade a student who makes these errors that the problems with his writing are all on the outside, or that he has no problems, may well be to perpetuate his confusion and deny him the ultimate freedom of deciding how and when and where he will use which language. For him, error is more than a mishap; it is a barrier that keeps him not only from writing something in formal English but from having something to write. In any event, students themselves are uneasy about encouragements to ignore the problem of error, often interpreting them as evasions of the hard work that lies before teachers and students if the craft of writing is ever to be mastered. Indeed, many students still insist, despite the miseries of their earlier encounters with grammar and despite the reluctance of teachers who have lost confidence in the power of grammatical study to affect writing, that they need more prescriptive grammar. Perhaps, as some would say, the propaganda of a long line of grammar teachers "took." But it may also be that grammar still symbolizes for some students one last chance to understand what is going on with written language so that they can control it rather than be controlled by it.

There is another reason why the phenomenon of error cannot be ignored at this level. It has to do with the writer's relationship to his audience, with what might be called the economics of energy in the writing situation. Although speakers and listeners, writers and readers, are in one sense engaged in a cooperative effort to understand one another, they are also in conflict over the amount of effort each will expend on the other. That is, the speaker or writer wants to say what he has to say with as little energy as possible and the listener or reader wants to understand with as little energy as possible. In a speech situation, the speaker has ways of encouraging or pressing for more energy than the listener might initially want to give. He can, for example, use attention-

getting gestures or grimaces, or he can play upon the social responsiveness of his listener; the listener, in turn, can query or quiz or withhold
his nods until he has received the "goods" he requires from the speaker.

Nothing like this open bargaining can go on in the writing situation,
where the writer cannot keep an eye on his reader nor depend upon
anything except words on a page to get him his due of attention. Thus
anything that facilitates the transfer of his meaning is important in this
tight economy of energy. Great writers, it is true, have drawn deeply
upon the energies of readers, holding them through pages of exasperating density or withholding from them conventional word order or
vocabulary or punctuation in order to refresh the language or create
new perceptions; but even here the reader expects his investment to pay
off in intellectual or emotional enrichment. He is, after all, a buyer in a
buyer's market.

Errors, however, are unintentional and unprofitable intrusions upon
the consciousness of the reader. They introduce in accidental ways
alternative forms in spots where usage has stabilized a particular form
(as is now true in spelling, for example, or in the familiar albeit
"illogical" inflections). They demand energy without giving any return
in meaning; they shift the reader's attention from where he is going
(meaning) to how he is getting there (code). In a better world, it is true,
readers might be more generous with their energies, pausing to divine
the meaning of a writer or mentally to edit the errors out of his text
without expecting to be rewarded for their efforts, but it would be fool-
hardy to bank on that kind of persistence except perhaps in English
teachers or good friends. (That errors carry messages which writers
can't afford to send is demonstrated by the amount of energy and
money individuals, business firms, publishing houses, etc., spend on
error removal, whether by correcting fluids, erasers, scrapped paper, or
proofreaders.)

All codes become codes by doing some things regularly and not
others, and it is not so much the ultimate logic of these regularities that
makes them obligatory but rather the fact that, logical or no, they have
become habitual to those who communicate within that code. Thus the
fact that in the general dialect the -s in *ten jobs* is a redundant form
merely repeating what a numerical adjective has already established
does not reduce the general reader's pause over *ten job*. The truth is that
even slight departures from a code cost the writer something, in whatever system he happens to be communicating, and given the hard

bargain he must drive with his reader, he usually cannot afford many of them.

This is not to say, of course, that the boundaries of error do not shift nor to suggest that certain battles along those borderlines are not worth waging. English has been robustly inventing itself for centuries—stretching and reshaping and enriching itself with every language and dialect it has encountered. Ironically, some of the very irregularities that students struggle with today are there because at some point along the way the English language yielded to another way of saying something.

But when we move out of the centuries and into Monday morning, into the life of the young man or woman sitting in a BW class, our linguistic contemplations are likely to hover over a more immediate reality—namely, the fact that a person who does not control the dominant code of literacy in a society that generates more writing than any society in history is likely to be pitched against more obstacles than are apparent to those who have already mastered that code. From such a vantage point, one feels the deep conserving pull of language, the force that has preserved variant dialects of English as well as the general dialect of literacy, and one knows that errors matter, knows further that a teacher who would work with BW students might well begin by trying to understand the logic of their mistakes in order to determine at what point or points along the developmental path error should or can become a subject for instruction. What I hope will emerge from this exploration into error is not a new way of sectioning off students' problems with writing but rather a readiness to look at these problems in a way that does not ignore the linguistic sophistication of the students nor yet underestimate the complexity of the task they face as they set about learning to write for college.

2
Handwriting and punctuation

The single most important fact about BW students is that, although they have been talking every day for a good many years, they have been writing infrequently, and then only in such artificial and strained situations that the communicative purpose of writing has rarely if ever seemed real. Compared with the 1,000 words a week that a British student is likely to have written in the equivalent of an American high school or even the 350 words a week that an American student in a middle-class high school is likely to have written, the basic writing student is more likely to have written 350 words a semester. It would not be unusual for him to have written nothing at all. He is often therefore still struggling with basic motor-mental coordinations that have long ago become unconscious for more practiced students. And as long as the so-called mechanical processes involved in writing are themselves highly conscious or even labored, the writer is not likely to have easy access to his thoughts. Thus matters like handwriting and punctuation and spelling become important, if only because without some measure of ease, without being able to assign some operations to habit, or even to indifference, the novice writer is cut off from thinking. "The first thing that happened to me was I ran into a wall," writes one student who recalled his struggle to break the error barrier. "I couldn't write because I didn't have the skills. I couldn't spell. I mean, words like *when* or *which*. Every word, I had to look up or get someone else to look up. It was like learning to type. For a while all you can do is watch the keys and your fingers. I did every paper over and over until finally I began to be able to think about what I was saying."

The physical act of writing, of moving the pen or pencil (or typewriter) across the page so as to form decipherable words without great effort, is of course fundamental to other writing skills. Yet students have often not mastered this skill by the end of high school. Thus it is not unusual to find among freshman essays a handwriting that belies the maturity of a student, reminding the reader instead of the labored cursive style of children. Often, but not always, the content that is carried in such writing is short and bare, reinforcing the impression of the reader that the writer is "slow" or intellectually immature. Yet the same student might be a spirited, cogent talker in class. His problem is that he has no access to his thoughts or personal style through the medium of writing and must appear, whenever he writes, as a child. Some BW students seem never to have made the transition from manuscript to cursive writing, a change that begins for most students around the third or fourth grade. And in both styles capital and lower-case letters are often mixed in unpredictable ways that appear to be related more to the ease with which certain letters are formed than to any conscious attempt at punctuation. Other students appear to have mastered the graphic demands of handwriting without coordinating the flow of script with the movement of thought, and their writing, with its "A for effort" legibility, often surprises the reader by its immature content. Sometimes a writer even reveals a flair for graphic art in his struggle with the written language. (One imagines the pleasure such an accomplishment would give to a student who was otherwise having a discouraging time with writing.) But the instances where eccentricity moves into illegibility are far more frequent. An individualized hand need not, of course, be illegible; it can be part of the expression of the writer. But when writing becomes so crabbed or slanted or blurred as to force the reader into puzzling out the shapes of letters, the patience of the reader and meaning of the writer are both lost.

Handwriting styles become extensions of ourselves and are therefore difficult to see, let alone change. Yet it is this "seeing" of the handwriting through other eyes that is the most important experience for the student. If he can see what others see, catch but a quick reflection of his writing in the mirror of other eyes, he is more likely to recognize the need to take pains, and it is this matter of taking pains rather than changing the writing style that is most often at issue. Projecting various writing styles on a screen, presenting materials on developmental stages in handwriting, or even getting into amateur handwriting analysis can help the student objectify his own writing style. It can even persuade a student who is camouflaging his uncertainties in spelling by blurring his script that he loses as much as he gains by such strategies.

Like error, poor handwriting of the sort I have been describing is not so much a cause of bad writing as an indication that the writer is not at home with this skill, that he is hindered not only by the difficulties of articulation that confront most writers but also by his stiffness with the pen. The answer to this is practice—writing and more writing, preferably in modes that encourage a flow of words (journals, free writing, notations or observations), until the pen seems a natural extension of the hand, and the hand of the mind itself.

Unfortunately few students from inferior high schools learn to type, and few classrooms are equipped with typewriters, even though the writing that people must do in the jobs they get after college must end up in typescript. For students with handwriting styles that impair their ability to communicate on paper, an intensive summer typing course is not impractical, particularly if the materials of instruction can also give the student practice in the spelling of difficult words or increase his awareness of the inflectional system of formal English. Such a course was given experimentally to twenty City College students during the summer of 1968. The students met for twenty-four evening sessions taught by regular typing instructors. Money was raised locally for the purchase of typewriters, and students were promised a typewriter if they passed the course. Of the twenty-five students, twenty completed the course with an average typing speed of forty. One student, a notably bad handwriter, proved to be exceedingly fleet and accurate as a typist, reaching a speed of fifty-eight words per minute within that short course. Subsequent checks with the students established that most of them went on to develop their skill and to rely on it for the preparation of academic papers.

Punctuation

The punctuation errors that commonly appear in BW papers reflect the students' inexperience with writing, and therefore with the punctuation code that serves to signal structural, semantic, and rhetorical meanings that would otherwise be missed by the reader. Although the full punctuation vocabulary of the code includes at least a dozen marks, the writer at this level uses only the three most common marks: the period, the comma, and the capital. Question marks, exclamation marks, or quotation marks appear infrequently, and often incorrectly; semicolons even less often; parentheses, hyphens, dashes almost never; and the special uses of such "academic" marks as ellipsis dots, brackets, and underlining are unknown. This means, of course, that the basic writer can say little through punctuation, whereas the experienced writer with a command of these slight notations adds both flexibility and meaning to his sentences. Parentheses and dashes, for example, help a writer overcome the linearity of sentences; the colon offers an economical way of presenting a series; and from the reader's point of view, punctuation provides a map for one who must otherwise drive blindly past the by-ways, intersections, and detours of a writer's thought.

Limited mainly to commas and periods, the inexperienced writer is further restricted by his uncertain use of these marks: commas appear at odd junctures within sentences, and both commas and periods mark off sentence terminations, or what appear to be terminations, for the writer frequently mistakes a fragment for a whole sentence or joins two sentences with a comma (comma splice) or with no punctuation at all (run-on). This difficulty with marking off the boundaries of sentences has led teachers to complain that their students "don't even know what an English sentence is." This is, of course, not so. These students, like other speakers, have been successfully communicating in sentences for many years. If we are to accept William Labov's research on the matter, in fact, they have probably been producing more "well-formed" sentences than their teachers.[1] What they have not been doing, however, is consciously marking off sentences according to grammatical

1. Labov writes, "Our own studies . . . of the grammaticality of everyday speech show that the great majority of utterances in all contexts are complete sentences, and most of the rest can be reduced to grammatical form by a small set of editing rules. The proportions of grammatical sentences vary with class backgrounds and styles. The highest percentage of well-formed sentences are found in casual speech, and working-class speakers use more well-formed sentences than middle-class speakers. The widespread myth that most speech is ungrammatical is no doubt based upon tapes made at learned conferences, where we obtain the maximum number of irreducibly ungrammatical sequences." *Language in the Inner City: Studies in the Black English Vernacular* (Philadelphia: University of Pennsylvania Press, 1972), p. 222.

structure, a highly abstract operation that often fragments the larger units writers seem to think in.

However unconventional a student's punctuation appears to be, it is always worth studying for the insights it gives into his perception of sentence boundaries and of specific punctuation marks. Thus although most writers at this level would say that periods are used at the ends of sentences, it appears from their punctuation habits that the writers often perceive sentences to be rhetorical units that are longer or shorter than the grammatical sentence. Furthermore there often appears to be a psychological resistance to the period—perhaps because it imposes an end on a unit the writer has usually had difficulty beginning or doesn't want to finish. It says that the writer must mobilize himself for another beginning, almost always a formidable task for an inexperienced writer. Commas, however, are not final, yet they hold things together. Besides, as one student who had randomly sprinkled commas throughout his essay explained, "They're so cheap!"

The question of *when* the punctuation code should become the subject of instruction depends upon how the teacher thinks students learn to write. But the question of *whether* the code should be learned loses much of its relevance when samples of writing rather than theories about self-expression are central to the debate. Then the paradox of options arising out of restrictions— the generative paradox of language itself—illuminates: without some convention for showing the groupings and relationships of words, for suggesting pace and intonation, the written sentence becomes a puzzle to the modern reader, and the writer, with "freedom" to do *anything* in the way of charting his reader's course through lines of words, must set about doing *something*, selecting some kind of systematic spacing or marking arrangement that will clarify his meaning. The code that now serves this purpose for most of the writing in this society (and here we can include even the writing of artists whose elaborations upon and departures from the code nonetheless depend upon it) is ready for use. In fact, it has been at least partially learned by BW students. The problem lies, however, in this partialness, in the writers' unawareness of a punctuation "system," in their fragments of misinformation that by now have often become trusted stratagems in the battle with the page (e.g., a comma where you breathe or in front of *that* or *and*), or in the surprising lacunae that raise the question, again and again, of what these students got for the twelve years they gave to schooling.

The following passages reflect some of the more common confusions about the marking off of sentences.

Passage 1

> The main point of this topic is that the Children an College students aren't learning how to read and write for that they will used later in life. I don't believe society has prepared me for the work I want to do that. is in education speaking, that my main point in being here, If this isn't a essay. of a thousand word's that because I don't have much to say. for it has been four year since I last wrote one, and by the time I am finish here I hope to be able to write an number of essay.

Here is a jumble of punctuation marks. Note first that the writer suggests in the opening sentence (patterned very closely after the wording of the essay question itself) that she understands the function of the period. But in the subsequent sentences, of which there are five (if one counts a compound sentence as containing two sentences separated by some mark of punctuation), only the final sentence gets the period in the right place. The other sentences expose two problems: an inclination to use the comma as a period

> I don't believe society has prepared me for the work I want to do that.
> is in education speaking, that my main point in being here,

and the inclination to use the period as a comma—that is, for subordinate junctures

> that. is in education speaking
> (that is, educationally speaking)
>
> If this isn't a essay.
>
> . . . I don't have much to say. for it has been . . .

Passage 2

> First of all the system, don't really care about the students, schools are always overcrowded and the students get the, impression that really there are some teachers, just like students just to Be there, and the children performing below par is mainly the parents fault too, they really don't stress How important is, and that when they go to school they should try to do the Best they can instead they are encourage to learned Basketball, But in all the fault would lie on the state and government officials, Because really they don't care about children Education they're more concerned about what's your color or do your family have a good Income? and really with all the pressure

society put on the children they don't have enough time to learned, But for the kids that are real Bright they can make it through, But what about the kids that need a little extra Time so with all this its too much, for them if a mother asked her child what did you learned today, the average child would say nothing Because there is always something going on Beside Educational, so when this kid is out of school he or she has nothing, Because all those school years were just problems society has push on the Kids, and when they hit the outside world they're not ready not because they' are dumb, But society has effect them on the wrong side, But who get the Blame? Always the children, if a kid could go to school and learned, without meeting society, they would come out a Better product, and could be ready to hit head on with society, over'all its all of our fault in one way or another, but to put it plain society is more the blame, But then again we the people make society up, but far as the children concerned not that much, so I would suggest that society get on the good foot, because whether they like or not we're the future

The writer of passage 2 appears not to have learned the convention for ending sentences. The capital B that dominates the passage probably reflects some difficulty with forming the lower-case *b* and has no significance as punctuation. Note, too, how the comma plays into the writer's aversion to closure, allowing him to create strings of conjunctions (mainly with *but*).

Passage 3

Education is a mean to the end although some people have their education and play down that doesn't mean that we the younger generation should just set and watch other people we want and education we got to fight for it, it is not easy but one person told me that any thing that is easy to get is not worth while having.

Yes I believed that their are some student who can't read text book, it is just that some people learn more than or I should say that some haven't got that much understanding about certain things, and his for us to try harder. Because with out an education we can hardly fine a good job, like me I know their are other means of being nurse like training programs but still want to finish my education, I know I haven't got enough this little that I now have I want to work upon it.

In passage 3, the writer has provided only two of the ten required terminal marks and here only where they are strongly evoked (i.e., to end the paragraph and to separate the *it* that ends one sentence from the *it* that begins the next one). In the second paragraph she introduces commas as terminal marks. The one period within the paragraph is used to set off a subordinate clause. The final period terminates the passage. Thus we again find evidence of a partially learned code where the meaning of a mark as basic as the period is unstable and where, as a result, no system of marking holds together.

At times a writer's punctuation seems utterly random, as when he punctuates parallel structures differently:

> The child grows older he goes to school. Learns to read and write the meaning which he had for a certain object, changes his basic ideas so that he does not have his original idea.

At other times he goes against the grain of the English sentence by inserting marks between words that are structurally bound to each other:

☐ The human race loses its capacity, to see and hear.

☐ Even before a child starts his, education . . .

☐ The infants sence of sight and hearing, are at their best early in life.

☐ Older people, look down upon young people. They go against, the constent nagging of parents.

☐ I agree with certain points that, has been stressed

☐ I however do not agree with a Statement that, has been made, that a youth becomes disinterested, in whatever he was.

☐ Unless the son accept, his father affliction of ideas upon him.

Still, a careful reading of an incorrectly punctuated passage often reflects a design which, once perceived, can be translated into conventional punctuation. The writer of Passage 4, for example, appears to have used periods and commas interchangeably as terminal marks, showing no awareness of their different functions:

Passage 4

> I remember working on a new puzzle father bott for me one summer. It was fun finding the different parts of the puzzle, this was an animal puzzle with jungle animal from the African continent. As I made progress on the puzzle, I discovered new animals. My mother came into the living room where I was working on my puzzle, She looked over the puzzle and said to me "are you having difficulties with this puzzle? I answered no ma. She look around for a while then she called my brother to come and help me anyway. This took all the fun out of this activity, I was angrey but no matter what I said and

did, mother always had the last word. I know my brother did not care to help me, he is three years older than I am and had his own intereses. After a while I became very dependent on my brother for almost everything, my brother too was very displease but he went along, and he told me, I am going to help you because mami wants it that way, and if I don't help you I wouldn't be able to go to the movie next saturday. I know my mother did not mean to harm me in any way, but I needed the time and independence to work out my own problems, I learned more when I did things on my own.

A closer look, however, suggests that the commas do serve a different purpose from the periods. Both marks, it is true, are used to terminate sentences, but the commas hold closely related sentences together whereas the periods mark the ends of the sentence clusters or terminate narrative sentences that advance the anecdote:

> *Narrative opening:* I remember working on a new puzzle father bott for me one summer.
>
> *Description of the puzzle:* It was fun finding the different parts of the puzzle, this was an animal puzzle with jungle animal from the African continent.
>
> *Narrative:* My mother came into the living room where I was working on my puzzle, She looked over the puzzle and said to me "are you having difficulties with this puzzle? I answered no ma. She look around for a while then she called my brother to come and help me anyway.
>
> *Writer's response:* This took all the fun out of this actiivty, I was angrey but no matter what I said and did, mother always had the last word.
>
> *Brother's attitude:* I know my brother did not care to help me, he is three years older than I am and had his own intereses.
>
> *Subsequent relations with brother:* After a while I became very dependent on my brother for almost everything, my brother too was very displease but he went along, and he told me, I am going to help you because mami wants it that way, and if I don't help you I wouldn't be able to go to the movie next saturday.
>
> *Writer's response:* I know my mother did not mean to harm me in any way, but I needed the time and independence to work out my own problems, I learned more when I did things on my own.

Here is another passage with a similar approach to periods and commas. It has three rhetorical clusters held together by commas and set off by periods. The first group announces the subject of the short passage; the second speaks of what the boy had to learn from his father; the third, of what both the boy and his father knew about birds:

Passage 5

> This is a short little essay, on A small young boy who's love for birds was so immence it was Pathetic, His Father was also a bird lover, and a bird watcher.
>
> However there was plenty that the boy had to learned about birds, And his father was ready to teach him all he knew, So he could grow up like his dad.
>
> The boy knew some things like telling certain birds apart by sizes and color like a blue Jay and a Sparrow for example, But he didn't know how to distinguwish them by sound, His father knew how each different bird sang, and the sounds it made.

Often, too, the spliced and fragmented units that BW students punctuate as single sentences make rhetorical sense:

- ☐ In her late teens my mother looked for enjoyment, I'm the end result.
- ☐ Grownups are to busy distinghishing, they haven't time to listen to nature.
- ☐ My parents never took Holidays or Vacations, lack of time or money.
- ☐ I guess my parents like to remind me of their past years. The tough years.
- ☐ People tell me I have the spirit of my father. The spirit to work and fight and stride for what I want. Although my father didn't get to reach his goal.

The impulse to use punctuation to reinforce the rhetorical design of a sentence or passage is very much in the spirit, if not always the letter, of punctuation practice. Yet elaborations of this kind should be deliberate, not accidental; they should show the writer to be extending, not ignoring, the vocabulary already available to him in conventional punctuation. BW students, for example, who learn the conventional use of semicolons, or colons, or non-restrictive commas, need no longer strain the resources of the comma for want of other marks. (The semicolon usually becomes epidemic when it is first learned, especially if the teacher mistakenly promotes it as a way out of comma splices rather than as one device for stressing a close or parallel thought relationship between sentences.)

But before the beginning writer explores his options for marking the ends of sentences or for indicating relationships within sentences, he needs to be more certain about where written sentences end. The fact that he produces sentences in speaking does not mean that he understands periods in writing. Like the centipede who could no longer walk after trying to analyze how he did it, the inexperienced writer often concludes that he cannot produce sentences, simply because he is uncertain either about the actual boundaries of the grammatical abstraction called a sentence or about the mark he should use to set it off. The second problem seldom, in fact, appears in isolation from the first (although occasionally a student mislearns his terms and goes through school calling commas periods without anyone's ever noticing). More often, the writer perceives periods as signals for major pauses and commas as signals for minor pauses, but he is not aware of the role that grammatical structure plays in determining which of the many pauses produced in speech get marked and which get ignored. Speech is, after all, an intermixture of sound and silences. As much as fifty percent or more of spontaneous speech is estimated to be non-speech. Pauses mark rates of respiration, set off certain words for rhetorical emphasis, facilitate phonological maneuvers, regulate the rhythms of thought and articulation, and suggest grammatical structure. Modern punctuation, however, provides no score for such a complex orchestration. What it does do is sharpen the sense of structure in a sentence, first by marking off its boundaries and second by showing how certain words, phrases, or clauses within the sentence are related. More simply, it helps a reader predict not so much *where* but *how* a sentence is leading him.

This is difficult for a writer to do without an analytical grasp of the sentence. Otherwise, he must go by what "feels" like a sentence, and here his intuitions, as we have seen, are frequently wrong. Rhetorically strong but grammatically dependent structures at the ends of sentences can "seem" independent:

☐ My parents are free and full people living inside a prison. A fortress so deeply embedded that it is barely recognizable.

☐ We would live off the earth, and nature. Living together to survive.

☐ You never had it so good, was often heard in my house, when things weren't going as well as they should. Especially when discussing such topics as unemployment.

☐ My parents have always lived in a cold water railroad flat. Not knowing when we would have heat and hot water. My mother had four children. Only because she had no choice.

☐ When I first came here I thought college was like you see on TV. Where everybody studies hard to get good grades. So when they get out they can become doctors or businessmen.

☐ I think this paragraph mean something else. The kind of education we get in the schools today. Which is really separate around race and class.

☐ He should have a taste of all these things. So that he can make up his own mine on what he want out of life.

☐ An intrusun on the part of the father, may changes the course of his life. Unless the son accept, his father affliction of ideas upon him.

Adverbial clauses at the beginnings of sentences often seem like sentences, perhaps because the writer does not hold in his mind the initial word that suspends the clause:

☐ If place two children together in a room, without any influencing their minds. The two small children would never known the difference, between each other.

☐ But I think if people could learn to think a little like children. This would be a better place to live.

☐ In this essay I have read. The main point of the story is, the jobs will require more reading skills.

☐ Because infants and adults differ due to the fact that grownups have already been exposed to the world. The infants don't know the bitterness.

The second part of a compound structure sometimes feels like a sentence:

☐ I agree that the little boy has seen beauty. But is confused with the question.

☐ I don't mean caring about coming to school on time. But caring about, why this student is out.

☐ By having a college education one not only becomes an expert in a particular field. But will learn a tremendous amount of disciplene. And the development of his friend.

Or a string of sentences can feel like a single sentence, as we have seen in the passages already quoted in this chapter.

Such an approach to punctuation defeats one of the main purposes of punctuation, which is to help the reader see in advance how the part he is about to read relates to what he has just read. If he sees a period, he prepares himself for a new subject; if he sees a comma, he withholds closure on the sentence in progress, etc. But when these marks are interchanged, transposed, or omitted, the code no longer works. In the writing of BW students, as the samples have shown, marks that conventionally signal the end of an independent predication are used within such predications:

☐ In otherwords, this person has a better chance to enter a career in for instance; show business if he so desires.

☐ The person should go to college. And enlargen his thoughts in many fields.

☐ According to the figures which were distributed. The people with little. Higher education have gotten more jobs.

☐ It is good for you to go to college and get a degree of some sort and be finish with. Because take for example. nursing or dietitics.

Marks that conventionally set off dependent units within a predication are given the value of periods, even as they continue their conventional functions:

A young person getting out of high school today, should go on for a college degree, even if the job he is preparing to take does not need a college degree, A college Education would further his knowledge in a variety of courses, he might even, decide to change his opinion after learning about the different fields in which he can chose.

Marks are omitted where they are needed:

☐ Yes because college would train you for the jobs like psychologists high school can't train you to be a psychologists.

☐ So you say to yourself maybe I should have gone to college but then not many colleges train you for such posts but some do I could have found one.

☐ In order to survive in the world today one should not only be concern with getting a job which there is demand for he should try to meet the needs of his fellow men by going to college a young person could get an increase his knowledge about the world he lived in and in a better way he will be of more service to his community, his ability to cope with people around him will be on a better basis.

Or marks appear regularly in places where they are uncalled for: commas in front of *and* and *but* without regard to the units being coordinated, before *that*, or between subjects and predicates (especially where some form of the verb *to be* is involved):[2]

☐ Grownups sometime overlook some of the thing, that infants are interest in.

☐ I will end by saying, that the writing and reading skills of today are behind what was expected.

☐ The main point of this essay, is high schools and colleges are not putting work out.

☐ An infants sense of sight and hearing, are at their best early in life.

Some of these inconsistencies, omissions, and inventions in punctuation can no doubt be blamed on carelessness. The small marks of punctuation, after all, don't look very important. They don't seem to say much either, at least nothing that the writer doesn't already know through his "writer's ear," which guides him in both the writing and reading of his own sentences. Nonetheless, there is a difference between the punctuation of a writer who knows but does not care and the writer who, no matter how careful he may be, lacks the information he needs to make secure judgments about written sentences. These judgments must grow out of a familiarity with the sentence as a grammatical unit and with the process whereby simple sentences are enlarged so as to include various types of subordinate structures. In other words, punctuation becomes a problem for the BW student, not because he has no competence with sentences at all but because the writing down of sentences introduces new competencies that he has not been taught, including not only a knowledge of the names and functions of the various marks but also an ability to manage the structures that writers depend upon to overcome the redundancy, fragmentation, and loose sequencing that are natural in speech. (This would include such structures as adverbial clauses and participial phrases in pre-subject positions, relative clauses, appositional constructions, and logical connectives like *therefore* or *however*.)

2. Although archaic now, the comma before *that* was once good usage ("It is true, that a little philosophy inclineth a man's minde to Atheisme . . ."—Francis Bacon). Students are interested to learn that their "errors" were once conventions. It reminds them, as they must often be reminded, that errors are not, after all, sins and that conventions are but agreements among people to do things in certain ways in order to make life easier.

Thus although punctuation is often set off in the *mechanics* section of handbooks and English courses, it should not be isolated in this way from the dynamics of composition, for the process whereby writers *mark* sentences is related to the process whereby they *make* them. The fact that BW students concern themselves mainly with terminal punctuation, using both commas and periods for the purpose, suggests that they do not perceive the written sentence as something that can be broken into or added onto for purposes of elaboration, modification, or side comment;[3] the fact that they punctuate so as to isolate clauses that are semantically bound to other clauses (e.g., clauses beginning with *if, when, even though,* etc.) suggests a difficulty with holding written sentences in mind when they contain more than one predication or even when one predication contains a compound subject or verb.

What one senses through such punctuation is a caution about losing control of the sentence by allowing it to become too long—too full, that is, of embedded structures, which to the unpracticed writer may well echo their deeper origins as sentences. Yet combined with this effort to simplify individual sentences grammatically by breaking them up into smaller segments is another effort to link sentences rhetorically by pressing commas into service as conjunctions, by overusing words like *and, but, that,* or *because,* or by ignoring terminal punctuation altogether:

Fragmenting
  □ If place two children together in a room, without any adults influencing their minds. The two small children would never known the difference, between each other. For example. Two infants are adopted by a Black and an White parents. The children can grow up thinking that they are the same. Now the black child is encountered by a bigot. He says, hay. boy or something The black child is aware, of the difference. As the father told him. The difference between a sparrow and a jay bird.

  □ I feel that For a young person. Who has Just completed High School and Wishes to attended College. To get a higher Education that this moved is a very wise one. I know For a Fact that there are people. Who have attended college and have recived a college degree. Who are

3. The superfluous commas that appear at odd junctures within sentences (between simple subject and predicate, for example) rarely serve to join subordinate parts to the sentence. Rather, they chop up the basic predication in distracting ways, reminding the teacher that punctuation is as much a matter of leaving *out* as putting *in*.

reciving the same paid as a high school graunted. To me I am attending college because I think it is a beutiful expreince. I also feel that it is a chance of a lifetime. To get more out of life and to better things for you in the Future.

Linking

☐ Education is a mean to the end although some people have their education and play dum that doesn't mean that we the younger generation should just set and watch other people we want and education we got to fight for it, it is not easy but one person told me that anything that is easy to get is not worth while having.

☐ I think it makes sence for a young preson getting out of high school to go on for a college degree. Because there are so mend thin'gs you can do with a degree you can get out and make more money than you would if you just whent for a job with a high school degree because that is not enough today because the things they want you to know you do not know this in high school because They do not teach you how to go out there and get a good paying job or if you have to know more than you know in high school.

With both strategies, writers appear to be using punctuation to solve larger problems in composition: the urge to cut sentences down reflects a need for practice with the various embedding operations that help make sentences clearer and more economical, albeit longer and more complex; the urge to string sentences together reflects a need for other ways of making links between sentences.

If this is so, the study of punctuation ought not to begin with the marks themselves but with the structures that elicit these marks: first, with the recognition and creation of simple subject and predicate phrases; second, with the embedding of sentences within sentences (focusing on *who, which, that, when,* and *if* forms); third, with the embedding of appositional forms; and fourth, with the embedding of *-ing* phrases. These combinations mastered, the student is not only prepared to face the punctuation "devils" but is also able to fit, by analogy, other punctuation situations into a frame. (He can, for example, learn that, for purposes of punctuation, *although, because,* and other adverbial clauses are in the same family as *if.*) As for the punctuation of these embedded units, it should become clearer to him after the embedding exercises that these units adhere to the sentence. He should, further, have no difficulty seeing the need for commas with pre-subject clauses and phrases or with appositives, for position rather than meaning makes their separation by commas necessary. Where meaning comes into play, however, as with relative clauses that are made restrictive or non-restrictive by the omission or use of commas, the student can be made aware that these distinctions exist but should not be expected to master them at the same time that he is learning to recognize the boundaries of sentences. (One of the first steps in teaching restrictive–non-restrictive distinctions must be to change the terminology, which is confusing to many because the prefix *non* seems to suggest *no*—that is, no commas—whereas it is the non-restrictive clause that requires commas. It may be better to talk about only one clause— the *extra* clause that gives extra but not essential information and therefore gets extra commas.)

To get at the second composing problem—the problem of rhetorical continuity between sentences—the student (aware of the grammatical boundaries of sentences after his work with embedding) needs to learn the different ways in which sentences can be made to transcend, rhetorically, their grammatical boundaries. The speaker stops when he has ended a unit of thought, not necessarily when he has ended a unit of grammar called the sentence, which in fact often falls far short of a complete thought. For many beginning writers, the need to mark off sentences inhibits the progress of their thoughts. In speech, they can produce sentences as easily and unconsciously as they can walk; in writing, they must stop to deliberate over what is and what is not a sentence. In the process, they break down the rhythm of their thought. As we have seen, writers at this level often seem to use commas to keep the thought between sentences running, but they make little use of the conventional connectives that are a distinguishing feature of analytical writing. The apprentice writer should first become aware of the basic options he has in connecting sentences. He cannot be expected to master at once the large vocabulary of logical connectives that are included in this system, but he should have clearly in mind—and in hand—the distinction between embedding and linking sentences, the one operation requiring a change within the sentence, the other a link or connection between two sentences. His experience with embedding should have given him a basic vocabulary of words that signal embedding, particularly those words that seem to invite the most fragments:

wh-words	although, though, even though
that	unless

if   since
because   so that

Because these words carry meanings that can easily blur or merge with the meanings of linking or connecting words that do not embed (e.g. when: then; even though: nevertheless; because: thus), students need other ways of remembering them. They can, of course, memorize them and run into only occasional confusion—as when a *so that* gets confused with a *so*—but if the concept of embedding is made clear and the student has performed a number of embedding exercises, the main embedding forms should be well known without memorization. It may also help to observe that embedding words are not moveable, whereas logical connectives like *thus, nevertheless,* or *then* need not appear at the heads of sentences.

Among the forms that link rather than embed, the writer should understand how to use the two forms that substitute for the period— the *,and* form (and, by analogy, the other coordinating conjunctions *but, for, or,* and *so*) and the semicolon. Unfortunately, *and* is more a habit than a carefully chosen coordinator. Like the comma in writing, the *and* serves to keep sentences going, especially in a narrative or summary where the basis of sequence (chronology or another writer's sequence) seems simple or pre-ordained and the writer senses no need to deliberate over connections:

> The paragraph says that children like to see other birds sing and they want to know the names of the different kind of birds and then they don't hear or see the birds and the father comes to the son and says that one of the bird is a sparrow and the other one is a jay but the boy wants to know which is the jay and which is the sparrow.

The difficulty with this all-purpose *and* is that it is easy on the writer but hard on the reader; it frees the writer from the work of getting his sentences to reflect the different levels of generalization that are implied in his thought, but instead imposes upon the reader the work of trying to divine what these relationships are. Thus the following revision of the above passage, in which the parts are rearranged and recast so as to point up the causal relationship between the child's response to birds and the father's effort at instruction, results in a clearer, although grammatically more complex, passage than the original:

> Children like to hear birds sing and to know the names of different birds, but when a father starts teaching his son the names of birds,

saying, "This is a sparrow and the other one is a jay," the son gets more interested in knowing the difference between sparrows and jays than in seeing or hearing birds.

Learning to use *and* (like learning to use commas) is in part, then, learning *not* to use it indiscriminately but only where the units being joined are structurally and rhetorically coordinate or where *and* functions less as a coordinator than as a kind of culminator (. . . and they lived happily ever after). This precision about the relationships between sentences, or between parts within sentences, is characteristic of analytical writing but not of talk, where there is little time for deliberations of this sort. And although talk has alternative ways of making connections—by intonation, pace, non-verbal gestures, and the dynamics of dialogue itself—it tends to go flat when it is transcribed on the page, where it seems to go on and on, leveling coordinate and subordinate thoughts, main and parenthetical structures, to one plane of discourse which the reader scans swiftly, looking for passages that catch his interest. But analytical writing is wrought so as to hold the reader, moment by moment, in the development of a thought, to capture, despite the linearity of the medium, the dimensions of an idea. The various embedding forms common to writing but infrequent in talk and the explicit connections that are required between sentences provide ways of making thoughts cohere at this complex level.

Thus the ubiquitous *and* has to be called into question wherever it appears. Is it pointing up a coordinate relationship or is it blurring a relationship of another sort? Are the structures that are joined by the *and* grammatically equal and of similar rhetorical weight? The question of coordinate status comes up not only in punctuating compound sentences but also in forming parallel units within sentences. The distinction, in fact, pervades the composing process, where the shape of paragraphs and essays is controlled by the writer's conscious movement between units of coordinate and subordinate value. The *and* strings are symptomatic of a style of communicating—and thinking—that is customary in speech, where thought seems to be almost simultaneous with speaking and the process of refinement or connection is part of the performance between speaker and interlocutor. As a result, the listener tolerates the use of *and* for a wide range of meanings. But writing begins, in a sense, where speech leaves off—with organizing, expanding, and making more explicit the stuff of dialogue so that the thought that is generated in speech can be given full and independent form.

This is not to suggest that the inexperienced writer must be expected to make an abrupt transition from writing talk to writing writing, but only that the difference between these two uses of language should be kept in mind, even as the student is engaged in free writing or other expressive exercises that are aimed at getting his writing to the point that it approximates his skill as a talker.

The rules that BW students have learned for punctuating *and* do not stand up well in practice. Some students have learned that it is safest to use no punctuation; others have learned to put a comma before all *ands;* and most have been warned against ever starting a sentence with *and* or *but*. Where the focus in punctuation is on sentence boundaries, the student should be helped to see that the comma before *and* has the significance of a period—that is, it signals the end of one sentence and the beginning of the next. Without it, the two sentences often collide, forcing the reader to retrace his steps. Thus the sentence "He likes his wife and other women like him" might be read at first glance as

He likes his wife and other women . . .

until the reader discovers that he has beheaded the next sentence by mistaking the function of *and* as a coordinator of two direct objects rather than two sentences. With the comma, the writer has a chance to prepare his reader for a new sentence. This, then, is a worthwhile rule to learn. As for beginning, rather than joining, sentences with *and*, the student, it is true, has been incorrectly taught to view this as an error. Usage clearly permits it. But until the student has stable criteria for recognizing the sentence, he is often likely to begin not a sentence but a fragment with *and* and then think that his error lies in using *and* rather than in failing to follow *and* with a sentence.

There is a nice distinction to be made between the *and* that serves as a fulcrum between two balanced units (My mother did domestic work, and my father ran an elevator) and the *and* that moves a passage forward or brings it to an end (My father grew so discouraged with his life in the city that he began to dream of running away. And that was what he finally did.), but the important lesson at this level is that both *,and* and *And* must be followed by sentences.[4]

Like the period and *,and,* the semicolon occurs between sentences, but unlike these two forms it is rarely used by BW students. Once

4. *And* represents in this discussion all the coordinating conjunctions. The use of the comma is in fact especially important with *for* because of the possible confusion with the preposition.

introduced, however, it often takes over, probably because, as its form suggests, it has the linking power of a comma and the terminating authority of a period. Given the difficulties of the unpracticed writer with both linking and sustaining sentences, the semicolon must appear as something of a bargain. Yet its value disappears if it is used indiscriminately to get around problems in punctuation. Explaining just when it does get used, however, is not easy. It is needed, of course, in a complex series where commas are used within the units in the series and semicolons between those units, but inexperienced writers seldom produce sentences of this kind. Explanations of when to use the semicolon instead of the period tend to be elusive. It is a mark that points up a fine connection between two sentences but one that is more easily understood by examples than by explanation. Discussions about why a writer has used a semicolon in a particular situation must become discussions about the relationships between ideas, and this, finally, is what analytical writing is intended to clarify.

The concern in analytical writing for signaling the way one sentence or paragraph is logically related to the statement or paragraph that precedes or follows it is reflected even more directly in the sizable vocabulary of logical connectives that writers in this mode generally use. Because of their heavy exposure to written language, much of it laboriously formal and "connected," academicians tend to talk like writers rather than, as their students do, write like talkers, and they are often not aware of the need to point out this feature of the analytical mode. Yet students must learn a basic vocabulary of logical connectives if they are to reduce the strain on commas and *and's*. Learning to use these connectives, they will find, is a matter not so much of learning to be logical as of learning how to signal the logic that is usually implicit in what they are saying, and although the full vocabulary is extensive, most of the words can be seen to signal roughly one of six types of logical relationships, each of which can be represented by one word.

Logical connective	*Similar connectives*
FURTHERMORE	also, besides, in addition, likewise, moreover, similarly, or other words suggesting an addition
HOWEVER	despite this, instead, nonetheless, nevertheless, on the other hand, still, and other words that reverse the logical direction of the sentence

THEREFORE   as a result, accordingly, because of this, consequently, hence, thus, and other words suggesting the last link in a chain of reasoning

FOR EXAMPLE   for instance, to illustrate

THAT IS   namely

THEN   afterwards, eventually, later, meanwhile, presently, sometime, soon, subsequently, thereafter, or other words suggesting a time relationship

To learn how to use these connectives, the student should see and hear them in the writing of others. They are, in a sense, idiomatic forms that occur in contexts too numerous to specify. The teacher, in conferences with the student, can note places where a logical connective would clarify the line of thought. Exercises are also useful when they encourage the student to deliberate over the logical relationship between two statements. In one such exercise, a student can be asked to generate a sentence following specific connectives:

Most students are in college in order to get good jobs when they get out; however, _____.

Most students are in college in order to get good jobs when they get out; for example, _____.

Most students are in college in order to get good jobs when they get out. Therefore, _____.

In another exercise, the student can be asked to supply a connective between two statements, preferably the statements of other writers so that the student can then compare his perception of the relationship with that of another writer.

Any man's death diminishes me because I am involved in mankind. _____ never send to know for whom the bell tolls. It tolls for thee.

In older literary English, as in current popular speech, two or three negatives were felt as stronger than a single negative; _____. a well-known writer could write in 1797, "I can't see no wit in her."

Under natural conditions, life is made possible for the pickerel by his capacity to recognize shiny, fluttery things as his food; _____ once in a while, the shiny, fluttery thing in the water may happen to be a lure instead of a minnow.

The student should be aware of the options he has in punctuating and placing these connectives, options that exist because the connectives are not structurally necessary to the sentence. The coordinating conjunctions, the period, and the semicolon are not moveable forms; they mark off grammatical boundaries. But logical connectives are moveable, their most common spots being at the beginning of the sentence when the preceding sentence is terminated by a semicolon and at varying points after the subject when the preceding sentence is terminated by a period. (Here the student needs practice because the insertion of these connectives affects both the rhythm and sense of sentences.)

This chapter has concentrated on the difficulties BW students have with terminal punctuation. To be sure, they share with writers at more advanced levels many other types of punctuation problems, among them the faulty (one comma missing) or missing punctuation of parenthetical elements and the missing comma following introductory elements, but these errors seldom distract readers as errors in terminal punctuation do. Furthermore, the experience of transforming sentences into various kinds of dependent structures prepares the student for this kind of punctuation. As for the many other uses of the comma, uses that generally overwhelm an inexperienced writer when he seeks guidance in a handbook and finds more reasons for commas than he had ever worried about, these are best taken up after the criteria for sentence boundaries are stable and the three main devices for marking these boundaries (period, coordinating conjunction, and semicolon) are in hand.

A word should be said, however, about the conventions of quotation and capitalization, which many BW students appear not to have learned. When, for example, a writer at this level finds himself faced with a quotation, he usually quotes it indirectly or allows the direct quotation to merge, unmarked, with the rest of the sentence. Sometimes dashes are called in to set off quoted material. And when quotation marks are used, the periods, commas, and capitals that also figure in the marking-off of quotations are either missing or in the wrong place.

Since the college student is often required to use quotations, the conventions for doing so are important. Clearly, the student at this stage is not ready to take up all the refinements of quotation that are called for in a research paper, but he does need to understand the basic ways of distinguishing in writing between his words and the words he attributes to someone else. He can begin by looking at passages that are cast in the form of dialogue—interviews, hearings, or plays—where quotation marks are not needed. He can try his hand at writing dialogues or interviews of his own. Then he can try, in the context of a summary, to quote passages from these dialogues, practicing the different placement of the "he said's" and the conventional punctuation around the quoted passages. Finally, he can move to indirect quotation, changing whatever pronouns and verb tenses he has to change in order to blend the quotation with his own sentence and placing quotes only around the words or phrases that are distinctively the possession of the other person. Congressional hearings are excellent for work on quotation, especially if parts of a hearing happen to be in the newspapers and the student can trace the movement of a quotation through each stage from the reproduction of direct testimony to the reporters' quotation of parts of the testimony to the editorial comment on the testimony.

With capitalization, most BW students are aware of the need to capitalize the first words of sentences and the names of people and places. True, their perceptions of what goes to make up a sentence are often off and they make very few specific references to people, places, books, organizations, etc., but these matters alone would not justify taking up capitalization at this point, where only the most basic encoding difficulties are being discussed.

However, the beginning writer's difficulties with capitalization do not show up in the omission of capitals where convention calls for them but rather in a superfluity of capitals in unexpected places, even at times in the middle of a word:

☐ Yes it does Because Befor I made up my mine to go on to college I went out looking for a job and it was hard the kid that had Been to college had first pick and uncollege got What was left and then most job Ask for a lest 2 year of college and You get pay more then a uncollege. Person Going to College You can take up what you want and went you go out looking for work you are in a better Position then Befor, and not al the time But some time You can Remar What you want and get in not just Be giving What they want you to have and Be UnEleclive you have know other chose. Young People Getting out of hight school should go on to college. I feel It is The Best Thing For All.

☐ In High School I took all of the Commercial courses and I' have been a Secretary working in a Hospital. College puts you ahead of those who have not gotten a College Education. After High School you are on your own; Most of the wanted jobs in the city just requires a high School Diploma; Especially in Hospitals where they are need most. In Some cases, the experience person has more priority then the College person has.

☐ I feel this for a person going to Become a nurses or Engineers it Not Necusarry they can take a short course In 3 mounts or so and they can Began working In today world the one whom go to college get lay-off first. But I feel if you always wanted to come something and you. had to go to college to get it. you might as well go. But College today it Really not need. Because while Riding the trains you see single saiding Earn College Many pay without four year's of college.

Some of these capitalizations suggest attempts at emphasis and some reflect regularized, non-standard styles of punctuation, but most of them seem, rather, to be linked to handwriting habits, to haptical rhythms that move the writer's hand at certain points into capital rather than lower-case forms, without any reference to meaning. In the first passage above, for example, the writer appears to favor the capital B in a number of different situations—with various parts of speech and after various letters. Of the nine words that start with B, only one is lower-case. Three words—*what*, *you*, and *be*—are consistently capitalized. Otherwise, the capitalized words seem to come in clusters, as if after producing one capital, the writer sympathetically shifted into more capitals and then returned to lower case. Students who use capitals in this idiosyncratic way are often not aware that they do it nor that readers find it distracting. Once aware of the habit, they must set about breaking it, mainly through careful proofreading, which eventually affects writing performance itself. Occasionally a student has been taught to capitalize for emphasis or has been influenced by sermon literature or Bible passages that follow seventeenth-century conventions of capitalization. With such a student, it becomes important to explain his "errors" in terms of the older convention and even to give him practice in modernizing the punctuation of earlier writers.

Suggestions for teaching

Codes, once they are mastered, seem simple—even at times universal. Thus people of remote tribes are confounded when outsiders do not speak their language; or Americans tend to increase the volume of their

English sentences in the hope of being understood in a foreign land. English teachers, too, are guilty of such provincialism when they expect quick proficiency from students who are barely acquainted with a code that teachers have taken years to absorb. The "simple" act of marking off sentences or articulating the relationships between sentences, for example, is not as simple as it appears to the person who has mastered that skill. Something about this convention poses difficulties for BW students. Some may see no importance in it, no gain in communication, and therefore no reason for taking note. Many have invested their ingenuity in a private system that must now be revised or even washed away by the demands of the conventional code. And most have been poorly instructed and rarely exercised.

All these possibilities must figure in the teaching of punctuation at this level. Students should be helped to understand, first of all, the need for punctuation, both as a score for intonations, pauses, and other vocal nuances and as a system of marks that help a reader predict grammatical structure. This understanding comes about when the writer is able to view his own work from the reader's perspective. It should not be surprising, however, that BW students, who have generally read very little and who have written only for teachers, have difficulty believing in a real audience. Various strategies can encourage this shift of perspective: exchange readings of student papers, an exposure to unpunctuated passages that students are required to read aloud, audiovisual demonstrations of the way a reader gets derailed by faulty punctuation.[5]

While this introductory work is going on, care should be taken to get the names of the marks straight. Students are sometimes confused about the names of the most common marks, such as the comma and the period. *Colon* and *semicolon* are easily interchanged, and operations such as *capitalizing* or *compounding* or *quotation* could as well come from the stock market as from a lesson on punctuation. It helps, when introducing these terms, to link them with homelier terms (the capital, or big letter; compound sentence, or a double sentence; parentheses, or

5. Because students are not in the habit of noticing punctuation, they may even need eye exercises that train them to pick up these details. Proofreaders, when they begin learning their trade, often suffer eye fatigue, not only from reading much more print than they are accustomed to reading but also from reading in a different way, a way that uses new muscles. The possibility of poor vision should not be discounted either. Many students at this level have undiagnosed health problems that begin to surface under the stress of college work.

the half-moon marks, etc.) or to write them on the board as they are mentioned.

If, through the careful observation of punctuation practice across a range of modes and historical periods, the student can begin to see that punctuation means something to significant numbers of people besides English teachers, that it can make writing easier to read and can even at times add a measure of precision that is not possible or practicable in talk, and if he can be shown, or led to discover for himself, that his punctuation does not take advantage of the code but rather confuses the reader by omissions, inconsistencies, and idiosyncrasies in relation to that code, he may be ready to invest some time in learning to punctuate.

The term *BW student* is an abstraction that can easily get in the way of teaching. Not all BW students have the same problems; not all students with the same problems have them for the same reasons. There are styles to being wrong. This is, perversely, where the individuality of inexperienced writers tends to show up, rather than in the genuine semantic, syntactic, and conceptual options that are available to the experienced writer. It becomes important, then, to do more than list, prescriptively, the ways in which the student breaks with the conventional code of punctuation. Rather, the teacher must try to decipher the individual student's code, examining samples of his writing as a scientist might, searching for patterns or explanations, listening to what the student says about punctuation, and creating situations in the classroom that encourage students to talk openly about what they don't understand. One of the great values of the decentralized classroom where students participate as teachers as well as learners is that it opens up the students' "secret" files of misinformation, confusion, humor, and linguistic insight to an extent that is not often possible in the traditional setting. However committed teachers are to starting from "scratch," they have difficulty deciding where "scratch" is without this kind of help from their students.

The point has already been made that punctuation is a response to sentence structure. It does not initiate forms so much as supply them in the wake of larger choices that affect the way a sentence is shaped. And if this is so, then the study of punctuation ought to be a study of sentence structure, not merely a definition of the marks themselves. To remind a student repeatedly that a period is used at the end of a sentence and then to illustrate this with a few isolated sentences is valueless if he is confused about sentence boundaries. What he needs is a sequence of lessons with accompanying exercises that clarify what is going on in sentences so that the rules of punctuation can be consistently applied. The following outline suggests steps for such a sequence.

I. The concept of a sentence
   A. The sound and look of English sentences, leading to observations on word order and the subject-predicate division in formal sentences
   B. Exercises in sentence recognition for both spoken and written sentences

II. Recognizing subjects and predicates
   A. Expanding kernel sentences
   B. Contracting long sentences (avoid atypical or highly complex sentences; narrative sentences from folk legends or well-formed sentences from student papers work best)
   C. Observations from the above exercises on the ways in which words or phrases get attached to (or embedded in) kernel sentences
      1. Position
         a. single-word adjectives
         b. appositional forms
      2. Suffixes signifying attachment
         a. *-ly*
         b. *-ing*
         c. *-ed*
      3. Embedding words
         a. *wh-* words
         b. *that*
         c. *if, although, whether*, etc.
         d. prepositions

III. Practicing basic types of embedding[6]
   A. Relative clauses (*who, which, that*)
      1. After subject
      2. At end of sentence

6. Relevant punctuation is introduced with each operation, but restrictive–nonrestrictive punctuation need not be mastered at this point.

B. Adverbial clauses (*when, if, because*)
   1. At beginning of sentence
   2. At end of sentence
C. Appositions
   1. After subject
   2. At end of sentence
D. Participial phrases (*-ing, -ed*)
   1. Before subject
   2. At end of sentence
E. Noun clauses
   1. As subjects
   2. As complements
   3. As objects of prepositions

IV. Recognizing fragments
   A. Recognizing and re-writing fragments from student papers (studied individually or with an overhead projector)
   B. Stylistic use of fragments
      1. Analysis of newspaper headlines to distinguish sentences from non-sentences

         Examples
         12 police officers facing cover-up trial
         Dean ends testimony; story unshaken
         Blooming Singapore: A clean, green, and straitlaced island state
         Nixon agrees to stop bombing Cambodia by August 15
         For Allende, 31 months of strife, inflation, crisis—and survival
         Letter of prosecutors and reply
         Jet to race moon's shadow to study the sun's corona
         June prices surged 6% for farm goods
                                    (New York *Times*, June 30, 1973)
      2. Analysis of deliberate fragments by accomplished writers
      3. Writing of a descriptive passage that contains deliberate fragments

V. Linking sentences
   A. Coordinate transformations
      1. Coordinating sentence elements with *and* and *or*
         a. Subjects
         b. Predicates
         c. Complements
         d. Prepositional phrases

        2. Coordinating sentences with *and, but, for, or,* and *so*

   B. The semicolon (see pp. 33–34)

   C. Logical connectives (see pp. 34–35)

VI. Application

   A. Student analysis of his punctuation habits, with examples from his own writing

   B. Preparation of check lists, mnemonic charts, or whatever else seems to serve the student in catching and correcting his own errors

VII. Capitalizing

   A. Basic capitalizing rules arrived at inductively through the study of selected passages

   B. Dictation exercises

   C. Recognition and correction of errors in capitalization (in exercises and in student's own writing)

VIII. Quoting

   A. Dialogue

   B. Direct quotation

   C. Indirect quotation

A sequence of this kind is intended to help a student reason rather than guess about the punctuation difficulties he encounters in his own writing, to understand the nature of an error when one is called to his attention, and to begin incorporating this conceptual knowledge into his habitual performance as a writer. Should it seem too elaborate a preparation for such modest goals, a teacher might do well to remember where twelve years of "simple" explanations left his student.

3
Syntax

Before a practiced writer begins a sentence, he has—or feels that he has—almost an infinite number of ways of saying what he has to say. But with each word he writes down, the field of choices narrows. The sentence seems to take its head and move with increasing predictability in the directions that idiom, syntax, and semantics leave open. The experienced writer responds to these constraints unconsciously, providing the words or structures that different contexts allow. He may have to struggle at times to write himself out of a syntactic or semantic corner of his own creation, but the sense of what he can and cannot do within the limits of the several codes that govern writing is certain. He struggles for aptness and meaning, not merely correctness. Syntax, for him, is largely a concern of style.

BW students at the beginning of their apprenticeship seldom enjoy this kind of ease with formal written sentences. For them, as for the foreign-language student, the question is rarely "How can I make this sentence better?" but "How can I make this sentence right?" Their concern is with the syntax of competence,[1] not of style, for they lack a sure sense of what the written code will allow. Much of this uneasiness,

---

1. I do not use the term *competence* here in the specialized sense of a competence/performance distinction where *competence* refers to what the student knows unconsciously about the underlying rules of the language and *performance* refers to what the student actually says or writes. I am thinking, rather, of competence in the general sense of performing correctly.

for the native speaker at least, can be blamed on the writing process itself, which, because it involves different coordinations from those of speech, creates a code-consciousness that can inhibit the writer from doing what he is in fact able to do in the more spontaneous situation of talk. But it is difficult to explain all his syntactical difficulties as accidents rather than as signs of his unfamiliarity with certain features of the code that governs formal written English.

This unfamiliarity with what might be called the dialect of formal writing leads some writers to affect the style without having mastered it. The result is an unconscious parody of that style, often a grotesque mixture of rudimentary errors, formal jargon, and strained syntax:

☐ . . . a young person could get an increase his knowledge about the world

Note here and in other sentences how the writer nominalizes his real verb in his effort to assume a formal style. As a speaker he would more likely have said, "A young person could learn more about the world."

☐ His ability to cope with people around him will be on a better basis. (He will cope better with other people.)

☐ Most of the more demanding jobs have many people at which their financial status is very low or about average.
(The jobs that are easy to get don't pay much.)

☐ According to this statement which projects there are more jobs available without college, was very obvious to me before enrolling.
(I knew before enrolling that there were more jobs for high-school graduates than for college graduates.)

☐ Although it is true from the information provided that most job opening would pertain to a nonprofessional level.
(. . . most job openings are for non-professionals.)

☐ However, I don't believe that a student whould determine whether or not he will to attend college chiefly on the basis of financial, but that of the importance of obtaining a qualified educational background, and the services he could be to his fellow men.
(A student shouldn't go to college in order to earn more money but to learn more and help others.)

☐ On the point assumed that infants have quality for excepting beauty more intellectual than grownups I fell are really true.

☐ In this ever more confusing world its my opinion that only the basic teaching are truely necessary for the child who will someday inter manhood, because most of his learnings will be done by his teachings and from that lanch [launch] pad we pressure [pursue] his on [own] life liberty and happiness and in doing so put forth his greates efforts.

Other writers, while they attempt no imitation of a mode they have not mastered, exceed the limits of their ability as writers in the effort to articulate a mature or subtle thought. In the following passage, for example, the writer has a complex thought to communicate and he holds on to it throughout the passage. Yet one senses the struggle he is having to articulate through the written medium:

> Not too many people acheve their degree in these fields so therfor you can say that, in a way they are an abundance of jobs for them, though it they are the jobs least demanded by. As in contrast to the Jobs most demanding it is because as I mentioned before if the quality of knowledge obtained and so forth. In comparing the status the persons with degrees in the least job demand would be highly regarded then to that if a person with the form of a job which was most demanding.

Note the difficulties the writer has with the forms for comparison and his consequent reluctance to depart from the wording of the essay question (*jobs in least demand*), which commits him to using these forms (*jobs least demanded by, as in contrast to, degrees in the least job demand, then to that*, etc.). Yet the idea he wants to articulate is both perceptive and complex:

> Not many people get college degrees. Those who do get their degrees have a chance to get the best jobs. Therefore, even though there are relatively few openings for good jobs, the number who qualify for them is also small. You could say, then, that people with degrees have an abundance of jobs to choose from. Furthermore, because the jobs that are easy to get require less knowledge, they also give less status.

In trying to analyze the difficulties that beset a writer of such a passage, a teacher is likely to find the familiar categories for classifying writing problems unsatisfactory. If syntax is understood to be a system for indicating the relationships between words in sentences, then almost any error except perhaps some misspellings reflects in some sense a syntactic problem. A comma splice, for example, misrepresents the grammatical independence of two sentences; a missing inflection creates an ambiguous relationship between a word and some other part of the sentence; even a carelessly omitted word can produce a major syntactic derailment. Yet it is important in helping a student master formal written English to try to classify the kinds of problems he has so that one can design lessons that meet his needs. This chapter is largely an effort to classify the syntactic problems noted in the placement essays of 4,000 BW students who ranked, as writers, in the bottom quarter of their freshman class. Two large categories of error emerged from this analysis: I called one *syntactic errors* and the other *common errors.* The latter category, which is discussed in the following chapter, covered most of the inflectional errors that trouble BW students. The *syntactic errors* were then organized under the following very general headings:

Accidental Errors
Blurred Patterns
Consolidation Errors
      Coordinate Consolidations
      Subordinate Consolidations
      Juxtaposition Consolidations
Inversions

These errors are described and illustrated in the following pages. In the last part of the chapter, I suggest ways that teachers might approach these difficulties with syntax.

Accidental errors

Syntax is generally, and loosely, used by teachers to mean the "big" problems in sentences—problems that keep a sentence from "working" or being understood as opposed to those that keep it from being appropriate to a specific situation (e.g. the double negative, while appropriate in some dialects and colloquial styles, is inappropriate in formal or erudite English). Some of the errors that seem to fit this category of syntax can, however, be quickly remedied by a reader who, upon perceiving that a sentence is not working, makes the needed repairs in his own mind and moves on. Nonetheless, the errors are disrupting, especially when an erroneous form sets up different syntactic constraints from the ones the writer is obeying. The erroneous use of *my* for *by* in the following sentence, for example, creates structural expectations that never develop:

> I feel that my extending their education it will provide with knowledge, so when they have got to make a decision they can think carefully and consider more than one viewpoint.

My leads the reader to expect a gerund subject for the clause "that my extending . . ." whereas the writer intends an adverbial structure, "by extending their education it will . . ."

Here are more errors of the same type:

☐ Life is really hard today so you can imagine what it will ☐ in   (be)
☐
the coming future and for us generation.   (our)

☐ But if they do they would ☐ much more stable be ready to   (be)
face the world.

☐
☐ They you realize that we probably went on to higher educa-   (then)
tion to achieve this position that he has obtained.

☐ Everyone should go to college even if they don't get a degree   (least)
at ☐ they can have a little more education.

☐ Young people should go to college because you ☐ get along   (can't)
in the world unless you have a good education.

☐ No ☐ should never think in turns of only this country.   (one)

☐ I probably feel lost without ☐. I suppose Ill miss ☐ for quiet   (it)
awhile.   (it)

☐ I still ☐ a person coming out of high school who wants to go   (think)
to college should still go . . .

☐ ☐ The majority of these job, one needs professional skills, in   (for)
order to obtain the job.

☐ A child possessing no feeling ☐ hate could be taught to hate   (of)
and have prejudice.

☐
☐ In the eyes on the person without a college degree ☐ is   (of)
wrong.   (this)

While skips and misses of this sort are often dense in BW papers, it is difficult to see a pattern to them. Generally they involve small words; sometimes they involve words that are known to be troublesome to many BW students (*be*, for example, or a modal auxiliary like *must* or *can*). Yet they are the kinds of errors that the writers usually catch themselves once they see them (not an easy skill for a beginning writer, who tends to see what he means rather than what he writes). Thus they are often syntactic errors that reflect a need for more efficient proofreading but not necessarily for lessons in sentence structure. Once again we are reminded that a student's inexperience with the physical act of writing affects not only his handwriting but his facility and efficiency with sentences themselves.

Blurred patterns

One of the difficulties in getting at syntactic problems (and perhaps one of the reasons for the broad use of the term for almost anything that goes wrong in a sentence) is that while some problems can be identified as problems attached to specific words or structures the writer is unaccustomed to using or writing and therefore needs to practice, many others occur in such a wide range of situations that a teacher despairs of taking them up one by one. (The student who is the victim of such an approach generally leaves the course believing that there is no end to the making and correcting of errors.) The problem of word skips and misses is such a problem: the difficulty is not so much in the specific words that get skipped as in the writer's failure to perceive skips on pages he has written; but once he can objectify his own page the errors disappear with dramatic speed since he already has criteria for correctness that he can trust. But where his criteria are not stable, and where there are no useful generalizations to be made that will cover many instances (as there are in areas like subject-verb agreement or pronoun case, which are not matters of idiom but of rules), he must either work on the errors as discrete problems or depend upon a less conscious acquisition of the correct forms through regular exposure to them in talk and reading.

This kind of problem is best illustrated in the following examples of *blurred patterns*, that is, of patterns that erroneously combine features from several patterns, creating a kind of syntactic dissonance:

☐ Statistics show that *on the average person* a high school diploma in a lifetime is worth about one hundred thousand dollars more than a person who has no diploma.
Several forms are blurred here: *on the average, a person . . . ; for the average person*, a high-school . . . Had the writer begun with the first option the form would have delivered to him the right subject for carrying off the comparison, which is not between a high-school diploma and a person, but between a person and a person.

☐ If they [jobs] descrease in a great number *At least I can say* is that I will have a college degree.
Blurred forms:

At least I can say that . . .
The least I can say is . . .

☐ I feel that if I had to go on to college instead of to work as I did I would *be more capable* to simply communicate to my fellow employers . . .
Blurred forms:
more able to communicate
more capable of communicating

☐ If a person feels that *by getting a college degree would* make him a better person although the jobs to fit his education might not be in demand of course it makes sense.
Blurred forms:
If a person feels that getting a college degree would . . .
If a person feels that by getting a college degree he would . . .

☐ I am also inclined to agree with the High School student because *noone makes but you* makes yourself successful.
Blurred forms:
No one but you makes . . .
No one makes yourself successful but you.

☐ By going to college a young person could *get an increase his knowledge* about the world he lived in.
Blurred forms:
could get an increase in . . .
could increase his knowledge

☐ *I do not think that there is anything to worry about* the jobs that are taught by colleagues and are not in demand.
Blurred forms:
I do not think there is anything to worry about.
I do not think a person needs to worry about the jobs that are taught.

☐ *To take speedwriting* you must go to a business school *for*.
Blurred forms:
To take speedwriting you must go to a business school.
You must go to a business school for speedwriting.

☐ You would *be most likely get* a better education.
Blurred forms:
You would most likely get . . .
You would be most likely to get . . .

One cannot assume that all blurred patterns of the kind illustrated above are patterns that the writer does not know or has never produced, especially in speech. Some of the blurs can be blamed, as word skips and misses usually are, on the manual process of writing, that is, on the ease with which the hand moves into familiar albeit unintentional patterns, especially when one pattern contains many of the same words or letters as another. But in other patterns where one form is more familiar than the other (as *at least I can say* is more familiar than *the least I can say*), the problem of interference is more complex and more difficult to get at by direct instruction.

Consolidation errors

Without a better understanding than we now have of the spoken language of the young men and women who are classified as basic writers and of the differences between written and spoken language, we cannot determine with accuracy what the students already know but cannot put into practice because of their stiffness or hesitancy with the medium of writing and what they do not know, or seldom use, and must in some way learn as part of the "dialect" of written formal English. If one is led by the kinds of errors that seem to dominate the writing of BW students, this much at least might be ventured: that while many of their problems with written English are obviously linked to the accidents of transcription in an unfamiliar medium, others seem to be rooted in real differences between spoken and written sentences, differences that are exaggerated when the writer's own speech is non-standard but are there for the standard speaker as well.

The differences arise, mainly, from the degree of consolidation each form of expression allows. Speech is more likely to follow normal word order and to tolerate a high level of redundancy and loose coordination. It is perfected in the dynamics of dialogue, not at the point of utterance. Writing, however, withholds utterance in order to perfect it. And "perfecting" in writing has much to do with the ability to consolidate sentences—that is, to subordinate, syntactically, some elements of an idea or statement to others and to conjoin other elements that are clearly of equal semantic weight.

Thus the attempts of students to consolidate sentences, even though the attempts lead to ungrammaticality, may show a responsiveness to the writing situation that should be encouraged and not checked by a permanent retreat into simple sentences where the subject always comes first and every possibility for subordination is lost. Students often complain about the gap between the "easy" sentences in their workbooks and the complicated ones they encounter in reading or that they generate in their writing, sentences they seem to need in order to express their meaning or pursue their thoughts but sentences that are difficult to manage without more experience with writing.

That the impulse to consolidate often exceeds the ability to do so is apparent in many of the sentences BW students write.[2] Sometimes the writer, in his effort (or hurry) to compress, leaves out a vital part of his statement:

☐ The most disadvantage and disappointment is *knowing and hoping* that somehow the field which one chose does not have an opening after college.

Here the writer intends to speak of two feelings—a feeling of disappointment at discovering that even with a college education there is no job and a feeling of hope that there will be a job. The gerund *knowing* needs to be completed by one clause (that the field does not have an opening); the gerund *hoping* by another (that there will be a job). Thus the consolidation the writer attempts by yoking *knowing* and *hoping* and then attaching them to the same complement cancels out his meaning.

☐ In High School you learn a lot for example Kindergarten which I took up in High School.

If the writer had written a second sentence rather than compressed the two points into one, the meaning would have survived: In high school you learn a lot. For example, I took up the study of kindergarten in high school.

☐ Presently due to the wage freeze and high unemployment, job are hard to find weather college graduate or not.

The omission here of a clause (whether a person is a *college graduate* or not) makes *college graduate* a kind of job.

☐ At this young age, children are always asking question. Depending on the answers the child will get thus creating his bias and prejudices.

Here the writer compresses two participial constructions into service as a sentence. The idea he seems to want to express requires a structure that will allow him, within a single predication, to say that one condition will produce one kind of result and another will produce another. The writer chooses the right structure (*depending on the answers he will get*) but does not carry through with it (*the child will turn out to be prejudiced or tolerant*).

☐ In my opinion the parents have to be more leaniang [lenient] with their children, to be free to express their opinions and thoughts.

The infinitive structure is mistakenly attached to *parents* because of the omission of an adverbial clause after *children* (so that the children can be free . . .).

☐ Although some people don't realize the pressures that are put upon a person when he is in school, then comes out graduating and cannot get a better job.

2. This is not to say, of course, that writers at this level do not also miss many opportunities for consolidation, as we have seen in the *and* and *but* chains illustrated in the preceding chapter.

A dependent clause (*although some people . . . school*) is joined here to the second half of a compound verb (the first half is missing, as is the independent clause). *Although some people don't realize it, pr ?ssures are put upon a person when he is in school. Then he comes out after graduating and cannot get a better job.*

Occasionally the writer simply abandons the task of consolidation, as this writer does in his effort to summarize within one sentence the stages of a child's life:

The main point of this paragraph is to show how a child is so sensitive in his/her first years of life and how life goes along throught the year, after being a child, and what come after. education etc.

At other times he seems to allow subordinate structures to tumble out on the page, obliging the reader to sort them out:

But many colleges have night classes so you could have worked and gone to college also pay for your education although some other programs to help pay on some where you don't pay or some where you don't pay at all so you were lazy.

(A person who wants to go to college but thinks he can't afford it has several choices: he can work and go to school in the evening; get help through some program; go to a free-tuition college. A person who doesn't go to college therefore is lazy, not deprived.)

And sometimes his stylistic stance lands him in syntactic situations that even a more experienced writer would have trouble with. Under the spell of a language he has read but not always understood or listened to and not often used, he begins his sentence with a structure he is not at home with and with formal-sounding words that are less precise than those he has easy access to:

Although it is true from the information provided that most job opening would pertain to a non-professional level, it is not for the amount of jobs that are to be available in the coming years to determine the amount of graduated high school student that should go on for a college degree, but to the individual that is seeking a higher degree of education in a feeld of his own interest.

The writer's choice of the unusual pattern "It is not for X to determine Y" gets him into a complex parallel arrangement that breaks down in the second clause. One suspects, further, that the selection of this pattern was encouraged by the tone of the opening clause with its awkward structure (*it is true from the information provided that . . .*) and its stiff vocabulary (*information provided, pertain to*). With more confidence, the writer might have trusted his real intuitions and headed his sentences more directly toward his meaning:

> True, most job openings will be in non-professional fields. But the number of job openings should not determine who goes on to college. If a person wants an education in a particular field, he should get it.

Coordinate consolidations

Sentences being the infinitely various creations they are, a teacher cannot hope to "cover" all the syntactically disorienting patterns an inexperienced writer might generate as he writes. It is possible, however, to generalize about some of these situations, for they arise frequently in the writing of BW students and are usually fundamental to the skill of consolidating sentences. Where, for example, a person has had little practice in articulating, formally, the relationships between sentences or between the parts of sentences, he is likely to depend in his writing upon a few all-purpose connectors like *and* or *but* or to use other means, such as juxtaposition, to express relationships. We have encountered before, in the chapter on punctuation, the linking *and's* and *but's* which serve to sustain the flow of sentences, even as they flatten the possibilities for subordination:

> You are told "wait" we'll get in touch with you" but by the tone of voice you know you'll never hear from them but after the first time you don't lose hope but when it has happened quite a few times you do. So you say to yourself maybe I should have gone to college but then not many colleges train you for such posts but some do I could have found one.

Coordinating conjunctions can also be used, however, to coordinate smaller units than sentences, and it is here that they serve to consolidate rather than merely link sentences. Thus the two sentences below can be consolidated without any loss of meaning:

> They believe they can become leaders in their field.
> They believe they can get good secure jobs.

> They believe they can become leaders in their field and get good secure jobs.

But this transformation involves the grafting of part of one sentence onto another, an adaptation that results in a syntactic derailment when the writer does not observe the grammatical constraint the *and* places upon his sentence. Thus, for example, he writes:

They believe they can become leaders in their field and a good secure job.

The writer begins the parallel structure with *leaders*, the complement of *become*. In doing so, he is constrained to provide another sentence, another verb, or another animate noun that will fit into the concept of people in general becoming certain kinds of people (*leaders, well-paid professionals*, etc.). His real intention, however, appears to have been to mention two things people think they can *do* once they are educated —become leaders and get secure jobs. Grammatically, in other words, the meaning required a compounding of verbs, not complements.

The problem with symmetrical constructions, of course, is that the boundaries of the symmetry are moveable. *And* can compound almost anything, and only by swift grammatical intuitions does a writer know what kind of boundary he is setting for himself. Even experienced writers find it necessary to scrutinize their sentences for broken parallels, and those special structures, such as *not only . . . but also*, which serve to hold elaborate coordinations, almost always demand a second look. These are balancing acts that, once again, point up the difference between spontaneous speech and the wrought language of the page. No wonder that inexperienced writers have difficulty with them.

Among BW students, parallels are often broken at the point where the verb enters (or ought to enter) a construction:

□ I agree on the fact that a father should share his son's experience and *to help* him when he is in need.

□ Boys and girls should see and hear so that nothing can come as a shock or *be flabbergasted*.

□ People are interested in better thing in just listen to poetry or *reading poetry*.

□ I have found more enjoyment in just *seeing something* I didn't know, than *to just going around* labling everything I seen.

□ No one can go through life *just listeneing to thing and and they never really understanding* what it means.

Lists are also common sites for broken coordination:

□ Good positions are only open to the one that have the ability of a leader, understanding of your fellow workers, and furthermore, *to invent* or to improve the working standards of one's company.

□ Parent positive thinking come when they tell you to get a haircut, a job, *who raise you*, and don't tell you know who the mother.

☐ Also people are taught the beauty of flowers, and animals, and *to listen* for sounds of nature.

☐ Their ages, many things have change. Like for instance clothing styles, hair-do styles and most of all, the way people think, act and present themselves *have changed a great deal.*
Note in the above example that the list which ends one predication interlocks with the next predication and becomes its subject.

That clauses, those familiar heralds of tangled syntax, often break up coordinate structures:

☐ I don't believe that a student should determine whether or not he will to attend college chiefly on the basis of financial, but that of the importance of obtaining a qualified educational background.

☐ I agree with the paragraph because it really gives the right opinions of infants and of their daily thoughts, which goes along inside them, and that it is right for the present to teach them more.

☐ . . . a job where I could meet people and help people and at the same time that something new happen every day.

Not only . . . but also structures usually go awry:

☐ This clearly not only makes it a disadvantage when competing with college students or grad, but also increasing disadvantaged to the student who holds a regular high school diploma.

☐ Students attending college are not only benefiting themselves but it will eventually benefit the community in which they live.

Even more difficult to balance are structures of comparison where elements that are grammatically balanced are semantically unbalanced (that is, where one element has more of the quality or thing than the other). The language provides a number of forms for managing comparisons, but inexperienced writers are not always at ease with them, as the following sentences indicate:

☐ When you do graduate from college with a degree your chances of getting the job you want is increased enormously *than that* of a high school student.
(your chances are increased over those . . .
your chances are better than those of . . .
you have a better chance than a high-school student has of . . .)

☐ In my opinion a employer would more readily accept a college graduate *quicker than* a high school graduate.
Redundant form.

☐ So they may wind up taking the *same* job a non-college graduate.
(same job as a non-college graduate
same job a non-college graduate would take)

☐ Our society is changing *then* it ever has.

☐ The employer wants someone with the most experience and skill *than* of one who just started.

☐ I feel it does make sense for a young person getting out of high school today to go on for a college degree, because where there are *the least demands* that people can follow up on something *that there are more* demands in the fields of experiates.

But difficulties with comparisons lie deeper than idiom. The writer must have in mind a point on which his comparison is based. Then he must show how the elements of his comparison differ in their relationship to that point. If he names the two elements in his comparison first (which might be natural to do since they are both on his mind as subjects), he cannot pursue the comparison easily in that sentence because the verb then serves both members of the comparison. In the following sentence, for example, a writer struggles several times to make the predicate serve his comparison, but each time, he can get it to serve only the second part of that comparison:

First try
> The life that my parents led and the life that I am going to lead *will reflect the opposite of them trying to maintain an image on the block.*

Second try
> The life that my parents led and the life I am going to lead *is the opposit of their struggle.*

Third try
> The life of my parents and the life I am going to lead *will be the opposit of their life styles.*

The writer is in trouble here for at least two reasons: his compound subject prohibits him from doing more than saying that his parents' life and his are different; the past tense in the first restrictive clause (*that my parents led*) and the future progressive tense of the second (*that I am going to lead*) set up a tense disagreement that cannot be resolved in the main verb.

When, however, a writer splits up his comparison, he is likely to lose one member or to introduce a new member that derails the comparison:

☐ I think that the main point of this paragraph is the in-born knowledge of an infant to an adult.

The comparison should be between a child's kind of of knowledge and an adult's kind, but the second member is lost.

☐ Statistics show that on the average person a high school diploma in a lifetime is worth about one hundred thousand dollars more than a person who has no diploma.

The writer intends to compare people with diplomas and people without diplomas, but he compares a high-school diploma with a person.

Subordinate consolidations

Coordination allows a writer to double sentence parts rather than whole sentences. It creates parallel structures which, while they make sentences more compact and simpler to understand, pose delicate problems for the writer, who must maintain the syntactic flow of one sentence as he introduces an element from another. This is especially difficult to do when a writer has written himself into an awkward sentence that makes the task of coordination even more complicated than it need be. (It is indeed hard, as we have already noted, to know just how much of the syntactic difficulty at this and other levels of student writing is rooted *not* in a writer's unfamiliarity with basic syntactic structures but in his attempt to use these structures in the formal register of textbooks and teachers, an attempt that often leads him into a wilderness of syntactic options with but a blurred sense of where he wants to go.)

Like coordination, subordination requires that the writer add parts to his base sentence. These additions, however, serve different purposes—either to qualify some element of the sentence, as an adjective or adverb might do, or to fill in (and fill out) the spots that a noun might occupy as subject, complement, or object of a preposition (appositional structures rarely occur at this stage). These consolidations require several things of the writer. If the dependent unit comes first in the sentence, the writer must suspend the independent unit in his mind while he qualifies it (as with introductory adverbial phrases and clauses). If the dependent unit comes between the subject and predicate of the base sentence (as with a relative clause after the subject), the writer must hold the main subject in his mind while he writes out the subject and predicate of the qualifying clause, and then he must return to the predicate of the base sentence. These operations require a memory for written words and grammatical structures that the inexperienced writer may not have. He hears what he says easily enough, but he does not as easily recall what he has written once his hand has moved on to another part of the sentence, and unlike the experienced writer, he is not in the habit of reviewing what he has written but instead moves headlong, as a speaker might, toward the open line, often forgetting the constraints he has set for himself a few words back. This difficulty with "hearing" what has been written leads to bewildering and grammatically unworkable sentences that belie the writer's skill with the language.

Usually such derailments occur at or near the junctions where subordinate and independent structures intersect. *Introductory adverbial elements*, for example, often cause the writer to lose his subject, or to think that he has already provided one:

☐ Even if a person graduated from high school who is going on to college to obtain a specific position in his career *should first know* how much in demand his possible future job really is.

☐ If he doesn't because the U.S. Labor Department say's their wouldn't be enough jobs opened, *is a waste* to society and a "cop-out" to humanity.

☐ According to the list of jobs, you are basing whether or not to go to college, *is a limited* list.

☐ For those people who do not want an education, but only a job, *should go* on to a training course.

☐ There may be a higher percentage of low paid and unskilled job openings and with young students getting out of high school *feel they* need fast cash they accept these jobs.

☐ Whereas if they continue their education and still get into a field they are not satisfied with *at least* have the advancement to work there a year or so and move on to better positions.

☐ As Dibs was in the beginning of the story *would make* it very hard for me to picture it as being myself.

☐ By doing this *is by* education and with an education your able to choose the job you want.

Ruptured as these sentences are, some of them could be returned to grammaticality simply by the removal of the adverbial term, as the revisions below demonstrate.

Even if a person graduated from high school who is going on to college to obtain a specific position in his career should first know . . .

For those people who do not want an education but only a job should go on a training course.

. . . with young students getting out of high school feel they need fast cash . . .

A few of the sentences, it is true, need more extensive repair, but all of them suggest that for an inexperienced writer the adverbial nuance, carried usually by a small word, tends to be obliterated or dimmed as the writer moves into his sentence. Often he seems to "hear" the subject of his sentence in the adverbial construction and therefore resists supplying another one. This fading of the introductory adverbial element may also explain why the same writers produce so many redundant adverbial structures.

A writer, for example, might use a redundant coordinating conjunction right after an adverbial clause:[3]

☐ *Even though* colleges do not train people for some jobs that are in demand, *but* they train people for other important jobs without which a society would find it difficult to exist.

☐ *Although* the U.S. Labor Department expects about 2.8 million jobs to open up each year during the mid-1970's, *but* the jobs that are going to be in most demand are for the most part, the jobs that colleges train people for.

Often the infinitive phrase that functions as an adverbial structure is reinforced at the end of a sentence by an *if* clause:

But *to become good* in anything I think you just have to work at it *if* you wish to achieve in a certain profession.

Or even more frequently, adverbial clauses pile up within a sentence, creating, if not a derailment, at least a disorienting sensation that the sentence is traveling on several tracks at the same time:

☐ *With the rise in the cost of living in order to get a good education* it will cost much more than it does at the present.

☐ *If this was true* I wouldn't be going to college myself, *if they couldn't train me for the career I wanted.*

3. Another possible explanation is that the writer feels a need for a balance of adverbial signals in both the dependent and independent clauses and therefore perceives the doubling of adverbs as a form of concord rather than as a redundancy.

□ All of the jobs that is kind of important don't have a good rating, like mechanics and repairmen, *when your car or* television break without them you would have to buy a new one *anytime something happens to it.*

□ This is the reason I think that young people should go to college *because you [can't] get along in the world* unless you have a good education *so that you can have a good and better job.*

As these disjunctures and redundancies demonstrate, subordinate structures do not guarantee consolidation. Introductory adverbial elements may as easily crowd out the subject or generate superfluous adverbial modifiers at the other end of a sentence. In other situations, *relative clauses,* which ought to link nouns to their modifiers, may in fact loosen or even derail sentences. And noun clauses pile up in ways that obfuscate rather than clarify sentence structure. *That* clauses are especially troublesome, whether they function as relative clauses or noun clauses. Like the coordinating conjunctions *and* and *but,* they too easily become grammatical fillers that blur rather than sharpen relationships, as these sentences illustrate:

□ Maybe if ones parents would have explained to them, as children that their is a time in everyone's life that you must make your own decisions and not try to get it from the next person, that maybe fewer of us would have been less weaker in trying to go through life in another persons shoulder. I am just proud to say, that I happen to be quite fortunate, that I consider myself one of the stronger humans in this weak world today.

□ If he or she feels that they would prefer going to college to take a course and major in something that has any doubt about whether or not they will be employed in the field that they have chosen then they should.

□ Then again there are more jobs of which I'm sure of that are going down in demand that you can choose of.

□ The US Labor Department show us that the highest number of openings will occur in fields that colleges do not train people for, does not stop my opinion that any person that wants to get a higher education should do so.

A closer look at these proliferations reveals that although *that* is frequently used, it is not accurately or, at times, correctly used. Often it blurs the relationship between clauses:

☐ Maybe if ones parents would have explained to them, as children that their is a time in everyone's life that [when] . . .

☐ I am just proud to say that I happen to be quite fortunate, that [because] . . .

☐ If he or she feels that they would prefer going to college to take a course and major in something that [but] has any doubts about . . .

☐ . . . does not stop my opinion, that any person that [who].

Often it is grammatically inappropriate:

☐ Maybe if ones parents would have explained to them . . . that you must make your own decision and not try to get it from the next person, *that* maybe fewer of us would . . .

Or it is missing where it is grammatically needed, as in this sentence where the opening independent clause must be made into a *that* clause if the verb *does* is to have a subject:

[the fact that] the U.S. Labor Department shows us that the highest number of openings will occur in fields that colleges do not trained people for, does not stop my opinion . . .

To make matters more difficult, inexperienced writers tend to begin their sentences with fillers such as "I think that . . ." or "It is my opinion that . . . ," the very structures that keep them from making a strong start with a real subject.[4] Thus the writer who wants to say that a high school graduate doesn't need a degree entangles himself in a sentence like this:

I think that a person who graduates from High School, is not necessary to get a degree.

Grammatically, he has reduced his central statement to a noun clause that serves as direct object to the filler *I think*, and in the process, he has lost his bearings. It happens often:

☐ In my opinion I believe that you there is no field that cannot be effected some sort of advancement that one maybe need a college degree to make it.

4. Some would argue, however, that inexperienced writers need the *I* to convey a stance or point of view and that these *I thinks* and *I feels* are therefore not necessarily fillers but indices of involvement. I am nonetheless inclined to interpret them as ritual disclaimers that "cover" the writer and preclude any judgment or criticism of what he says. No one else, he seems to be saying, needs to think what *he* thinks.

(A person with a college degree has a better chance for advancement
in any field.)

☐ For example, as it have been stated that secretaries will be one of the
highest opening for the 1970.

(The highest number of openings in the 1970's will be for secretaries.)

☐ This is true in a since to the writter of the article that many of people
today that are being trained on the job or in a special school for these
kind of high paying jobs that was once held by college grads are not
being taken over by high school grads.

(What the writer said is true. High school graduates today get trained
on the job for high paying jobs that were once held by college grads.)

☐ My own opinion about the airlines hiring mechanics, is that I doubt
very much, due to the fact that they'll usually rehire the people they
layed off first.

(The airlines will probably rehire the mechanics they laid off before
they will hire new mechanics.)

Who clauses appear less often than *that* clauses; they are, in fact,
often displaced by them, *that* being an uninflected, and therefore safer,
relativizer. In sentences such as the following (a *who* string with a by
now familiar kind of derailment) we see that the writer feels no constraint about using *who* and *that* interchangeably:

I am a 1968 High School graduate *that* has been in the army and
who has met quite a few people who as I are High School graduates
feel that going to a trade school is much better than going to college.

And here a writer simply transplants a whole formula in the hope,
perhaps, of getting the *who* inflection right:

. . . but someone has to come out in the open and discuss it to whom
it may concern.

But of the *wh-* subordinations, *which* is unquestionably the most
used and misused. Like *that*, it functions as a catch-all subordinator:

It was great to learn Staniflovsky's method *which* I know I just
spelled his name wrong. As Marlon Brando always uses the method
and many other professional actors and actresses. All he talked about
was actors and actresses *which* he wished he was a professional
actor. He loved the theater so all he talked about was actors, actresses
movies, plays. *which* after a while became interesting to me because
that's all he ever knew and I had him for 5 days a week.

The first *which* in the above passage "covers" for the inversion *whose name I know,* which rarely occurs correctly at this stage. The second *which* seems to be "covering" for *because.* The last clause (*I had him for five days a week*) is probably intended to be a second reason for the subject's being interesting (and *because* I had him for five days a week).

But *which,* while serviceable as a subject or direct object in a subordinate clause (*The paper, which comes in the morning . . . , The paper, which I get in the morning*), is often linked with a preposition (the paper *in which* I read the announcement, or *to which* I subscribe, or *for which* I pay, or *from which* I get my ideas, etc.). Largely idioms of the written language, these various forms of *which* are confusing to many inexperienced writers, who are likely to use the form (either with or without a preposition) in settings where no form of *which* will work:

☐ Society has set up certain limits of education *which* every citizen has to meet their standards.
Which is an inverted direct object but the writer has not "heard" it and goes on to provide another direct object (*their standards*).

☐ Most of the more demanding jobs have many people *at which* their financial status is very low or about average.
Whose would work here, of course, but the writer is not likely to be comfortable with it.

☐ It is a thing which gives one self a sense of accomplishment. Especially to the poor *which* I fall in that category.
Here *which* cannot serve as subordinator because the clause that follows will not accept a complement.

☐ And you don't always go out for the odds you go out for the ambition *in which* the field that you want to work in.

☐ I intend to go to college to try to find another field *in which* to take.

☐ I am going to attend City College after graduation taking a course in Industrial Arts *which* after I complete the course I wish to become a professionally trained teacher.

As many of the above examples illustrate, writers tend to bind *which* to prepositions even when *which* alone seems clearly appropriate:

☐ The most disadvantage and disappointment is knowing and hoping that somehow the field *in which* one chose does not have an opening after college.

☐ You know what you want and you can just about demand the price *in which* you think you should receive.

- □ ... but because of public pressure he has to fulfill 4 years of studies *of which* he cannot earn a living by when he leaves college.
- □ The reason comes out, is that they can't find job *in which* they would like to do.
- □ The child will get is education *of which*, I feel, the father will have little to do with in the child's development into an adolescent.
- □ America started with violence and fought and drove the indians off land *in which* was theirs.

Finally, in situations where a preposition is bound to a word (as in *involved in* or *sure of*) and the writer has the option of either leaving the phrase as it is and using *which* or splitting the phrase and placing the preposition before *which*, the writer is likely to take up *both* options, producing an unwanted redundancy:

- □ They felt a person with a college Ed. can handle more easily the problems that arise in the type of work *in which* you are involved *in*.
- □ And there are so many fields *from which to choose from* which a student never really knows.
- □ Then again there are more jobs *of which* I'm sure *of* that are not going down in demand.
- □ The college bound student would like to find out *in which* field he or she would be most interested *in*.

Whether they use the structures effectively or not, writers at this level are clearly pressed by the force of their own thoughts and the dynamics of writing to make use of the devices for consolidation that the language offers them. Some of these devices are uncommon in daily speech because of the many other ways speech has of indicating relationships (tempo, pitch, emphasis, juxtaposition, etc.) and because of the relative speed at which speech must be produced, but they are evoked by the writing situation, by the silence of the composing process, which urges the writer into specificity and coherence because he can't be certain otherwise that his reader will know what he means. Some of the devices seem "unnatural" because they are not used in the writer's mother tongue, which, despite years of school English, may continue to be the language he is "at home" with. Some devices are initiated because the writer is straining to sound formal and in the process gets himself into deeper syntactic waters than he can negotiate without a further development of his memory for written words and structures.

Juxtaposition consolidations

Unlike the elementary-school writers with whom these writers are some-times carelessly compared, the young adult is not content with "Dick and Jane" sentences nor does he characteristically write them. His difficulty appears, rather, to grow out of an imbalance between his mature perceptions and his rudimentary skills in writing. As we have seen, this imbalance leads both to an overuse of some relationship words (*and* and *that,* for example) and to an abortive use of others. Or it can encourage the writer to rely on mere juxtaposition as a way of consolidating his statements. In the following sentence, for example, the writer has modified the noun *job* by the simple expedient of placing his adjectival elements after the noun, a "logical" strategy but not, un-fortunately, a conventional one unless he makes use of certain forms that attach such elements to the sentence:

> Now mostly every job you go to get *worthwhile or making a decent salary something to live off* is asking for a college degree.

A similar problem arises in this sentence, where the writer's thought calls for some kind of appositional structure that will further define "intellectual period." For want of such a structure, he relies on juxta-position alone:

> I think the author tried to show, that dued to the intellectual period in which we live *the need to categorize things in every respect of life* we tend to lose the natral beauty of what is happening around us.

In another kind of juxtaposition, the writer announces his topic, often a rather elaborate one, and then follows this announcement with a sentence that does not seem to be grammatically linked to the topic announcement. With this device, he is able to center the attention of his reader on the real subject of his discourse and then go on to make statements about it. Unfortunately, he often leaves his reader behind him, hunting for a verb:

☐ The jobs that's are listed in the paper, I feel you need a college degree.

☐ Retail buying and merchandizing, there is a tremendous demand.

☐ A young man would like to become a mechanic or a repairman, there is a special training.

☐ A country with 200 million or more mouths to feed and no food to feed them, then people will start to steal, rob, and kill for food to eat.

☐ A sturdy tall trees that stood saluting, the roots came up and it looks as though it standing like a old men with a cane.

☐ The job that my mother has, I know I could never be satisfied with it.

Even more familiar is the topic announcement followed by a reinforcing pronoun which serves as the grammatical subject of the sentence. Here, because the pronoun represents the topic, the confusion for the reader is mild. Furthermore, the pattern is common enough in speech to sound merely inappropriate for formal discourse:

☐ The people *they* go to school to look for a husband.

☐ But as I grew older, those same friends I grew up with *they* despised me.

☐ The boys father *he* has a job and a family to take care of.

We see in this pattern, once again, the tendency to shorten the span between subject and verb by introducing what in formal English is perceived as a redundant subject. In other sentences where adverbial clauses precede the subject, we have seen the tendency to reach into the adverbial clause for the subject of the independent clause. The inexperienced writer, it would appear, does not want to wander too far from his subject, yet the complex structures his thoughts evoke require that he do so. This is particularly true of the subordinate clause, which, except for its subordinating signal, is another sentence and easily entangled with the base, or independent, clause. Yet shorter modifiers such as appositives, verbal phrases, or adjectives are apparently more difficult to produce. In any event, they appear less often. Introductory participial phrases are rare, as are gerund phrases in the subject position. Adjectives more often appear on the right rather than the left of subjects (*the job that is high-paying* rather than *the high-paying job*). Infinitives, when they do not immediately follow a verb or even in some instances when they do, seem to cause many different types of errors. Not infrequently the structure is missing where it is needed (*It is important for young people attend college*) and often it is inflected as if it were a finite verb (see the next chapter for a fuller discussion of these difficulties).

Inversions[5]

As we have seen, the inexperienced adult writer often has difficulty managing the subordinate structures he introduces into his senténces. They obstruct in a variety of ways his progress from subject to verb, posing additional subjects or verbs that must in some way be incorporated into the base sentence without distorting it. We have seen, further, that whether these subordinate structures come before the subject (as with adverbial clauses) or interrupt the progressions from subject to verb (as with relative clauses) or function within the base sentence as subjects or complements (as with noun clauses), they often fracture rather than consolidate a sentence. They add to the number of predications the writer must hold in his mind as he creates his sentence. They pull him, in a sense, from the solo of his base sentence to a complex orchestration of related structures that can easily overpower him grammatically.

There remains another kind of distraction, one that arises not so much because the writer is *adding* to his sentence but because he is *rearranging* it, changing the direction of that habitual flow from subject to verb to complement. Expertly managed, rearrangements of the sentence can gain for the writer a measure of emphasis or variety or grace, but they require a facility with sentence parts and a familiarity with the patterns of inversion that are common in formal writing. The writer, for example, who for good stylistic reasons begins a predication with a direct object is likely to produce it again in its "natural" place:

□ It is my belief that *what you do* you should be praised for *it*.

□ *The things they want you to know* you do not know *this* in high school.

The same type of difficulty often appears where relative pronouns serve as inverted direct objects:

□ I am getting able to discuss many differents points of view in this course *which* I could not do *it* before.

5. Had there been many instances of faultily constructed questions, they would have been discussed in this section. However, neither direct nor indirect questions figured significantly among the syntactic errors found in the placement essays. In part, this may be because the topic and mode did not elicit question forms. A teacher can expect to find some students, however, who, influenced by their own dialects, carry over the inversions of direct questions into indirect questions (*we asked him when would he come home* rather than *when he would come home*).

◻ So in my senior year he finally got a drama course *which* he finally talked me into and many other people from my junior year to take *it* as an elective in my second year.

If he begins with one of the set forms for inverting some part of the sentence, he does not always stay with it:

◻ Not almost all the time when we get out of college we find the job we wish.

The writer of the above sentence has missed the structure *not always do*, which requires a subject-verb inversion. In the sentences below, the writers have difficulty with the unusual *the more the merrier* pattern:

◻ The more education that one gets its better for them the more experience they get.

◻ I feel that the more educated a person is how much faster he'll get a job.

One of the most common inverting devices is the expletive *it is*, which enables a writer to place his subject after the verb. The structure is familiar to the inexperienced writer in such set forms as "It is said that . . ." or "It is believed that . . ." Yet it can also be troublesome. Since the pronoun *it* figures in other types of problems, teachers tend to lump all *it* errors into one group, even when the causes and solutions of those errors may be very different. Something must first be said, therefore, about the other functions of *it*.

Part of the trouble with the word stems from its vagueness. Like other pronouns, *it* refers to something that has already been mentioned, but unlike *he* or *she*, it can refer to any *thing* in the world as well as to some beings (an animal, for example, or even a child when the sex is unknown or of no importance to the context). Beyond this, it can refer to ideas or situations or even to something in the mind of the writer that never quite gets stated on the page. (Certain idiomatic expressions illustrate this vagueness—"It may rain today." "How far is it to Wall Street?" "It's late." "Let him have it.") In analytical writing, where inanimate nouns and abstract terms tend to be more frequent than in talk or written narrative, the word *it*, with its broad range of designata and slight semantic weight, easily becomes a free-floating substitute for thoughts that the writer neglects to articulate and that the reader must usually strain to reach if he can:

1. With all the jobs available, he will have to know more of *it* because there is a great demand for *it*.
   it = the knowledge that is acquired in college
2. Students attenting colleges are not only benefiting themselves but *it* will eventually benefit the community in which they live.
   it = the act of attending college
3. Many people are worried about the problem of racism. But also there are those who pretend *it*.
   it = to be worried

BW students are not the only students who have difficulty mooring *it* to the page. But their writing does reveal another use of *it* (and other pronouns), in a seemingly redundant position after the subject and before the verb:

4. But college today *it* really not need.
5. I think college *it* one of the best thing for your future.

This appears to be part of the familiar topic/comment pattern heard in talk (*My brother, he . . . ; Vivian, she . . .*).

When the distance between subject and predicate increases (as when, for example, a *that* clause or an infinitive construction forms the subject), the writer is often likely to use *it* not simply to re-emphasize or classify his subject but to recapture it:

6. I think this passage is stating that the Reading skills that a high school graduate should have, *it* is below their average.
7. All the knowledge you receive from going to college be it for academic commercial or general use, *it* should be enjoyable.
8. The programs that are available now, *it* enable you to go to school and support a family.

In the examples above, *it* functions as a pronoun, referring back specifically to real subjects:

Sentence 4	college . . . it
Sentence 5	college . . . it
Sentence 6	reading skills . . . it
Sentence 7	knowledge . . . it
Sentence 8	programs . . . it

In each of these sentences, the substitution of some form of the verb *to be* for *it* would solve the problem of redundancy (But college today *is* really not needed). Yet this "simple" change may be resisted by the writer if he perceives that change as a weakening of the link between subject and predicate.

The two problems with *it* that have been touched upon so far are different kinds of problems requiring different strategies. The first (sentences 1, 2, 3) is the problem of a loose or inadequately articulated relationship between pronoun and antecedent; the second (sentences 4, 5, 6, 7, 8) is an apparently redundant relationship between pronoun and antecedent. The first creates a semantic problem—the problem of determining what the pronoun means; the second, a word-order problem—the problem of processing a sentence that produces a duplicate subject: the full subject and a pronominal substitute side by side. Clearly the writer's perception of the copula as weak or redundant increases the error "static" around *it* structures and possibly encourages the introduction of *it* to reinforce the subject in sentences where subjects are long.

The word *it* functions not only as a pronoun, however, referring back to something already mentioned, but as a kind of structural device that points ahead to a subject when it is placed after the verb. In this function, *it* is semantically washed out and serves merely to fill a grammatical slot until the real subject comes along. As a "dummy" or "anticipatory" subject, it combines with a verb—the verb *is*—and enables the writer to place a long subject at the end of a sentence:

☐ To go on to college after finishing high school is important.
It is important to go on to college after high school.
☐ Whether you go to college or not after you have finished high school isn't important.
It isn't important whether you go to college or not after you finish high school.
☐ That you go to college after you finish high school is important.
It is important that you go to college after you finish high school.

Some students get into difficulty with this structure. They may, for example, create a sentence that requires the "dummy" *it* and then not produce it:

☐ It is said that ☐ is important to be able to get jobs in certain fields.
Note the correct use of *it is* at the beginning of the sentence where it appears in a set form.
☐ Many young people today believe ☐ is essential to succeed in this society.
☐ In the eyes of the person without a college degree ☐ is wrong to give them a job.

Or they may, in casting about for a way to attach an extended subject to its predicate, put the expletive structure at the end rather than the beginning of the predication:

> I feel this for a person going to College to Become a nurses or engineers □ it not necessary.

Two operations would be needed to improve this sentence:

1. The deletion of "I feel this," a common filler that commits the writer at the outset to the very kind of syntactic constraint he has difficulty managing in writing, although it is common enough in speech.
2. The introduction of the expletive at the beginning of the sentence and the restoration of the remaining part of the sentence as is: *It is not necessary for a person going to college to become a nurse or engineer.*

The reasons for these difficulties are various. Students whose mother tongues make no use of such a structure as the expletive nor of the copula have a double difficulty in learning it—the *it* carries no semantic weight and the *is* is redundant. The use in Black English Vernacular of *it is* where the formal dialect uses *there is* (*It's not enough food to go around*), while it does not seem to surface at this level in students' writing, may well create ambiguities that inhibit writers from using *it is* in places where it would help smooth out the sentence. For the same reason, sentences beginning with the expletive *there is* are often unsuccessful:

> □ There is always before entering an academic high school you could see what special vocational and technical high school have to offer you.
>
> □ And there can be in some specialize fields they may pay for your living quarters, meals, expenses.
>
> Note that in both sentences the expletive has had no influence on the sentence. In fact, if it were deleted the sentences would be grammatically correct.

The causes and cures of syntactic errors

Young men and women who have spoken years of sentences cannot be said to be ignorant of sentences. What the material in this chapter does suggest, however, is that when academically ill-prepared young adults write, which they rarely do except in an academic situation, they often mismanage complexity. This mismanagement gets explained in different ways. One explanation focuses on what the student has not internalized in the way of *language patterns* characteristic of written English, another on his unfamiliarity with the *composing process*, and another on his *attitude* toward himself within an academic setting. And each of these explanations suggests a pedagogy: the pedagogy that stresses grammar, whether in the abstract or as a set of forms to be generated through practice with sentences, tends to assume that students do not have command of many of the forms required in written English and must therefore learn them through explicit instruction; the pedagogy that stresses process (pre-writing, free writing, composing, re-scanning, proofreading, etc.) tends to minimize the value of grammatical and rhetorical study and assume, rather, that students already "know" the wanted forms but cannot produce them, nor anything resembling their own "voices," until they are encouraged to *behave* as writers; the pedagogy that stresses the therapeutic value of writing and seeks the affective response to whatever is read or discussed tends to see *confidence* as central to the writing act and to dismiss concerns with form or process as incidental to the students' discovery of themselves as individuals with ideas, points of view, and memories that are worth writing about. A teacher should not have to choose from among these pedagogies, for each addresses but one part of the problem.

First, the inexperienced writer is indeed not likely to have command of the language he needs to bring off the consolidations that are called for in writing. If, as we have said, writing presses the writer toward greater explicitness than he would require of himself in speech, and if that explicitness is realized through various types of consolidations—syntactic and semantic—the person who has done little writing may not be able to use some or many of the forms that facilitate consolidation. This inadequacy is reflected in the students' difficulties with vocabulary and sentence structure.

It is difficult to know what proportion of the syntactic difficulties at this level, in fact, arise solely from vocabulary, that is, from the writer's felt need for a particular word or phrase which he doesn't know or hesitates to produce because he is uncertain of its allowable contexts or of its spelling. Without the "right" word, he often cannot collapse sentences or clauses in ways that preserve his meaning and must thus choose a circuitous syntactic route to his meaning. (The person who has not learned the word "dregs," as Moffett notes, must speak of "what is left in the cup after you finish drinking.")[6]

Often the consolidating word is not missing from the writer's vocabulary but is simply less accessible than a clause; the writer, that is, cannot "calculate" with words swiftly enough to make the most efficient choice. The writer who became entangled in

> The government set up certain jobs which don't required much training to place them in it.

might have had an easier time had a suitable adjective such as *semi-skilled* come to mind. (The government set up semi-skilled jobs for them.) Or the writer who wrote

> The employer doesn't want someone who has just started who doesn't have any experience with the job . . .

could have avoided both relative clauses had he thought of *beginner.*

At other times, when the correction of a faulty sentence requires the writer to substitute a new word because the original word cannot be made to shift forms, the writer may not have on tap the word that will get him out of the difficulty. The student who wrote

> I did not like anything about the class. His boring lectures. Those stupid conferences. The homework assignments were always too long. The movies we went to see were out of the Dark Ages.

may have had to break the parallel structure he started because he did not have readily at hand an adjective for *assignments that were too long* (too-long assignments?) or *movies that were out of the Dark Ages* (Dark Ages movies?). With alternatives, the parallel structure might have been sustained:

> His boring lectures. Those stupid conferences. Tedious homework assignments. Outdated movies.

The imprecise *stupid* may also have been a syntactic compromise because the student could not see how his real meaning (that he couldn't get anything out of the conferences because someone else was always waiting to get in, that the professor always seemed cold and indifferent, and that the conferences never resulted in any improvement) could be condensed to *hurried, cold, unproductive* conferences. Similarly, heavily nominalized sentences, those breeders of ungrammaticality, are often

6. James Moffett, *Teaching the Universe of Discourse* (Boston: Houghton Mifflin, 1968).

difficult to turn around because the writer cannot come up with an appropriate verb. If, for example, the student who writes

> The evasion of responsibility on the part of citizens of today . . . will result in the downfall of democratic civilization.

wants to make *civilization* his subject, he will have a hard time proceeding with the sentence unless *collapse* is in his active vocabulary, for he cannot say "our civilization will downfall" or "fall down."[7]

If we extend our meaning of "vocabulary" to include not only the writer's stock of different words but also his agility in shifting word forms to meet the demands of syntax, then vocabulary is an even more pervasive problem than a vocabulary count would suggest. Whether the student does not know the forms (in the sense that he does not habitually produce them in speech) or whether in his concentration on getting all the letters of words down on the page he forgets the grammatical constraints of his sentence and simply writes the form that comes most easily, inappropriate word forms are among the most common errors writers make at this stage:

☐ People are judged by what they *product* on the job.

☐ She tells the *difference* changes that the women has experienced.

☐ It is protecting familyhood of which I am a *strongly belief*.

☐ It is a big *uncertain* at the moment so I would *strong* suggest to go to college.

☐ A person who is more *knowledge* . . .

☐ They work without *supervise*.

☐ It is very smart and *intelligence*.

☐ I believe that college can be a further *rewarding* because we are always seeking knowledge.

Still another kind of syntactic problem arises when the student knows the bare word but has no sense of the kinds of relationships that word is permitted with other words in the sentence. (This way of "not knowing" words is encouraged in most vocabulary books, including the thesaurus, and in subject areas that stress objective tests.) The student who wrote

> The man grew up in a maladjusted environment.

7. I am indebted to Sarah D'Eloia for this and the preceding example. I am also indebted to her for the many fresh and illuminating views of student sentences I have gained from her in our discussions over the years about student writing.

intended to suggest, as he later explained, that it was the environment and not the man himself that had caused the maladjustment. Reasoning thus, the writer had placed the adjective in front of the word he wanted it to modify. He was, in short, observing a rule about the position of adjectives in relation to the words they modify, a rule that would have been applicable had he been writing about a *healthy environment* or a *dangerous environment*. What he hadn't counted on was the semantic constraints of the word itself, which because it denoted a response to an environment was semantically bound to the subject, *man*.

When students run into such difficulties with words, they are likely to be confused or even annoyed by a teacher's correction, viewing it at first as an arbitrary correction or even an abrogation of the rules they have already learned. It becomes important therefore for a teacher to try to explain why a certain word won't work in a particular setting—to ponder over the student's choice, demonstrating its semantic and syntactic limits or contrasting it with other words that do not create the same constraints. Otherwise the student will miss the most important point: that while language itself is far more complex than he had realized, it is still influenced by rules and patterns that can be learned in the way that other rules and patterns were learned—by producing sentences and then correcting them.

Vocabulary, then, impinges upon syntax in at least three situations: a student may not know the word that would enable him to consolidate his sentences; he may not know the grammatically appropriate form of that word for his sentence; or he may not know its allowable contexts. None of these difficulties are likely to disappear quickly in response to explicit instruction. Vocabulary grows slowly, with the accretion of contexts acquired as a result of reading, and, if the student is lucky, of exchanges with his teachers.[8] Word-class distinctions, while they can be worked on profitably in systematic ways, with explanations and drills that heighten the student's awareness of words as units with detachable parts that carry grammatical meaning, are only gradually incorporated into the sentences students write themselves. And finally, the allowable contexts of individual words are usually learned, as so much of language is learned, by making mistakes not by memorizing rules. But unlike the child, who is surrounded by adult speech and able

8. For an illuminating analysis of the use of language for learning, see Douglas Barnes, *Language, the Learner and the School* (Harmondsworth, Eng.: Penguin Books, 1969).

therefore to check his utterances against theirs, the apprentice writer has more need of a teacher who can explain to him why words that seem right to him won't work in particular sentences. These explanations inevitably involve grammatical as well as semantic concepts and are much easier to give if the student has some knowledge of the parts and basic patterns of the sentence. (Whatever its direct influence on writing, a rudimentary grasp of such grammatical concepts as subject, verb, object, indirect object, modifier, etc. is almost indispensable if *one intends to talk* with students about their sentences.)

Sentence structure seems easier to get at than vocabulary, especially since the appearance of transformational sentence-combining exercises of the sort described by Mellon in his work on syntactic fluency and subsequently modified by O'Hare (who achieved similar results without the grammatical terminology that Mellon built into his approach).[9] The acquisition of mature structures merely increases the possibility of a student's making the best choice *consistent with his purpose*. (There is nothing intrinsically immature about a coordination nor mature about an ablative absolute without reference to intended meaning.) If that purpose is lost sight of in the rush to sound mature or academic, the writer is in danger of self-consciously decorating his thoughts rather than developing them.

Still, the writers whose sentences we have considered in this chapter are clearly reaching beyond the simple sentence—attempting, often without success, to articulate through structure and the idioms of relationship such connections as sameness and difference, causality, temporality, condition, importance, or attribute. The practice of consciously transforming sentences from simple to complex structures (and vice versa), of compounding the parts of sentences, of transforming independent clauses into dependent clauses, of collapsing clauses into phrases or words helps the student cope with complexity in much the same way as finger exercises in piano or bar exercises in ballet enable performers to work out specific kinds of coordination that must be virtually habitual before the performer is free to interpret or even execute a total composition. The analogy weakens, of course, when we remember that the writer is not performing someone else's composition, that his performance *is* the composition, and that he cannot therefore

9. John C. Mellon, *Transformational Sentence-Combining*, Research Report #10 (Urbana, Ill.: National Council of Teachers of English, 1969). Frank O'Hare, *Sentence Combining*, Research Report #15 (Urbana, Ill.: NCTE, 1971).

as easily isolate technique from meaning. Indeed, should he try to do so, his technique will also be affected. Nonetheless, sentence-combining offers perhaps the closest thing to finger exercises for the inexperienced writer. Whereas traditional grammar study classifies the parts of the sentence, sentence-combining requires the student to generate complex sentences out of kernel sentences. Thus the student who must create

> The blunt nose of the Hindenburg bobbed up, hung a moment in the air, and then crumpled toward the field.

out of

> The blunt nose of the Hindenburg bobbed up.
> The blunt nose hung a moment in the air.
> Then it crumpled toward the field.

is solving a grammatical problem at a deeper level than the student who is required to identify each member of the compound predicate in that sentence.[10] With some regulation of the kind and amount of transforming a student does, it is possible to help him move toward complexity without losing grammatical control of the sentence. (What the combining exercises often demonstrate, interestingly, is that the student has already internalized the syntactical forms he needs for complex sentences but that he is "all thumbs" when he tries to get them into written form.) Indeed, the process sharpens his sense of the simple sentence as the basic, subterranean form out of which surface complexity arises, and this insight gives him a strategy for untangling any sentence that goes wrong, whether simple or complex.

To revise a sentence a writer must have a way, a place, a strategy for breaking into it, but beginning writers tend to experience their sentences as unmanageable streams of words which, once set in motion, cannot be turned back. Thus injunctions to revise or reword or even proofread passages often produce merely neater copies of the same sentences, not

10. O'Hare, *Sentence Combining*, p. 93. For a collection of sentence-combining exercises, see William Strong, *Sentence Combining: A Composing Book* (New York: Random House, 1973). Frank O'Hare in his workbook *Sentencecraft* (Lexington, Mass.: Ginn and Co., 1975) not only moves systematically through the basic combinations but also incorporates writing assignments with each lesson. For a multi-media approach to sentence-building which concentrates on the transformations BW students are likely to have most difficulty with, see the videotape series The English Modules, written by Sarah D'Eloia, Barbara Gray, Blanche Skurnick, Mina Shaughnessy, and Alice Trillin and produced by the New York Network, an affiliate of the State University of New York, 60 East 42nd Street, New York, N.Y. 10017.

because the student is recalcitrant but because he does not "see" the parts within his sentences that need re-working. He sees no seams nor joints nor points of intersection—only irrevocable wholes.

Here the problem of unfamiliar forms merges with the second pedagogical problem—that *the beginning writer does not know how writers behave.* Unaware of the ways in which writing is different from speaking, he imposes the conditions of speech upon writing. As an extension of speech, writing does, of course, draw heavily upon a writer's competencies as a speaker—his grammatical intuitions, his vocabulary, his strategies for making and ordering statements, etc., but it also demands new competencies, namely the skills of the encoding process (handwriting, spelling, punctuation) and the skill of objectifying a statement, of looking at it, changing it by additions, subtractions, substitutions, or inversions, taking the time to get as close a fit as possible between what he means and what he says on paper. Writers who are not aware of this tend to think that the point in writing is to get everything right the first time and that the need to change things is a mark of the amateur. (Thus a student who saw a manuscript page of Richard Wright's *Native Son,* with all its original deletions and substitutions, concluded that Wright couldn't have been much of a writer if he made all those "mistakes.")

Teachers themselves promote this narrow and inhibiting view of perfection by ignoring all stages of the writing process except the last, where formal correctness becomes important, and by confronting students with models of good writing by well-known writers without ever mentioning the messy process that leads to clarity. The messiness is indeed writing—the record of a remarkable interplay between the writer as creator and the writer as reader. No sooner has the writer written down what he thinks he means than he is asking himself whether he understands what he said. "How do I know what I think," wrote W. H. Auden, "until I see what I say?" This interplay, the distinctive opportunity in writing, has implications for syntax. If a writer is not worried about being wrong, if he sees a chance for repairing and perfecting his copy at a later point before anyone sees it, he will be free to think about what he means and not worry so much about the way he is saying things, a worry that almost inevitably cuts him off from his best grammatical intuitions. Furthermore, by withholding closure on his sentences, he is more likely to work on them and, in the process, begin to be aware of his power to make choices (semantic and organizational) that bring him closer and closer to his intended meaning.

The ability to re-scan and re-work sentences, however, assumes several things: a memory for unheard sentences, an ability to store verbal patterns visually from left to right, as in reading, and beyond this, an ability to suspend closure on those patterns until, through additions, deletions, substitutions, or rearrangements, the words fit the intended meaning. Young adults who may have impressive memories for what they have heard or watched in life or on film may have short memory spans for written sentences simply because they have not read or written enough to develop that kind of memory. Thus a student who remembers Tom Seaver's earned-run averages or O. J. Simpson's rushing averages over the years and can use those data to make informed guesses about trading possibilities or contract negotiations may, nonetheless, forget the subject of his sentence as his eyes and hand move across the line or on to another page. His movement is headlong, like someone making his way through a lush forest that closes behind him as he moves ahead. Any pattern that counters this pitch forward (the adjective in front of the noun instead of after it, in the complement position, the subject postponed by an expletive or an adverbial clause, etc.) is likely to be avoided or mismanaged, and any behavior that turns him back, as re-scanning, rewording, and proofreading do, is against the grain and must be practiced.

Being able to re-scan and re-work sentences also assumes that the writer is conscious of what he wants to say; otherwise he cannot judge how close he has come to saying it. This consciousness (or conviction) of what one means is difficult to describe. It seems to exist at some subterranean level of language—but yet to need words to coax it to the surface, where it is communicable, not only to others but, in a different sense, to the writer himself. Since teachers can read only words, not minds, they cannot judge the "fit" between what a student intends and what he has written. But inexperienced writers also have trouble locating their purposes. Often in fact they think of purpose as what someone else wants of them. Usually they have not been taught to notice their responses to things nor to value these responses as possible content for academic statements. As a result, they are in the habit of discarding what they need most to be able to write—their felt thoughts— and trying instead to approximate the meaning they *think* is expected of them. For them, the problem is not so much finding topics to write on as gaining access habitually to their own responses, their own thoughts, whatever the topic they are writing on. College assignments, and in fact most writing "assignments" in life (except for some self-employed writers), are stipulative. The autonomy of the writer lies in his knowing what he thinks (or perhaps even before that, knowing *that* he thinks), not in his choosing to think on one or two subjects. Without this conviction that he has "something to mean," the writer cannot carry on the kind of conversation with himself that leads to writing. Either he will be blocked from writing or he will allow his words to run on, like an idling engine, disengaged from personal thought or purpose.

To overcome such difficulties, the composition course should be the place where the writer not only writes but experiences in a conscious, orderly way the stages of the composing process itself. English teachers have been trained to look for and at the end product (the completed theme) without questioning the writer's way of composing it (unless, that is, the question of plagiarism arises). But the beginning writer, like any apprentice, is ignorant of process, with the result that he usually perceives writing as a single act, a gamble with words, rather than a deliberate process whereby meaning is crafted, stage by stage. Indeed, beginning writers often blame themselves for having to revise or correct sentences or for taking a long time to get started or even for not being able to start at all—problems only too familiar to the professional writer as well. With some insight into the methods of other writers, they can begin to exploit those halts and hesitations rather than feel embarrassed about them.

The subject of how writers work, where and how they get their ideas, how they nurse them into form—including their idiosyncratic preferences for certain kinds of paper or pens or tables or times of day, as well as the routines they follow for arriving at final copy—such information is important to the beginning writer.[11] It reveals the mess and privacy of the behavior called writing, and beneath that, a sequence of concentrations that seem implicit in the act of writing:

1. Getting the thought—recognizing it, first, and then exploring it

11. The *Paris Review* series Writers at Work is an excellent source of information on the composing habits of a wide range of modern writers. (Viking/ Compass, First Series, 1957, Second Series, 1963, Third Series, 1967.) See also Janet Emig, *The Composing Processes of Twelfth Graders* (Urbana, Ill.: NCTE, 1971) and "The Uses of the Unconscious in Composing," *College Composition and Communication*, April 1964, pp. 1–4.

enough to estimate one's resources (motivational and informational) for writing about it.

2. Getting the thought down—proceeding, that is, into the thick of the idea, holding on to it even as the act of articulation refines and changes it.

3. Readying the written statement for other eyes, a matter of catching whatever in the content or form is likely to deflect the reader's attention from the writer's meaning.

Students usually have difficulties with each of these steps in the composing process. They seldom, as we have mentioned, know what they ought to—or want to—write about. They have not been trained to recognize or respect their own intellectual vibrations, those inner promptings that generally reveal to writers where their best energies lie. More often, their training has been in the opposite direction—to try to understand or catch the sense of what someone else wanted them to do, as if the theme they were to write existed elsewhere in perfect form and their task was to approximate it.

Paradoxically, we tend to discover what we as individuals have to say by talking with others. Here, in the give-and-take of discussion, we see our experiences in larger contexts: what seemed idiosyncratic or unimportant before now illuminates a general truth; what seemed obvious must now be defended; what seemed inexplicable now begins to make sense. Ideas come out of the dialogue we sustain with others and with ourselves. Without these dialogues, thoughts run dry and judgment falters. Even accomplished writers, deep into the sense of their subjects, doubt at moments the worth of what they are saying and wait uneasily to be judged by their readers. The student who has been systematically isolated as a writer both from his own responses as a thinker and speaker and from the resources of others not only needs these other voices but needs to become conscious of his own. Until this happens, he is locked into a linguistically barren situation, forced to say something when he thinks he has nothing to say. No wonder, then, that "getting started" is the most difficult of all the writing problems. No wonder that injunctions to "develop" or "expand" are interpreted as license to "pad." Without strategies for generating real thought, without an audience he cares to write for, the writer must eke out his first sentence by means of redundancy and digression, strategies that inevitably disengage him from his grammatical intuitions as well as his thought.

Precisely because writing is a social act, a kind of synthesis that is reached through the dialectic of discussion, the teaching of writing must often begin with the experience of dialogue and end with the experience of a real audience, not only of teachers but of peers. Yet classrooms in their usual asymmetrical arrangements with the teacher on one side, talking, and the students on the other, listening—or looking at the backs of other students' heads—do not breed discussion. Neither do the counter-classrooms that abandon procedures and objectives under the illusion that freedom is something people simply fall into after authoritarian structures crumble. What is needed is a classroom model that grants teachers the responsibility for content and procedure but at the same time grants students the kind of social independence they need in order to think and speak and write for themselves.

Useful models already exist. M. L. J. Abercrombie, searching for a way of teaching that would stimulate independent thought among science students in England, has developed a model for small-group teaching (and many insights into that method) that is adaptable to the teaching of writing. Kenneth Bruffee, drawing upon Abercrombie's experience and upon the work of others in small-group dynamics, has written persuasively about collaborative learning and has developed a writing workshop at Brooklyn College that uses this method in the training of tutors and tutees.[12] Betty Rizzo, working with students at City College who failed two or even three semesters of conventional remediation, has developed a model for peer teaching in small groups that has had impressive results.[13]

All these approaches share several features. They break the class up or limit the class initially to small groups (six to twelve students) that work on carefully prepared assignments; the assignments generally pose specific problems or assign tasks that students work on individually first and then collaboratively; the teacher plans the assignments and acts as a resource person during the class sessions, sometimes giving information when students ask for it, sometimes entering into the discussion in order to summarize or sharpen the group's awareness of where their discussion is going or of how seemingly contradictory or irrelevant comments are related to the comments of others. The method

12. See M. L. J. Abercrombie, *The Anatomy of Judgment* (New York: Basic Books, 1960) and Kenneth Bruffee, "The Way Out: A Critical Survey of Innovations in College Teaching," *College English*, January, 1970, pp. 457–70.

13. Betty Rizzo, "Student Teaching in English 1," paper delivered at the National Convention of the College English Association, Philadelphia, April 1974.

requires many adjustments for teachers and students, but when skill-fully used can change the dynamics of classroom behavior in remarkably productive ways.

When the writer moves from spoken to written discourse, he faces a formidable task of synthesis. Somehow he must sort and link and refine his thoughts along the lines that serve his individual purpose—a purpose that is itself influenced by the act of articulation. At this point, he needs the help of his teacher or an expert tutor who can serve (as a trusted friend or editor might serve the professional writer) as another pair of eyes and another set of responses. But teachers customarily "correct" papers rather than read them. Whereas the ordinary reader tries to understand what he is reading, the writing teacher, like a lawyer examining a client's document for all possible ambiguities and misin-terpretations, tries to see what keeps the paper from being understood or accepted. Unfortunately he habitually makes this evaluation *after* the student has finished writing his paper, not during the composing process. Like most writers, the student writer reaches closure on what he has written once he has put it into circulation (that is, into the teacher's hands for grading). Some authors resist reading their books once they are in print: the imperfections they may find are no longer in their control, so why suffer. Similarly apprentice writers tend to gloss over the painstaking corrections and suggestions of their teachers be-cause they cannot mobilize themselves to work on something they regard as finished. The teacher may view a theme pedagogically, as a stepping stone to the next theme; the student, however, like most writers, is more likely to regard the work he has just completed as a discrete creation, important for itself but not particularly interesting when viewed in the context of his "works" for the semester.

If the teacher is to act as editor rather than reviewer, he needs to con-fer with the student while his paper is in progress. He needs to remem-ber, too, that his purpose is to recommend or prescribe *in the interest of the student's purpose or intent*, to find out, through questions, through collaborative re-phrasing, through talk, what the purpose is and to be wary of substituting his stylistic preferences for those of his students, riding (and writing) roughshod over the student's meaning in the in-terest of grace or economy or ferreting out errors without commenting upon or even noticing what the writer is getting at, as if thought were merely the means for eliciting grammatical forms.

Finally, when the student has reached the limit of his thoughts, or more likely, his time, he must be able to prepare his written statement for other eyes. Unfortunately, proofreading, the central skill for this stage of the writing process, is one of the "simple" skills students seldom learn. It is important for syntax not only because it enables the writer to correct himself but because it frees him while he is writing from the inhibiting worry about being wrong. But it is a way of reading that must be learned, not merely enjoined or, worse, taken over by the teacher. Seeing things is always a selective activity—a matter of *not* seeing some things in order to see others. In proofreading the reader must be trained to look consciously at what he would normally need to ignore—features of the code itself. In some instances, as with syntax or inflections, he must often re-code the written statement into speech before he can determine whether he has written what he intended; in others, as with punctuation or spelling, he must consciously review the rules that govern those conventions. Many of the errors we have considered in this chapter would never have been produced in speech by the writers, yet the writers missed seeing them on the page. They could not objectify their own product in this way, although they may well have caught similar errors written by their peers. Nor are they likely to learn how to do this so long as teachers keep marking the errors for them rather than training them to see for themselves.

Our concern with process merges easily with the third pedagogical problem—*that the student lacks confidence in himself in academic situations and fears that writing will not only expose but magnify his inadequacies.* Such a feeling is antithetical to the impulse that leads people to write. From its origin, writing has been a way of protecting important facts, events, or creations from the transformations of time and space. It is, above all, an act of confidence, an assertion of the importance of what has gone on inside the writer, an exhibition of his thoughts or experiences. The student who mistrusts his thoughts or cannot locate them is hardly in a position to write about them. And little about the academic situation he is caught in is likely to reduce his self-doubts. Self-doubt may indeed be the lesson he has learned in school.

For what, after all, are the conditions under which the academic writer is expected to perform? They are, as we have said, stipulative—restricted usually to a certain topic and mode and often, as in the essay question, to the point of view that has been promoted in class lectures.

They are for the most part unmotivating conditions—messages that the writer has no impulse to send and that the reader (teacher) probably would not choose to read if he were not being paid to be an examiner. They ignore, in short, the conditions that would ordinarily give rise to writing, and while many students have developed strategies for writing under these conditions, the inexperienced writer is undone by them. Cut off from the impulse to say something, or from the sense that anything he might say is important to anyone else, he is automatically cut off from the grammatical intuitions that would serve him in a truly communicative situation. Thus his real problems with syntax are exacerbated by the conditions under which he must write. Uncertain of what to say, he avoids crisp beginnings with real subjects and starts instead with empty fillers (*it is my opinion that, in this world today, it is believed that*). He avoids active verbs (preferring *make application to* to *apply to* or *which are an interference against* to *which interfere with*) or backs off in other ways, both syntactically and semantically, from his statements:

□ I feel that college education is basically used for men and women to face problems.
(College helps men and women face problems.)
□ I don't believe that a student should determine whether or not to attend college chiefly on the basis of financial but that of the importance of obtaining qualified educational background.
(A student should not go to college to earn more money but to get an education.)
□ By paying directly it is assured that we get better service.
(By paying directly, we get better service.)
□ His ability to cope with people around him will be on a better basis.
(He will cope better with other people.)

Unwittingly, and out of a tentativeness that is not of his making, the inexperienced writer draws upon the same passive constructions, the same circumlocutions and evasions as the bureaucrat, who uses these syntactic strategies deliberately, as a way of blurring or suppressing information.[14] How ironic it would be if so-called "remedial" English

14. "Mull the marvelous language," writes Wilfred Sheed of the Watergate hearings, "not just the familiar examples but the whole cunningly flaccid tone of it: 'I am hopeful that' for 'I hope'; he is 'supportive of,' 'dependent on,' 'cognizant that.' The bureaucratic mind recoils from the active verbs because they fix responsibility. So, too, 'I was wrong' becomes 'my judgment was incorrect.' The petty official abandoning ship becomes passive in every pore, barely breathing: perhaps we'll take him for a passenger" ("The Good Word," *New York Times Book Review*, December 9, 1973).

were to produce no more than a mastery of bureaucratic syntax! Yet without reforming the conditions under which students are expected to write, particularly during the early stages of their apprenticeship, it is difficult to see how they will ever learn—or want to learn—to write well.

We see then that many syntactic difficulties are rooted in the differences between writing and speaking—in the fact that writing serves a different purpose from speech, that it tends to exploit syntactic possibilities in language that speech either need not or cannot exploit, that it demands coordinations of hand and eye that a speaker does not automatically control and that inhibit the production of grammatically sound sentences (even, at times, where relatively simple predications are involved), that it is created through a process that is both more extended and conscious than the process whereby speech is created, and finally, that it removes the writer from the supports of dialogue and puts him on his own in ways that even experienced writers find formidable.

If it is true that many of the difficulties we see at the surface of sentences are caused by the effort to recode speech into writing rather than by an ignorance of common syntactic patterns, then the first objective in the improvement of written syntax ought to be to give the student access in writing to what he already knows as a speaker. This means practice; it means more writing than the student has ever done before. We have as yet no adequate record of the speech repertory of the students whose written language we have been analyzing, but the obvious sophistication of so many of these students as speakers and the general understanding we have from linguists about language acquisition suggest that many of their syntactic problems will disappear simply with more writing. This seems rather obvious, yet the amount of writing required of students not only in English courses but in their other courses as well is, if anything, dwindling, for the very reason that their minimal skills require more work of their teachers. In most colleges, writing instruction is confined to freshman English courses, where students are expected to write about ten essays a semester or, generously, about 500 to 800 words a week. For the apprentice writer, 1,500 to 2,000 words a week is not unrealistic. But even this is not enough. Ways ought to be found to increase students' involvement with writing across the curriculum. This does not mean simply persuading more teachers in other subjects to require term papers but making writing a more integral part of the learning process in all courses. Writing is, after all, a learning tool as well as a way of demonstrating what has been learned. It captures ideas before they are lost in the hubbub of discourse; it encourages precision; it requires, even in the less autonomous work of taking down lecture or reading notes, that the writer make judgments about what is essential, and finally, it lodges information at deeper levels of memory that can be reached by more passive modes of learning. The lecture notes students take, the passages they choose to transcribe from their reading, the jottings they make on their own ideas or observations —these and other *in situ* formulations are also writing, and teachers who regard term papers as barren exercises or who resent any editorial time they must give to them can still build writing into their courses. They can require that students keep efficient class notes or commonplace books or journals and they can encourage in countless ways the habit of writing things down (but not necessarily "up" as finished products).

To further integrate writing into the curriculum, courses can be formally linked so that the academic content of one course can serve the writing course as well, thereby relieving the writing teacher of the task of fabricating writing situations and at the same time encouraging the content teacher to plan more occasions for writing. Speech, reading, and writing courses can be taught collaboratively, thereby increasing the possibility of reinforcement rather than redundancy in language instruction and tripling the amount of time to be spent on language skills in one semester. Or the entire cluster of language skills courses can be linked to one or two content courses, thereby providing a semester's program that coordinates performance with content. Administratively looser arrangements are also possible. Kenneth Bruffee, for example, has developed at Brooklyn College a writing cooperative in which member teachers agree to assign in their freshman classes one or two essays early in the semester, and writing teachers agree to accept and work on these assignments in their courses as well.[15]

Conclusion

The emphasis in this chapter on process and practice rather than on direct grammatical instruction as a way of improving syntax implies that the learners know more about sentences than they can initially

15. See *CADRE, Newsletter of the Freshman Writing Program at Brooklyn College*, Fall 1973.

demonstrate as writers. Yet we have also said that the effort to translate the "inner" speech of thought into written language taxes and ultimately extends the writer's syntactic resourcefulness. Just how and when this happens we do not know. Direct intervention in the form of drills or grammatical explanations may help where a student's ability to handle a specific pattern is in question (patterns of comparison, for example, or certain uses of *which*) or where common operations habitually disorient him (creating parallel structures or spanning introductory dependent clauses). Pattern practice and sentence-combining exercises can increase the frequency of "mature" sentences, if we mean by "maturity" a readiness to produce complex subordinations but not necessarily the ability to make judgments about the appropriateness of those structures in particular settings. One suspects, however, that the greatest gains are made in those moments—or hours—when the writer, in his effort to say what he has in mind, comes to terms with the exasperating literalism of the medium, a literalism imposed by the need to get all the letters of words down on the page, to get words in the right place, to point up relationships between words and between sentences so that the reader can follow the flow of thought, to be sensitive to the neutral possibilities of words so as to avoid the distortions and misunderstandings that occur when readers are led to make the wrong choices of meaning. This is more than exercise; it is a wrestling with Jacob's angel to claim one's meaning within the constraints of a specific situation. Here, to extend considerations of syntax over large numbers of predications, to distinguish between subordinate and coordinate relationships, to ponder over syntactic options is to be engaged in thinking at a level of abstraction and with a degree of deliberation that is certain to affect not only a student's writing but his thinking as well.

It is the business of a writing class to make writing more than an exercise, for only as a writer, rather than as an exerciser, can a student develop the verbal responsiveness to his own thoughts and to the demands of his reader that produces genuinely mature syntax. As we have seen, many non-grammatical conditions and considerations enter into such an achievement—the amount of writing (and reading) students do, the preconceptions they have about good and bad writing, their attitudes toward themselves as writers, their composing habits, and the connections they make with ideas and audiences. These, then, become matters that a teacher of young adults must consider if he would influence in any lasting way the syntax of his students' sentences.

4
Common errors

When a writer breaks the rules of word order that govern the English sentence, he usually disturbs the reader at a deep level, forcing him to re-cast mentally the deviant sentence before he can proceed to the next one. As we saw in the last chapter, however, the source of such ungrammaticality among the student writers we are considering is often located at what might be called the surface of their performance—in their inexperience with writing rather than with the language itself. On the other hand, the grammatically less important errors these students frequently make in their efforts to write formal English, errors that do not seriously impair meaning, are often rooted in language habits and systems that go back to their childhoods and continue, despite years of formal instruction, to influence their performance as adult writers.

These errors, since they usually affect ordinary features of written English, are easy to spot and, for English teachers, almost irresistible to correct. Yet despite the amount of time teachers have spent doing this, the errors cling—often remaining with the writer long after more important difficulties have disappeared. The stubbornness of these problems and the economics of getting rid of them (the cost of the letter s in remedial writing programs, for example, would be worth exploring) raise questions about the nature of the errors and the wisdom of trying to clear them completely from a student's writing before moving on to other things.

They are errors that usually surprise or even alarm a college teacher the first time he sees them in a group of freshman themes, for they differ not simply in frequency but in type from the errors he is prepared to find in freshman writing (i.e., the familiar verb form errors, tense switches across sentences, pronoun case, dangling modifiers, broken parallels, etc.). Indeed, unless the teacher has had some experience teaching English to the foreign-born, it may be some time before it occurs to him that the errors he is encountering, while they may not disturb the sense of a message deeply, seem often to him to cut across the "Englishness" of English, producing deviant forms in spots where the so-called "native" speaker rarely seems to err—in, for example, the inflection of regular verbs (especially those endings involving the letters -s and -ed) and of nouns (both with the plural and possessive forms), the basic verb combinations in tense formation, the use of the article, and even the two-part nature (subject-verb) of predication in formal English.

Linguists, in their studies of the origins and features of Black English Vernacular, have greatly increased our understanding of the sources of such errors among native-born black students. What has not been noted as often, however, is the extent to which errors of this type *also* show up among non-black students who are native Americans with twelve years of schooling but who have grown up under the influence of another language or dialect besides formal English. Here, for example, are passages written by three native-born Americans who had twelve years of school in New York City: the first a Jewish student whose mother tongue was Yiddish, the second an Irish-American student, and the third a Chinese-American student:

> It is my feeling that is worthwhile for a young person to go to college for a degree. College is not only suppose to gave a high paying job, but well arounded education and understanding of the fine thing in the life. For young person to be with its peers, it gaves better understanding people.

> My parent were both born in a small town in Ireland, which far better or worse was untouch by modurn science. This was not a hinderance to any of the mother at that time. They were all experience with the proper knowledge of childbirth. One thing that was very influenced to my life occur the man and woman decided to marry.

Engineer and mechanic are rated fourth and fifth. When they should be rated in first and second because engineers helps to build better machine and car and other thing and mechanics are their to repairs all these new equipment.

Such writers, however different their linguistic backgrounds, are clearly colliding with many of the same stubborn contours of formal English (note in the above example, the common difficulties with -ed and -s) that are also troublesome to students learning English as a second language. At the same time, however, the native-born students differ from the second-language students in significant ways: they have usually experienced little or no success with written English in school, which is often not so of foreign-born students in relation to their native languages; they have not identified the real reasons for their lack of success in writing, having usually perceived themselves (and having been perceived by their teachers as well) as native speakers of English who for some reason use "bad" English; and finally, perhaps most importantly, they have been functioning in English for years, understanding the English of people in their communities and being understood by them in the full range of situations that give rise to speech, and managing, although usually in more restricted or restricting ways, to hold jobs, get diplomas, and talk with a variety of "outsiders." At a disadvantage primarily as writers or readers, such students seem at times to be revealing through their writing grammatical problems with formal English that are no longer even apparent in their classroom speech. One must of course be alert to the possibility that writing, by making the language of the student visible rather than audible, exposes what might otherwise be hidden by phonetic blurring and the tendency of listeners to hear what is not pronounced—the -ed, for example, in *supposed to* or the possessive *s* in *my girl friend's song.*

If the students whose writing we are considering do indeed have this quasi-foreign relationship to the language they are learning to write, the teacher is in the position, first, of having to teach features of English he has seldom had to think about, features whose complexity and irregularity or arbitrariness have been masked by habit, and second, of having to search out the logic of his students' preferences for erroneous forms. Here he will find that much of value can be extrapolated from linguists' studies of the speech of children and younger adults and from contrastive studies of English and relevant source languages. Still, the student from the kind of language background we are describing who has finished high school and become a freshman in college can be expected to have already made many shifts in the direction of standard English, however unsatisfactory his skills might seem to an English teacher, and a list of his difficulties with written English will not usually include all the contrasting features from his first language. Indeed, it may omit some of the most obvious characteristics of the source language: negative concord (as in the double negative of "It won't make no difference"), for example, is not a high-frequency error in the writing of BW students even though it is a common feature in BEV, Spanish, and other European languages represented in the population. A highly stigmatized form, it is apparently replaced much earlier than other dialect forms by the standard form when the student finds himself in a formal speech situation.

It is difficult to know, of course, how many errors, while not directly attributable to first-language interference, are nonetheless an indirect result of the students' uneasiness with or misunderstanding of specific features of the formal code. In at least one study of the dialect mixture among a remedial group of City College freshmen, there was found to be a high correlation between the scores on a test designed to elicit non-standard features and placement in the first level of remediation *even though* these non-standard features did not appear in the students' placement compositions, which were designated "remedial" for other reasons.[1] Either they had learned the standard forms or they had learned to avoid using the non-standard forms in certain situations.

Even after we subtract, however, for the disappearance of certain features of the first language and the masking of others, we are left with a sizable list of erroneous forms that reflect more reason than randomness once we are sensitive to the complex and even ingenious ways in which people acquire second languages or dialects. It is the purpose of this chapter to identify the most common of these errors, suggesting wherever possible the logic behind them, and to recommend ways of helping a student recognize and correct them.

Verbs

Verbs probably create more difficulty for writers at this stage than any other part of the grammatical system. This is not surprising when one

1. Daisy Crystal, "Dialect Mixture and Sorting Out the Concept of Freshman Remediation," *The Florida FL Reporter* (Spring/Fall, 1972).

considers the many ways in which verbs can go wrong in formal English. The most common verb, *to be*, has eight forms, five of them bearing no resemblance to the stem, and one of them (*was, were*) requiring a change of form to indicate number in the past tense, the only such concord in the system. This key verb functions not only as a main verb in many sentences but also as an auxiliary verb in the progressive tense and in passive constructions. Like *to be*, the verb *to do*, which serves not only as an important main verb but as the key word in forming questions with most finite verbs, is formed irregularly. Then there are all the other irregular verbs of English—the oldest verbs of the language —whose "regularities" have been rubbed off by the centuries.

But even the "regularities" can be troublesome to the BW student. The inflections of the "regular" verbs (*-ed, -d, -t*) are easily lost in speech, especially where a speaker's mother tongue has given him no or limited experience with such an inflection. Add to this already bewildering assortment the periphrastic forms required to indicate tense (and the complex interrelationships of tense within and between sentences), and one marvels at even the partial mastery of the formal verb system that students from other language backgrounds demonstrate.

As English teachers know, the irregularities of verbs and the fine discriminations made possible through the tense system pose difficulties for so-called native speakers of standard English. There is probably not a college handbook in print that does not list the parts of the main irregular verbs or attempt, once again, to distinguish between *lie* and *lay*, *rise* and *raise*, or *sit* and *set*, or reiterate the distinctions between tenses and devise exercises for avoiding illogical tense shifts. Such books, however, are less likely to take note of the kinds of verb problems BW students run into in their efforts to master formal English. "Regular verbs," writes the author of one handbook, "give no trouble to anyone." The teacher of BW students needs but one set of themes to discover otherwise.

Problems distinctive to this group arise in three general areas: inflections, periphrasis, and time relationships. These are overlapping areas, yet the operations involved in each of them are different. With inflection, the writer's attention is on the word, usually the end of the word; with phrasal verbs, the writer must concern himself not only with the ends of words but with words that precede the main verb and are themselves often inflected; with time and mood relationships the writer has to make certain that the forms he is using are logically related and semantically appropriate to the statement he is making. Students whose mother tongues either do not have these features or have alternative ways of creating tense distinctions or have the features in some contexts and not in others can be expected to have difficulty remembering them or believing that they are important in getting their meaning across. This is especially true where the unlearned form serves no semantic purpose in standard English—that is, where it is redundant.

The letter -s in the third-person singular present tense is the best example of such a redundancy. Except for the inflections that indicate number in the first and third persons indicative in the present and past tense of *to be*, this letter is the only inflection that survives an older system which distinguished number in all tenses and moods. Uniformly called for with all verbs in the third-person singular present indicative, it would seem to be an easy inflection to remember, despite its anomalous role in the present verb system. Yet the letter -s will simply not stick in the minds or habits of a wide range of students. One can only conclude, when intelligent people have such difficulty mastering a "simple" feature of a language, that the feature is not simple.

Most BW students partially control the -s form, but their use of it is not habitual, and with certain words it can be habitually absent—particularly with words like *makes, finds,* or *expects,* where the two final consonants are both voiced or both voiceless. Thus in the sentence

They do [what] *pleases* them which *make* life great.

the writer has added the -s inflection where there is no consonant cluster but has omitted it where there is.

However, the problem is clearly more than a phonological one for most students, as is often illustrated by the presence of the plural -s for nouns and the absence of the -s for verbs in the same sentence.

- ☐ The boy hear birds. The boy's father want to show other things besides birds. It good that the boy like birds.
- ☐ There is alot of things a baby see diferently from a grownup.
- ☐ The adult feel it is good that the child is taking an interest in nature for future accomplishments.

At least two other reasons for the -s difficulty must be added to the phonological: that the -s serves no purpose, the number of the subject already being indicated by the subject itself or by a limiting adjective; and that the stem form of the verb often appears after a third-person subject in contexts that are difficult for a learner to distinguish from the third-person present indicative. The first reason suggests why students have so little motivation to master the form, and the second reason suggests why they have so much difficulty mastering it even when they try. For while the rule for adding -s to the verb stem is without exception, there are conditions that must exist *before* the rule can be applied—namely, that the subject be a certain person and number and that the predication be in a certain mood and tense. Unless the student can make these abstract discriminations, he is likely to be confused by the many occurrences of the stem form of the verb after third-person-singular subjects, a confusion that is reinforced by the tendency of teachers to stress the third-person-singular condition for the rule but to ignore the fact that the learner often *hears* third-person-singular subjects followed by stem-form verbs. He hears this most commonly in questions that begin with *does*, where the -s form *precedes* the subject and the stem follows the subject:

Does *he want* a course in biology?

A somewhat similar confusion can result from questions that begin with modal verbs or even in statements using modal verbs:

Can *she run* as fast as her brother?
She can *run* faster.

These verbs are in themselves difficult for many students to "fit" into the verb system as it is usually presented to them. The verbs do not carry time-meaning nor do they combine with verbs so as to indicate past time, as other auxiliaries do. They may therefore seem to the student to meet the requirement for present tense of the -s rule. The following student sentence suggests this kind of confusion:

He can *make* up his own mind on what *he want* out of life.

Add to this the probability that *can* in spoken sentences such as "She can run faster" is likely to be unstressed to the point of becoming attached to the subject as a contraction (*shé-cn' rún fástĕr*) and therefore to be perceived as analogous to *she run faster*. There are many other situations in which the student might perceive a third-person-singular subject as being linked to a present-tense verb. In the sentence

She can do everything but smile.

the student is likely to hear a connection between *she* and *smile*. And how is he to explain a contradiction such as the following, where the non-finite nature of the second verb is masked by the absence of the infinitive signal (*to*), making it appear to the student that the stem form is acceptable with a singular third-person subject:

> She makes the student laugh.

Without even considering the semantic complication of having to use -*s* to indicate plurality with nouns and singularity with certain verbs, we begin to see the difficulties this "simple" inflection poses for students who are not in the habit of using it.

The -*ed* inflection raises similar difficulties: it is often redundant (although not always); phonetically it often disappears (as in *walked downtown, he locked the door, used to go*); and it is not highly predictable, being the regular way of indicating past tense or forming a past participle in a verb system that relies heavily on a relatively small number of irregular verbs. In addition, it is required in a variety of grammatical settings—in past, present perfect, and past perfect tenses (*married, has married, had married*); in a variety of passive structures, including finite verb forms (*he is married, he has been married, he will have been married*, etc.) and passive infinitive phrases (*to be married, to have been married*, etc.); in attributive positions in noun phrases (*the married man*); and in both predicative adjunct positions (*The man is married* and *Married, the man now lives in the suburbs*).

For a small number of writers at this level, the -*ed* inflection is rejected in almost every situation:

> When he was finish □ I return □ to find out why my combatants has left me like that. I ask □ them all why and they all had the same answer. Their were scare □. I would has been scare □ myself.

For most writers, however, the -*ed* is more likely to appear in some situations than in others. Although it is a form in flux among these writers, it is stabilized (in writing) in the direction of the standard form wherever the main verb is carrying a simple narrative line. But it is frequently rejected in situations where auxiliary verbs precede the main verb (especially in passive constructions) or where, through passive transformations, the verb has become an adjective:

With perfect tense
> □ There are many students who *have drop* out of high school.

□ I will like to be a person that *have study* more than high school cours.

□ I*'ve experience* it myself.

With passive voice

□ One should not *be force* to go.

□ He *wasn't train* for a job. He *was train* to go on to college.

□ Stenographers soon will *be replace* by speedwriting.

□ The jobs that are going to *be demand* you have only *been train*.

With past participle as adjective

□ It has to be of a strong and *determine* character.

□ They are not *qualify* students for college.

□ He was a *frighten* man.

□ They are looking for college *train* jobs.

In teaching the use of inflections such as -s or -ed, teachers tend to concentrate on those situations where the inflections are required, even though the student is often just as troubled by situations where they are *not* required. The ability to think analogically is central to language-learning, but it can also multiply errors in those situations where the rule has exceptions and the analogy therefore breaks down. Thus a student who has learned that

auxiliary + regular verb stem → -ed
(have)   (walk)   (have walked)

might reason that

can + walk → can walked

or the student who has learned

You study today. You studi*ed* yesterday.

may decide that he should also write

Do you study math every day? Did you studi*ed* math every day?

unless he has learned that certain auxiliaries combine with the stem form—the future and modal auxiliaries (*shall, will, would, could, may, can, must,* etc.). And here spoken English may often blur the distinction, since familiar modal auxiliaries like *could* or *must* frequently contract with *have* in such a way as to slight the *have* and stress the juxtaposition of auxiliary and inflected verb (*must've walked, could've danced*). As the sentences below suggest, however, not all of these erroneous -ed inflections have phonological explanations. Rather, they seem to reflect analogical thinking that simply happens not to work in formal English:

☐ We can always *used* it in another field.

☐ Machines *can* easily *performed* many manual labors.

☐ Children *will listened* to the parents to a certain extend.

☐ If you look sometime at the statistics *you'll decided* not to go to college.

☐ People *would received* the smallest salary.

☐ Quite a few college grads have been out of work because the jobs that they *would liked to* do was not in demand.

☐ A person *shouldn't jeaperdized* his or her changes of starting right.

☐ My mother made him stand by me *should* I *needed* help.

When learners move into uncertain territory, they tend to go by the "rules," even where the rules lead them to produce forms that sound completely wrong. Their intuitions having proved wrong in so many instances, they may even conclude that "sounding wrong" is a sign of being right. Yet without the help of their intuitions they must depend upon rules that rarely if ever cover all the situations they are likely to create in their natural use of the language. Thus one can expect many errors to crop up with those forms that are linguistically too mercurial to be held by work-a-day rules.

The infinitive is such a form. Distinguished by the marker *to* in some instances, it can also appear without it in a variety of situations—with future and modal auxiliaries, with *do* and *did*, with sentences where it is an objective complement (*I watched her go*) or where it follows certain words (*He does nothing but study*). There are, furthermore, situations where it would seem, by analogy, to be appropriate but where it is non-grammatical or where *to* shifts meaning. One can say, for example, that someone *ceased to sing* but not that he *finished to sing*; and *to stop to think* is not analogous to *to start to think*, the first meaning to stop *in order to* think, and the second meaning to begin *the activity of* thinking. In all these situations the infinitive takes the stem or first-person form of the verb (creating, as we have seen, a problem for students who are learning the -*ed* inflections). But it has also acquired in linguistically more recent times a number of expanded tenses in which the main verb *is* inflected (*to be asked, to be asking, to have asked, to have been asked*, etc.).

Thus we have in the infinitive a form that is difficult for a learner to predict—sometimes it appears with *to*; sometimes it does not and when it does not it appears to the student to be inflectable; in some situations it seems to depart from the inflectional rule that governs the use of other auxiliaries; at other times it seems to follow that rule. The following errors reflect the responses of learners to this unpredictability:

Inflection with to

- ☐ The question cannot be generalized *to fited* all people.
- ☐ There was plenty the boy had *to learned* about birds.
- ☐ We sould be taught how *to decided* for ourselves
- ☐ Today our generation, unable *to felt* the monstruosity of the depression years, do not fear tomorrow as much as our parents did.
- ☐ Adults feel its imperative *to explains* things to children.

Erroneous omission of to *with and without inflections*

- ☐ He'll help you *decided* maybe what your objective is.
- ☐ I believe it is important for young people getting out of high school today *attend* college.
- ☐ Music helps *relaxed* us or to stimulate us into dancing.
- ☐ I began *learned* more about myself. I began to feel proud of myself. Note the correct use of infinitive forms as well in the last two examples.

The *-ing* inflection, like the *-ed* inflection, is rarely fully pronounced in ordinary speech (*I'm goin' to town*). Many of the errors with this form may therefore be phonologically rather than grammatically based. The most common error with this inflection, for example, occurs with verbs whose past participles end in *-en* (*given*), a sound very close to, and in some dialects identical with, *-in* (*goin'*). The writer may reason that since the spoken *goin'* becomes *going* in writing, then the spoken *given* becomes *giving*.

Thus we find:

- ☐ This is one responsibility *giving* to you in college.
- ☐ By this I mean you can find a job with a good pay and holidays and vacation *giving* to you.
- ☐ In a sence he is gifted because he has been *giving* the opportunity of nature.
- ☐ The labor Dept. census was *taking* in 1970. This is now 1970, the economy action has *taking* changes in the past year.

Errors in which the *-ing* is omitted or confused with *-ed* suggest, however, a wider confusion about inflection than can be explained by phonology alone:

- ☐ ... with the idea of *become* and experts in it.
- ☐ Every day man is *come* up with new type of materials.
- ☐ By *go* to college I would have a greater chance to be the person I would like to be.
- ☐ Going to college after high school is not like *get* a job.
- ☐ After he has fully *completing* his studies, he will get a job.
- ☐ *Surrounded* the playgrounds were wire fence.

Modal auxiliaries complicate the problem of inflection by *not* combining with inflected forms. Other auxiliaries are troublesome not only because they *do* combine with inflected forms but because they are themselves inflected. Thus *have* is inflected for number in the third person, but students tend to reject *has* for *have*, whether as an auxiliary or a main verb:

- ☐ He is more sure of his work and *have* confidence of performing the work to its top quality.
- ☐ It *have* always been that way that some find it obligatory to interpret something to others.

Have is particularly confusing to students when it is used in a combination of *have* as auxiliary and *have* as a main verb, producing such riddles as *have had* or *had had*. Students who hear but do not habitually use these forms often get them wrong:

- ☐ A college trained person would be picked over a high school student who *has* not *have had* the benefits of college training.
- ☐ The good father in my opinion is justified for his efforts to make sure the little boy knew that the bird had definite names. However, he *might have had* understood the different colors of birds.

The auxiliary *do* creates yet another complication: like the other modals, it combines with a verb stem; *unlike* the other modals, it is itself inflected for number:

Auxiliary	*Main verb*
modal (uninflected) +	verb (stem form) = He might go.
regular auxiliary (inflected) +	verb (inflected) = He has gone.
do (inflected) +	verb (stem form) = He does go.

The student who does not habitually indicate tense through inflection or whose verb-phrase system differs from that of formal English must reason his way through what seems to him a periphrastic maze, and if he is not aware of the difference between *do* and the other auxiliaries, he might quite rationally assume that *do* should be followed by inflected forms:

☐ The highest number of openings will occur in fields that colleges *do not trained* people for.

☐ This opportunity *does* not *happens* every day.

☐ The government set up certain jobs which *don't required* much training.

☐ I don't think it makes sense for a person to go to college for something that *doesn't required* a college degree. If a person does decide to go to college for one of the jobs that *don't required* a degree . . . Note correct as well as incorrect use of *do* in this passage.

Both as an auxiliary and a main verb, *to be* is often wrongly inflected for number (the singular forms *is* and *was* being favored over *are* and *were*). In addition, this verb is often missing in grammatical contexts where formal English requires it, a clear consequence of interference from languages such as Chinese or BEV that permit sentences without verbs. Such omissions occur before predicate nouns and adjectives (*What the sense of going? You very busy on the job*), after filler subjects, or expletives (*It because of the time I live in. A child begin to feel that it true.*), and in verb phrases where *be* is an auxiliary (*As long as this country continues to move in the manner it moving . . . So you enjoying what you doing plus you getting about $150,000 a year*).

Finally, we must add to these difficulties with regular inflections and basic verb phrases a number of irregular verbs whose forms are often erroneously regularized.

☐ My older brothers and sisters *founded* life not very much different.

☐ Now you wish you had *stucked* to your job.

Or mixed:

☐ It should be something you saw once. I didn't go around labling everything I *seen*.

Or ignored in preference to the stem form:

☐ We sometimes have to have things *show* to us.

☐ People have not *make* up their minds.

☐ When they first *build* the park it was a nice new park.

In considering the difficulties students have with the forms of verbs we should not forget that the forms often carry little meaning for writers whose native languages or dialects do not make the same tense distinctions or make them in different ways. The student often works at such forms as he might a mathematical formula, without any attention to semantic context, only to find that he has used a standard form in the wrong place. Student A, for example, in the passage below has not yet learned *how* to form the perfect tenses; Student B has not learned the *context* for the past perfect tense:

Student A
> I feel that if I *had go* on to college instead of to work as I did I would be more capable to simply communicate to my fellow employers in a more open-minded way and maybe they *would have realize* how close-minded they were.

Student B
> Engineering is an old profession. I think that engineers *had done* a great deal for modern man.

The erroneous shifting of tenses, both within and between sentences, appears to be a different order of problem from the tense shifts that are common among more experienced writers who forget (especially in narrative passages) to sustain the tense they start out with. The examples below suggest, rather, a confusion about tense meanings:

☐ When we *are* first born and we *began* to recognize things which we have no knowledge of, it seems very beautiful, but as we *grow* older we *began* to know the difference then problems *begin* to arise.

☐ Then the good father *came* along and *feels* he should share the experience.

☐ I *will like* to be a person who *have study* more than high school.

☐ In the middle of this park *lies* a lake which *was* about three fourth of a mile.

We have been considering common verb errors one by one, noting not only the errors but some of the reasoning that may be behind them. This rather orderly way of looking at errors does not prepare a teacher, however, for the kind of palimpsest he is likely to find in an actual theme, where regular forms intermingle with deviant forms, and a few dialect features that go back to the writer's childhood mix with a scattering of hypercorrections that would strike any speaker of English (including the student himself) as odd. Thus although students may, for example, reject -*ed* in various settings for linguistically logical or understandable reasons, the fact that they do not do so habitually makes their errors appear random or illogical. In the following passage, for example, a number of problems collide:

> I feel that no education *is wasted*. If it is not *use* in the specialty that we *were trained*, we can always *used* it in another *relatived* field.

Here we have evidence that the writer knows how to use the -*ed* in passive phrases (*is wasted, were trained*). The verb *use*, however, often appears in student writing without the -*ed* so that the omission in *is not use* is not surprising. Yet in the same sentence we can find *can always used*, which appears to be a hypercorrection rooted in the mistaken (but common) notion that modal auxiliaries must be followed by the past-tense form. The final error is not an -*ed* error but a vocabulary error, the -*ed* having been added correctly to make a word that doesn't exist.

This sense of a language in flux dominates the writing at this level. The student who in one sentence writes correctly ". . . who at least had 2 years of college" will write in another sentence "You *would had stayed* in school." In one sentence appears a dialect form that is rarely heard even among children followed by a most peculiar hypercorrection that one might never have heard (I don't understand why the child has to see and hear things as *he* father *dids*). Correct and erroneous forms of the same word or phrase will appear in different parts of the same sentence (Money is the only thing that if it is saved *would save* them in case something like the depression *would ever happened*). And not infrequently two forms will appear side by side, as if the writer could not finally make a choice (I think it *do does* make sense to learning as much as you can; I think it *is would be* advisable).[2]

These fluctuations in form are not haphazard, although they may seem to be at first glance. They suggest, rather, that in moving into formal English a learner does not move evenly on all fronts. Sometimes habit will control his choice in the direction of his mother tongue, leading him to use a form that is present in that tongue but absent in formal

2. The appearance of double modal forms, however, may also reflect the influence of a southern dialect, as in *may can do it, might could do it, I used to could,* or *I should ought to do it.*

English (negative concord, for example) or to omit a form that is required in formal English but not in his mother tongue (the *s* inflection, for example). At other times, the need to make choices within some kind of conceptual frame rather than haphazardly will lead him to simplify the grammar in the interest of greater predictability (as with the inflection of the main verb in modal tenses). He will be aided in this not only by his own powers of reasoning but by the simplifications of classroom grammar, which seem often to function for the learner as highway signals too often do for the driver, giving him abundant information where he doesn't need it and then abandoning him at the crossroads.

There is no point in discouraging a learner from making these premature formulations. He will make them anyway, sensing that mastery lies in the direction of generalization rather than memorization. Language, it is true, is too mercurial and rich and centuried to allow for easy predictions, yet the native-born speaker of English has, after all, already absorbed the English language in all its essentials. He is simply stuck at a number of secondary points where habit does not serve him. And here he may need help of various kinds—grammatical explanations, practice, or simply time to absorb those features of the language that resist schematization. More will be said toward the end of the chapter about these strategies. For now it is important to note how often the errors students make with verbs, no matter how peculiar they may sound to a teacher, are the result not of carelessness or irrationality but of *thinking*. Part of the task of helping such students master the formal verb system therefore depends upon being able to trace the line of reasoning that has led to erroneous choices rather than upon unloading on the student's memory an indifferent bulk of information about verbs, only part of which relates to his difficulties. "We done all the conjugations of the verbs for a semester," wrote a student after completing a course that had worked exclusively on abstract grammar, "but I haven't did any writing yet."

Nouns

Nouns are inflected to indicate number and possession, and although there are a number of rules for pluralizing nouns (requiring stem changes with words that end in -*f*, -*fe*, or -*y*, changes of the stem vowel in key words like *woman-women*, Latin and Greek endings for a number of words, and no inflections for others, as with *sheep* or *fish*), they would seem to be easier to master than more complicated number-tense rules that govern verbs. Still many errors occur with nouns, most of them involving the letter *-s*. And once again, the rejection of that letter, this time to mark plurality rather than singularity (as in the verb) or to indicate possession, has both phonological and grammatical explanations which are reinforced by the predominance of the stem form of the noun in standard English.

The sound of the terminal *-s* is easily lost in speech, especially where mother-tongue influence leads the speaker to reject certain sounds because they are too difficult to pronounce (as with *-sts* or *-sks* endings in words like *wrists* or *desks*). In the following passage, for example, the writer applies one rule for pluralizing a noun that requires even a change in the stem form (*laboratories*) and yet omits the *-s* on two words that would be more difficult to pronounce (*-sts* in *scientists*):

> In the depth of the ocean *scientist* will be exploring with underground *laboratories*, *biologist* will be trying to understand our wild life and preserve our natural habitat.

But where this disinclination to pronounce *-s* is reinforced by a different system for indicating plurality or possession (as in Chinese or BEV), the *-s* is even more likely to be rejected. Teachers whose experience has been entirely with standard English forms are often so attuned to the pluralizing force of *-s* that they mistakenly assume that students who do not use the *-s* lack the *concept* of plurality rather than the habit of using a particular form to indicate that plurality. A closer look at their students' writing will generally reveal that the students are in fact using the pluralizing *s* in many contexts but avoiding it in settings where it would seem to the teacher most needed, that is, in phrases where the plurality is made explicit by a quantifier:

□ for at least four year of college   □ in many field

□ 2.8 million job each year   □ these program

□ these two suggestion   □ some year back

Such a pattern suggests that where plurality is indicated in some other way, these writers feel no need for the pluralizing *-s*. Like the third-person *-s* on the verb, it appears to them to be redundant, despite the static its absence in these particular contexts might create for English teachers. Thus this sentence is not as inconsistent in the matter of plural forms as it might appear:

> Your would be wasting your time by going to college for four, five, six *year* when the jobs are in the *fields* that require a minimum training.

For the student who has been corrected often for "missing" -*s*'s without having felt the need for them in the formal system, the habit of using -*s*'s in some places and not in others can appear to be quite random. In some sentences the plural form of a verb, or pronoun, or some other contextual clue may still make the plural marker seem redundant. Thus:

☐ Life is fill of *up* and *down* and it is up to you to make the best of *them*.

☐ When a man starts to question its not for beauty but for the how and why *thing* do what it is *they* do.

☐ Also by going to college you have the opportunity to learn the legal *aspects* of *thing*.

But the reasoning behind other inconsistencies is not clear:

☐ I also think that all *colleges* and *universities* should provide *course* for those *field* that are creating a great many *jobs*.

☐ If we did not have *engineers* we would not have *subways car*, *light* and the *thing* we use in every day life.

Some hypercorrections suggest real confusion about when and where to add the -*s*:

☐ The jobs that are going to be in most *demands* . . .
Despite the familiar expression—*in most demand*—the writer appears to have responded to the plural sense of *most*.

☐ It is a temporary *things*.

Certain irregular plural forms are mixed or missing, particularly the forms for child and woman:

☐ The *childs* do not understand the grownups.

☐ Todays women are confused. She realized her roles as a *women* but also she herself as a *women*.

And finally, it often becomes apparent when a student is asked to read his paper aloud that the plural forms are in fact sometimes present in his spoken English but absent in his writing. Where there are discrepancies between spoken and written forms we might expect the language skill acquired last (i.e., writing) to reflect later stages of the student's spoken language. Yet the reverse situation has been noted among students at much earlier ages. Thus a ten-year-old student who wrote "I like going to school here because there are air-conditioner, squirrel, and crow" supplied the plural -s's when asked to read his passage out loud. When asked to repeat "squirrel" he clearly pronounced the missing -s; yet when asked what the last letter in the word was, he said "l."

Where students have been influenced by a language that has no form comparable to the 's (BEV, for example, depends upon juxtaposition to indicate possession—Mary house; Chinese uses a special word, de, following the word that would have 's in formal English; Spanish indicates possession by de preceding the owner), the resistance to pronouncing the final s is reinforced by a contrasting grammatical pattern. Two types of problems result: the 's is simply ignored in favor of juxtaposition, a pattern which could be seen as analogous to noun compounds such as school bus, child welfare, student activities, etc.:

☐ in today world

☐ over 42% of this nation youths

☐ these people beliefs are of the early middle ages

☐ a parent positive thinking

or the 's is used indiscriminately to mark possession, plurality in the noun, or even singularity in the verb:

☐ I think that grownups are just as creative and cheerful as baby's but one thing a baby's sight's and sounds are or can't be expressed by an older person.

☐ the next ten year's

☐ two college diploma's

☐ because it help's the mass production of this country

☐ Their life were completely different from mine's, that kids my age's think different . . .

The distinction between the plural and singular possessive is peculiar to writing. A speaker cannot indicate, except by context, whether he is talking about the girl's clothes or the girls' clothes. To master this, the writer must be able to distinguish between the stem and plural forms of nouns. Even then, the rule has important exceptions since a number of common words do not form their plurals by adding -s to the stem (*children, men, people,* etc.). The plural form plus apostrophe (*girls'*) rarely appears in writing at this stage, and to the student who perceives the 's as redundant, this even finer distinction between plural and singular possessives must indeed seem fussy. The rule, if it is to be taken up at this point, should be simplified as much as possible and applied in a way that clarifies rather than complicates the problem:

1. Add 's to all singular nouns;
2. Add 's to plural nouns that don't end in -s;
3. Add an apostrophe alone to plural nouns that end in -s.

Word to be marked for possessive	's		Application
girl	X		the girl's house
girls		X	the girls' house
child			
children			
actress			
actresses			
Marvina			
person			
people			
man			
men			
etc.			

When a student omits s regularly as a plural and possessive marker, there is usually no point in repeatedly reminding him to put the s in. Instead, he needs to be on a surer footing with nouns—that is, be able to recognize them first and then understand the rules for marking them. And because abstract definitions of parts of speech are too mercurial for such purposes, the student should have a more dependable way of identifying nouns. Here, word lists of the sort that Fries uses in his discussion of parts of speech are effective.[3] Columns of words belonging to Class 1 (nouns) are listed beside contrasting forms (verbs and adjectives) of the same word. Thus:

Class 1	Class 2	Class 1	Class 3
arrival	arrive	bigness	big
refusal	refuse	activity	active
departure	depart	truth	true
delivery	deliver	idealism	ideal

etc.

By exposure to large numbers of nouns, the student begins to sense what they are. Then if additional tests for nouns can be added—i.e., that they sound "right" with determiners (*the, a/an, my, your, each,* etc.) or with prepositions (*in, on, for,* etc.) in front of them or some form of the verb *be* after them—the *s*-rule for adding the meaning of "more than one" to nouns or for indicating the meaning "possession" or "related to" is easier to apply.

Pronouns

The formal English pronoun system is more complicated than need be for the purpose of communicating. Possession could, for example, be shown by juxtaposition, as it is with some nouns in formal English (*child welfare*) and regularly in BEV (*in they house*). The fact that *his* can serve both for *his house* and *this is his* suggests that there is no need for *yours, ours,* and *theirs* (a pattern that students often extend to *mine*—as in *a habit of mines*). Finally, the existence of some pronouns that do not change form to indicate number (you), gender (they, you), or objective case (it, you) establish that it would be possible in English to determine number, gender, and objective case by context and sentence position alone. Such anomalies and redundancies do not (and need not) swiftly disappear from natural languages simply because they pose difficulties for learners, but teachers who see the gaps and illogicalities in what they are teaching are more likely to respect and understand their students' reasons for being wrong. As should now be clear, being wrong is often synonymous with being linguistically consistent or efficient at those points where the language is not.

Learners who experience forms as redundant or inconsistent are likely

3. Charles Fries, *The Structure of English* (New York: Harcourt, 1952), Chapter 7.

to disregard them at least some of the time. And where this tendency is widespread, cutting across dialects and registers, it usually means that the redundant form is losing ground. For example, the *who-whom* distinction, now in flux even among the well-educated, does not seem to warrant the attention that English teachers often give it, particularly at the basic level of instruction. The absence, however, of other forms, perhaps equally redundant, may cut deep into the average reader's sense of the way things ought to sound in formal English.

Two errors of this order should be noted under pronouns: the use of juxtaposition rather than a special form for indicating possession and the apparent disregard for number and person in matching pronouns with their antecedents. We have already encountered juxtaposition as a way of construing possession with certain noun compounds, and even the regular way of adding *'s* or the apostrophe alone to the noun stem involves but a slight alteration of the noun. Most pronouns, however, change their forms notably in order to indicate possession:

I—my	we—our
he, she—his, hers	they—their

All these forms are known and used by writers at this level; however, students who have been strongly influenced by a language or dialect that shows possession by juxtaposition and who have done little reading or writing will often prefer juxtaposition with *they* to the regular possessive form, *their*, and, very rarely, a student will favor *he* to *his*:

☐ They don't see and hear things the same way as *they* children do.

☐ I may not be saying how I want to follow the footsteps of my parents exactly, but I am showing *they* morality and determination.

☐ . . . a child has to see and hear things as *he* father dids.

The second problem, that of agreement with antecedents, is of course rooted in the nature of the pronoun, which depends upon other words (antecedents) for its meaning and is bound by those words in specific ways—namely by number, person, and gender. But students often resist these structures. In particular, they have a tendency to accept *they* (and *their*) or *he* as all-purpose pronouns that can refer to singular or plural antecedents of both genders. The tendency points up a gap in the pronoun system itself, which recognizes gender in the third-person singular (*he, she*) but ignores it in the plural (*they*), thereby necessitating the use of either *he* or the awkward *he or she* when the antecedent is singular and of unknown gender (as nouns often are in analytical writing—*a person, a student, a teacher,* etc.). Thus some writers will use *they* without a feeling for its plurality or with the feeling that certain words commonly used in abstract discourse, such as *person,* are like collective nouns in that they refer not so much to individuals but to a group of individuals about whom the writer is generalizing:

- ☐ It's really up to the *person, they* would have to think it over.
- ☐ A young *person* in our society is accustomed to whering long hair. Rather than be called square *they* go against the constant nagging of parents.
- ☐ A high school *graduate* today should continue *their* education.
- ☐ The *teacher* really has your career in *there* hands.
- ☐ But if a *person* was to receive a BA this could provide *him or her* with advance knowledge that would prove beneficial to *them* in *their* profession.

Other writers will perceive *he* or *he or she* as plural in certain contexts:

- ☐ More and more *students* would go to college for ... training that might make it easier to get a good job in the field *he* was trained for.
- ☐ They children accept things *they* see without being told *he* should accept it.
- ☐ Many college *dropouts* learn ways to make money just as if *he* had gone to college for four years.
- ☐ Many *students* today may not be sure of *himself.*
- ☐ Today employers are hiring the high school *graduates* to send *him* to a professional trade school.
- ☐ The person would be able to cope with life at a much higher scale than if *he or she* didn't continue *their* education.
- ☐ If *he or she* wishes to go on even though they won't get a job ...
- ☐ *People* should go on to get a college education in the field that *he or she* is best at.

Still others resist the convention of assigning singular forms to indefinite pronouns like *one, anyone, everyone,* or *everybody.* Often, as in the first three sentences, the forms fluctuate between *he* and *they*:

- ☐ It is still important for *someone* to go to college to get a better education and to learn more so that *they* can get a higher pay, When *they* still want to be a salesperson or something else then *he* should quit college and find someplace else where they will train *him* for that particular job.

☐ One can get the job *he* want and have most of the things *they* need.

☐ I think the main point of this paragraph is the natural sense of when one is young, to interpret things *they* see and hear as an art and beauty. When *one* starts *his* education it seems that *they* lose the meaning of hearing and seeing.

☐ If *someone* wants to be an architect, a sociologist or a physicist *they* should not be too optimistic.

☐ *Everyone* is entitled to *their* own opinions of their goals, but I think *one* should be suaded to believe that *they* arent capable of becoming someone important.

Unwanted shifts in person are almost invariably movements from first- or third-person pronouns to the second person, *you.*

☐ A lot of people have been told if *they* want a good job *you* have to stay in school.

☐ The reason *I* came to college is because its the only place where to future your education and have a secure job promising to *you* for the rest of the future *I* might go into.

☐ If *we* came out of our shells we'll fine a lot of interesting things about *yourself.*

These shifts, disorienting to a reader, usually go unnoticed by the writer until someone points them out. Shifts in person are not uncommon among more practiced writers, but they are more likely to occur between passages rather than within sentences. Often such shifts reflect an unstable sense of the writer-audience relationship, with the shift to *you* signifying a more direct sense of audience. Shifts of the kind illustrated above, however, suggest that the *you* that intrudes is the generalized *you* of adages ("You can fool some of the people some of the time . . . ," etc.) and is no more direct than such third-person words as *person, one, he,* or *they.* If so, the writer may well not feel the dissonance of a shift from *they* to *you.* (The *I-we-you* shifts, however, are difficult to explain in this way since they produce an unmistakable shift in person.)

But behind this range of specific errors in pronoun reference lie the common roots of error that we have already touched upon in our discussions of other errors. There is, first, the natural linguistic impulse to reduce complexity without impairing communication. And for the student whose criteria for redundancy may be drawn from a different language or vernacular, this may result in the omission or simplification of forms (e.g., the omission of the possessive pronoun or the copula or the interchanging of certain conjunctions or pronouns) that, while they may be grammatically redundant, are deep in the grain of formal English. Second, there is the perceptual problem of remembering what has been written in sentences so that no vital part of a sentence is omitted and the sentence itself can be laced together by the various agreements of number, tense, person, and gender. And third, there is the nature of the analytical mode, which pushes writers out of reportage (description and narrative), where experience grounds their generalizations, into vaguer statements about a *person* or *they* or *one*, which are more difficult to control, or even care about.

Instruction in pronouns for such students must go beyond the conventional kind of lesson in which the three persons are identified as *I*—the person talking, *you*—the person I talk to, and *he, she,* or *it*—the person being talked about. Since the third person gives the most difficulty and is, furthermore, the most confusing with its irregular treatment of gender (*he, she* in the singular, *they* in the plural), it makes sense to begin with the third-person pronouns, giving special lessons on the correct use of that family of generalized pronouns so commonly used in abstract discourse (*he, one, everyone,* etc.). For students who favor juxtaposition to a possessive pronoun, the basis of the preference should be explained and the student given many opportunities to work contrastively with both forms. Finally, the grammatical principle of concord or agreement must be graphically demonstrated so as to heighten the student's awareness of the grammatical web he spins as he moves from left to right across the page. This can be done simply by having the student for a time circle each pronoun he uses and draw a line to its antecedent, or more elaborately by audio-visual demonstrations.

Subject-verb agreement

The filament that links subjects to predicates in formal English is number, and while it could be (and is) argued that word order and context suffice to give any native reader or listener a sense of the relation between subject and predicate, readers continue to be distracted by errors in subject-verb agreement. Clearly redundancy is no reason for a reader's dismissing errors, even though it is often good reason for a writer's making them.

Writers who by habit ignore the -s inflection, whether with the noun or the verb, or who use that inflection erratically without an under-standing of the inflectional system in formal English, will inevitably make more errors in agreement than the general writer, whose main problems with agreement arise when subjects get separated from predicates by intervening phrases or clauses or when certain refinements of agreement have not been mastered (e.g., *everyone is, one of those people who are, criteria are, either my brother or his friends are*).

The agreement difficulties of the students we are describing begin at an earlier point, with the entire convention of matching up subjects and predicates by means, largely, of one shifting letter (-s) which they tend not to perceive as important. Thus even in sentences where an error appears to be caused by the writer's unfamiliarity with a secondary rule of agreement, one is never certain. In this sentence, for example,

> Take a stenographer or a secretary that don't need to go on to college . . .

the erroneous use of *don't* could be explained by the student's ignorance of the rule for counting compound subjects that are joined by *or* rather than *and*. More likely, however, the writer has perceived the singularity of a secretary *or* a stenographer but accepts *don't* for both plural and singular forms, as the writers of the following sentences have done:

☐ Sometime I say to myself that it really *don't* matter whether you go to college or not.

☐ I think that a person that *don't* go to college, *don't* have the opportunity to have a better life.

☐ More education *don't* hurt anybody.

☐ A person who is more knowledge or had some degree of higher education sometimes *don't* make it.

Similarly, in sentences that begin with *there is*, the writer may, like most other writers who get into difficulty with this pattern, simply fail to anticipate the number of his subject and slip into *there is* without thinking. But there is also a good chance that the writer we are describing would not change his verbs in the following sentences, even if the sentences were reversed:

☐ It is believed that there *is* other *forms* of life.

☐ There *is* only 97,000 *openings* per year.

☐ For every one job there *is* about five *people* going for it.

Not only is *there are* more difficult to produce in speech than *there is* but students report that *are* seems "stiff" and "distant" to them. They tend to avoid it in other situations as well.

☐ Most of the *jobs* that will be existing *is* for stenographers and secretaries.

☐ The *ads* one sees in a newspaper *is* asking for someone who's in college.

Have is another verb that cuts across distinctions of number:

☐ My father *have* four brother and three sisters. My mother *have* seven brothers.

☐ As it *have* been stated . . .

☐ The need for college in certain fields *have* drop.

And finally, we have the overriding aversion to -*s* with regular verbs, which produces many agreement errors:

☐ Thats why this *person need* to get a degree.

☐ Once *he get* into college he will get to the heart of these fields.

☐ It also depend on the person what *he want* to do when he get out of high school.

☐ Every day *man progress* a little more.

☐ The *future belong* to the well-trained and educated.

All these errors—the preference for certain plural forms like *don't* and *have* with plural and singular subjects, the preference for *is* where *are* is required, the rejection of -*s*, sometimes with plural subjects and more often with singular verbs, and the unpredictable hypercorrections that arise from a writer's efforts to conform to a system he is not clear about—come under the heading of subject-verb agreement errors. Not infrequently, many of them pile up in one sentence or a short passage:

A college degree *help* [1] one attain more than just a degree but *broadens* [2] their outlook on life. *Student* [3] then become more confident in *themselves* [4] and the field they have chosen.

1. incorrect omission of -*s* (verb)

2. correct use of -s (verb)
3. incorrect omission of -s (noun)
4. correct use of -s (pronoun)

> Take a student who *want* [1] to become a mechanic, can't he take some course that *intrest* [2] him besides machines or cars. School *are* [3] the best years of your life ... A student goes back to school to get the material he or she *needs* [4] to advance to the position they *wants* [5] which *mean* [6] more jobs have to be produced.

1,2,6. incorrect omission of -s (verb)
    3. hypercorrection with *are*
    4. correct use of -s on verb
    5. hypercorrection with -s on plural verb

Such passages reveal more confusion than a teacher's marginal notation (the familiar "Agr.!") is likely to dispel. If the agreement errors are to be taken up at all at this point, the approach must be basic. The student must first learn what the word *agreement* means in grammatical talk, for otherwise he will have but a vague sense of its application to subjects and verbs. The word *number* must itself be explained, since the student does not automatically translate the word into *one* or *more than one*. The student must be able to recognize subjects and be able to separate the nucleus of a subject phrase from its surrounding modifiers. He must know the intricacies of counting subjects and then of identifying verbs and knowing their singular and plural forms. He must have, in short, something approaching a short course in grammar if he is to move with certainty into the territory of agreement with the modest goal of being able to correct during proofreading the agreement errors he makes while writing.

Limits to correctness

When agreement errors merge with other common errors of the sort we have been discussing in this chapter, the question arises in the minds of most teachers of just how, when, and even whether error of this magnitude can be brought under control. Here, in this short but full orchestration of error, the conscientious teacher stops to ask (if only himself) whether anything he can do will make much difference:

> The majority of the student [1] *alway* [2] major in some kinds of field [3] that will help them in the near future. Some of them end up working

in factory [4] because of their education. Sometime [5] I say to myself that it really don't [6] matter whether you go to college or not because people with college degree [7] can't even get a good job. Some countrie [8] or manufacture [9] will not hired [10] them because they feel that they will only work for two month [11] and then leaves [12] and they [13] company maybe just lost money.

Of the eighty-nine words in this passage, thirteen (14.6 per cent) are wrong. This is a discouraging number of erroneous forms. Yet a closer look reveals that ten of these errors reflect difficulties with the one letter *s* (1, 2, 3, 4, 5, 7, 8, 9, 11, 12). Two are common verb-form errors (6, 10), at least one of which the student could easily learn to correct (*will not hired*). And the final error (13) is the use of juxtaposition to indicate possession. In other words, three basic problems are reflected in this passage, all of them common to large numbers of writers who err not for want of intelligence or care but because of opposing language habits and analogical thinking. The student who learned to make these errors reveals, through them, all the linguistic sophistication he needs to correct them. The issue is not his capacity to master the unfamiliar forms of formal English but 1. the priority this kind of problem ought to have in the larger scheme of learning to write and 2. the willingness of the student to concentrate his energies on the goal of writing formal English.

Correctness and writing progress
On the first issue, the relationship of grammaticality to improvement in writing, there is much disagreement. Some would insist that if error becomes a subject for instruction it will quickly loom in the writer's consciousness as a central problem in writing, whereas writing is about much more than that. Furthermore, such a concentration is believed to impede the writer's development, even in relation to the reduction of error, producing highly self-conscious and hypercorrected writing that moves him even further from his resources as a native speaker of English. Others would insist that the student cannot be released into the written language until he is more certain of the code, that in fact the mastery of a common code precedes the development of an individual "voice." Furthermore, they would argue that whether his teacher concentrates on form or not, the student knows that things don't come out right for him when he writes and that more often than not he is likely to write something that, for reasons he cannot understand, will

be considered wrong and will put him at a disadvantage with his reader. Subject to the whims of language and English teachers and stocked with an assortment of grammatical superstitions and rules of thumb that have filtered through to him in the course of twelve years of schooling, he needs more than anything to get his grammatical bearings so that he can reason rather than hazard his way through his difficulties.

As yet we lack developmental models for the maturation of writing skills among young, native-speaking adults and can only theorize about the adaptability of other models for these students (Piaget's model for the acquisition of language among children, for example, or the models that have been developed in second-language teaching), who until recently have been written off as learners of the eleventh hour whose appearance on the developmental continuum has been judged too late to make much difference. Lacking a model, we cannot say with certainty just what progress in writing ought to look like for BW students, and more particularly how the elimination of error is related to their over-all improvement. Meanwhile, teachers, trained usually to evaluate writing by absolute rather than developmental standards, rarely ask how realistic it is to concentrate on certain errors during the early stages of writing instruction. Taking all errors to be the province of remedial English, they doom their students and themselves to a sense of failure when they garner but a limited crop of correct forms by the end of a semester. And how are they to interpret the phenomenon of *increased* error at the end of a semester of writing except as a sign of ineducability, even though it is not unusual for people acquiring a skill to get "worse" before they get better and for writers to err more as they venture more?

This absolute standard of correctness that has come to be associated with English teachers often precludes their asking another important question—not only how realistic it is to expect beginning writers to learn what many English teachers want them to learn in the time allotted to them for writing (usually no more than four contact hours a week) but how many readers are likely to have the same sensitivity to error as English teachers have. While we must dismiss as irresponsibly romantic the view that error is not important at all and that readers can "catch the meaning" in error-laden writing if they try, we should also be wary of any view that results in setting tasks for beginning writers that few besides English teachers would consider important. In short, a teacher must ask not only what *he* wants but what the student is most ready to do and what, from a reader's viewpoint, is most important. Here it becomes difficult to make absolute statements. Adept as teachers may be at noting how far students fall short of a standard called "good writing" (even here there is wide disagreement), this is not the same as tracing the path that leads to such writing; we know that errors carry messages but we can make only rough guesses about the importance and nature of these messages. But within the limits created by our ignorance and the complexity of the writing situation, we must develop a fresh perspective on error. Teachers must do something on Monday morning, and this reality forces them either to do what *their* teachers did on Monday morning or to invent English composition anew out of their understanding of the craft and their observations of students learning to write. The two propositions on error that follow come largely out of the effort to follow the second alternative:

1. *Errors count but not as much as most English teachers think.* For many reasons, English teachers are inclined to exaggerate the seriousness of error. Since the birth of the composition course in American education, the English teacher has been viewed as the custodian of "refined" usage. It has been his, more often her, responsibility to press upon a linguistic culture of kaleidoscopic variety a model of good English that would not only improve communication but communicate social and educational distinctions that the society deemed significant. But distinctions of the latter sort are usually made in linguistically unimportant ways—that is, they involve changes that would not in themselves impair communication. Like the pronunciation of *shibboleth* (or the proper use of *who/whom*), they hinge upon subtle differences that do not seem in themselves important. Yet the consequences of ignoring these distinctions have seemed serious in a country as socially mobile as this society has until recently imagined itself to be.

This emphasis upon propriety in the interest not of communication but of status has narrowed and debased the teaching of writing, encouraging at least two tendencies in teachers—a tendency to view the work of their students microscopically, with an eye for forms but with little interest in what was being said, and a tendency to develop a repugnance for error that has made erring students feel like pariahs and allowed teachers of mediocre talent too many easy victories. The fact that graduate schools, aware that their students would spend a good part of their professional lives teaching freshman English, made no effort to train students to teach writing (or to write themselves) only guaranteed that English teachers would be the last to see the limitations of the prescriptive approach to writing.

Many influences have combined, however, to expose these limitations. A revolution in social awareness has increased our interest in and respect for linguistic variety. A deeper, and more cynical, understanding of success in America has reduced our confidence in "good" English as a key to advancement. A strong egalitarian thrust within higher education has not only brought a new kind of student into the four-year college but has caused the community colleges to flourish throughout the country, and wherever the new students have arrived in substantial numbers English teachers have begun to realize that little in their background has prepared them to teach writing to someone who has not already learned how to do it. Confident in the past that students who could not master certain "simple" features of English usage were probably not "bright" enough (a much-used term) to stay in college, they now begin to wonder, when large numbers of intelligent young men and women fail to learn a simple lesson, whether the lesson is indeed so simple. And once having asked this fruitful question their own revolution as teachers of English usually begins. It is a revolution that leads not inevitably or finally to a rejection of all rules and standards, which would be to deny the very point that is finally being made about language, namely that it is variously shaped by situations and bound by conventions, none of which is inferior to the others but none of which, also, can substitute for the others. But it does produce a different view of error and of the students who make errors. That view might be compared to the view a teacher is more likely to have toward a foreign student learning English: his errors reflect upon his linguistic situation, not upon his educability; he is granted by his teacher the capability of mastering English but is expected in the course of doing so to make errors in English; and certain errors, characteristic errors for natives of his language who are acquiring English as a second language, are tolerated far into and even beyond the period of formal instruction simply because they must be rubbed off by time.

Often, English teachers with the backgrounds I have described have difficulty making this kind of adjustment to error, but teachers in other disciplines are generally more intent upon getting at the heart of what a student is saying and therefore deliberately edit out errors as they read.

Indeed, so complete is the indifference of some teachers to form that their attitude seems irresponsible rather than tolerant. ("I just want to find out what they learned," goes the disclaimer. "I'm not an English teacher.")

Someplace between the rigid prescriptions of the unregenerated English teacher and the loose permissions of the uninterested professor lies a territory of tolerable error. The territory is not well or easily mapped but its borders can be guessed at.[4] In an essay of 300 words an average academic reader is likely to tolerate between five and six basic errors of the kind we have been describing in this chapter before committing a writer to a semester of work on errors (a beginning BW student makes between ten and thirty). He will tolerate far more spelling and punctuation errors, provided they are the writer's only problems and the errors are familiar (*recieving* for *receiving*, for example, is less disorienting than *duagter* for *daughter*). The static around some errors is greater than that around others—an agreement error caused by the intervention of modifying phrases or clauses between subject and verb is not as serious as one where subject and verb are juxtaposed (as in *he say*). A regular pattern of error with one feature (a missing *-ed* ending on most verb phrases, for example) seems easier to accept than an assortment of *-s* problems of the kind illustrated on pages 117–18. Certain erroneous verb forms (*done* for *did*, for example, or *seen* for *saw*) are more distracting than others. Nonetheless, it is the number of serious errors that seems to make the crucial difference for readers, shifting their attention from the meaning to the form of things and, beyond that, to questions about the writer's broader competencies.

2. *The teacher should keep in mind the cost to himself and the student of mastering certain forms and be ready to cut his losses when the investment seems no longer commensurate with the return.* As we have seen, common errors persist because they make some kind of linguistic sense to the writer or because they are so habitual as to be

4. The guesses on tolerable error given here are based upon my analysis of 311 freshman placement essays written in the spring of 1973 at City College and read by two groups of readers, the first group for the purpose of deciding which of three classes the essay belonged to (1—needs to work on correction of errors, 2—no serious problems with error but needs to work on organization and development, 3—needs no work on general composition but probably needs help preparing long academic papers), the second group for a breakdown of the number and types of errors in each essay. Readers in both groups were English teachers, but they were selected for their moderate views on error and encouraged to read as if they were teachers in other subject areas.

untouched by what the student has learned from his teachers. It is the beauty of teaching young adults, however, that matters of great complexity can be made conceptually clear so that the student has a way of thinking about a problem that will eventually generate the correct answer. Cognition in this sense means that he has grasped the nature of the problem but not that he is ready to be right all the time. As in mathematics, the right answer is not always as important as the right route to an answer. Teachers who understand this are less likely to feel discouraged when students who have seemingly understood a lesson and done all the exercises go on to make the same mistakes in their writing. The gap between cognition and practice can be wide—sometimes wider than a semester—but eventually a student can learn to correct in his own writing what he has learned to correct in someone else's. His failure to do so immediately does not necessarily call for a repetition of the lesson but for more opportunity to apply the lesson to his own writing, preferably without any more teacher intervention except for a check in the margin or a general direction to edit the essay for the troublesome feature.

Finally, it is possible that residual traces of a common error will remain in a student's writing far beyond his course in English or even beyond college. It is hard to believe that the world will be much the worse for such an imperfection. And the writer ought to be reassured, if he has not already intuited this for himself, that a common error here and there is not likely to keep an otherwise good writer down—except perhaps in freshman English.

Student motivation and correctness
The motivation to learn what a teacher has decided ought to be and can be learned has often been considered, along with native intelligence, the equipment a student should bring with him to class: the teacher's job is to help the student learn; the student's job is to want to learn. This comforting formulation of a teacher's responsibility, however, ignores the subtle but pervasive ways in which teaching influences and even generates motivation. Indeed, unless the teacher is able to do so in the work on common errors, he is not likely to make much headway, because students are rarely ready at the outset to commit their long-term energies to the understanding and correction of errors.

There are several reasons for this. Probably the most obvious one is that errors seem to demand more concentration than they are worth.

Students who are learning a language for the first time depend upon their teachers to select those features of the language that are important to learn. They are not certain how much they have to know in order to say something intelligible. Native-born speakers of English who are learning formal written English already know that they can communicate in English and this gives them a momentum with the language that makes classroom work on errors drag. Whereas the student learning a second language will stretch his competence with the new language when he writes a short paragraph, incorporating the forms he has just learned, the native speaker learning another dialect of his language (as formal writing might be considered to be) is prepared at the outset to rush into English, scattering as he goes a wide range of variant or erroneous forms. Paradoxically, his knowledge of English enables him to err profusely, and since he has acquired the language without direct instruction, he has more difficulty than the second-language student in looking at what he writes analytically. We might say, then, that for the purposes of correcting errors, our student knows too much to be patient.

To the extent that he *is* motivated to learn about his common errors, he is usually negatively motivated, that is, he wishes to avoid the punishment of a bad grade, or, more broadly, the social penalty that comes from not being able to use the prestigious dialect. Such motivation carries a student through the beginning of a course but not always to the end of it. If, in addition to this kind of motive, however, the student has a career goal that calls for writing skill or even if he is in a career program that requires a passing grade in writing, however irrelevant that skill seems to him, he usually has the fuel he needs to get through the course. Nonetheless, the strongest learning energies are generated by the desire rather than the obligation to learn something. Gardner and Lambert in their research on attitudes and motivation in second-language learning distinguish between instrumental and integrative motives for learning a language, the first stemming from the recognition of a practical use for the language and the second from an active desire to identify with the cultural group that uses the language. While both attitudes will serve the language learner, the authors conclude that "learners who identify with the cultural group represented by a foreign or second language are likely to enjoy an advantage in attempts to master that language. Their motivation to learn the language appears to stem from and be sustained by the desire to identify."[5]

When we remember the ways in which the majority society has impinged upon the lives of most BW students and when we recall the student's distrust of teachers and their language, engendered over years of schooling, it is difficult to see how the desire to identify with the majority culture, and therefore its public language, could possibly have survived into young adulthood. At best we might expect deeply ambivalent feelings about "making it" in a course that teaches what is perceived as an alien dialect. Even the instrumental motive is likely to be weak among students who are not yet in the habit of seeing themselves in careers. Add to this the reckless predictions of futurists (or even administrators who begrudge the expense of skills instruction) who would have us believe that by the time today's students leave college people will be talking on telephones or into tapes or hopping on planes to deliver all their messages, and we see that the motivation to concentrate on writing itself, let alone on the mere correction of errors, needs reinforcement.

If we subtract for these attitudes of mistrust and indifference that students are likely to bring to class, we are left with at least three potential sources of motivation:

1. If students understand why they are being asked to learn something and if the reasons given do not conflict with deeper needs for self-respect and loyalty to their group (whether that be an economic, racial, or ethnic group), they are disposed to learn it. This means that teachers cannot assume that students are fired to write correct English, particularly if the students have reason to believe that the mastery of this version of English cancels out (or ought to cancel out) the language they use with their family and friends. What teachers can assume, however, is that if a case can be made for the mastery of formal written English as the language of public transactions—educational, civic, and professional—and if the phenomenon of dialects and registers can be introduced in such a way as to explain language variety and illuminate for the individual student the nature of his own difficulties with formal English, a student is more inclined to commit his energies to learning it. Students who have been using English all their lives find it difficult to

5. R. C. Gardner and W. E. Lambert, *Attitudes and Motivation in Second-Language Learning* (Rowley, Mass.: Newbury House, 1972), p. 130.

believe that they weren't intelligent enough to learn it, especially when other young adults who appear no more intelligent than they have learned it. What they need to understand is that they *have* learned a variety of English that differs in systematic ways from formal written English and serves them in ways that formal English cannot.

What generally emerges from such an exploration of language variety, provided it is a genuine exploration and not simply a quick pitch for getting on with the job of learning "good" English, is a sense of the students' own ambivalent feelings about their English and about their ability to learn to write well. Invariably students who are asked on the first day to indicate anonymously whether they think they can get an A in the course say they can't, and their reason is usually that they're not "good" at English. When asked to rank a number of passages written in different dialects and registers, they tend to rank passages written in variant forms of English below the passages written in formal English, even when the former is a description by Mark Twain and the latter is a passage obscured by officialese. These responses may well be aimed at pleasing the teacher. Even so, they reflect at least a deeply ambivalent attitude toward written English—when it is said to be good, it usually sounds bad (i.e., wrong-sounding and stiff), and when it sounds bad to others, it is usually good (right-sounding and alive).

Without a clearer understanding of the reasons behind language variations and of the difference between being effective in any dialect and being right according to the conventions of a particular dialect, the student is not psychologically ready to work on common errors in formal English. Readiness implies a respect for one's own linguistic aptitude and a confidence that the act of mastering a second variety of English is neither a disloyal nor destructive act but in fact a claim upon a wider culture, not only to acquire its network language but to improve upon it. We need no reminder of the state of public language nor of the implications this has—not only for a democracy but for less exalted causes such as textbooks that students (and teachers) want to read or letters and instructions that meet the modest criterion of the Admiralty Pilots during wartime: that they be intelligible to a tired man reading in a bad light. I am surely not the first to have sensed, in working with the new students on their writing, a directness and freshness of response that will eventually strengthen the public language even as it represents them in the larger world.[6]

2. Linguistic data are interesting to students in and of themselves. The detection of patterns, the discrimination among forms, and the application of rules to a range of situations are self-sustaining activities. Like taking machines apart or playing intricate games, they tease and challenge the brain, creating tensions and surprises that need no outside encouragement. What is needed, however, is a teacher who is prepared to expose students to linguistic data and allow them, wherever possible, to observe the phenomenon being studied and arrive through these observations at their own grammatical formulations. This takes time and ingenuity and it is not always the quickest way to get at common errors, but there is probably no more certain way to increase the resourcefulness of a student than to introduce him to linguistic concepts that enable him to see the fragments of his troubles with formal English in a larger frame.

3. The discovery by a student that he can do something he thought he couldn't releases the energy to do it. Students who make many errors feel helpless about correcting them. Error has them in its power, forcing them to hide or bluff or feign indifference but never to attack. The teacher must encourage an aggressive attitude toward error and then provide a strategy for its defeat, one that allows the student to count his victories as he goes and thereby grow in confidence. This means letting the student in on what is happening—setting a reasonable limit to what he needs to accomplish (the reduction of errors per 300 words from fifteen to six in one semester, for example), helping him classify the kinds of errors he makes most often (the discovery that although he has twenty errors he has only five problems is in itself encouraging to a student), and then planning instruction so that success is built into each lesson and the student can see that he is finally beginning to cope with errors.

The alternative course of ignoring error for fear of inhibiting the writer even more or of assuming that errors will wear off as the student writes more is finally giving error more power than it is due. The "mystery" of error is what most intimidates students—the worry that

6. For excellent material on the fallen state of public language, see Hugh Rank, ed., *Language and Public Policy* (Urbana, Ill.: National Council of Teachers of English, 1974).

errors just "happen" without a person's knowing how or when—and while we have already noted that some errors can be expected to persist even after instruction, most of them finally come under the control of the writer once he has learned to look at them analytically during the proofreading stage of composition. Freedom from error is finally a matter of understanding error, not of getting special dispensations to err simply because writing formal English is thought to be beyond the capabilities or interests of certain students.

Suggestions for reducing error

We come finally to the question of how to help students reduce their errors to a level that is tolerable to their readers, and here the individual talents and training of teachers, the learning styles of students, the time allowed in a writing program or department for the mastery of grammatical forms, and a variety of other considerations preclude my recommending The Way or The Book or The Grammar. Still, it has been my opportunity to observe over the past seven years a number of successful and some unsuccessful teachers concentrating on the kinds of difficulties I have been describing in this chapter, and these observations, rather than any systematic research on the matter, are the source of the recommendations that follow.

1. Where the intent is to spot and correct errors, grammar (which is used here to mean any effort to focus upon the formal properties of sentences) provides a useful way of looking at sentences. Correcting errors is an editorial rather than a composing skill and requires the writer to notice features of the sentence he would ordinarily have to ignore while composing. "The aim of a skillful performance," Michael Polanyi writes, "is achieved by the observance of a set of rules which are not known as such to the person following them."[7] Thus composing requires the writer to forget about the details that a proofreader must scrutinize. When he has finished, however, he needs new eyes that enable him to concentrate upon those formal relationships that, while related to his meaning, have not until this point been at the center of his attention. He must shift his orientation to the foreground. Grammar offers a way of looking at sentences that makes it easier to notice the kinds of details that figure in errors. It reorganizes the sentence along priorities that happen to serve the needs of proofreaders.

7. *Personal Knowledge* (New York: Harper and Row, 1958), p. 49.

Like most native speakers, these students have acquired grammatical control of the language without English teachers or grammar books, and the effort to perceive forms rather than meaning, or more accurately, to perceive forms as another kind of meaning, goes against the grain. Time spent at the outset of instruction in clarifying the nature of this shift in perspective is well invested. Students rarely see any connection between the language they use (which they consider ungrammatical) and the grammar they study. One suspects that they think of grammar as a network of rules and prohibitions which exist outside the language and are imposed like laws on errant writers.

Actually, the students themselves are their best sources of information about grammar. Despite their difficulties with common errors, their intuitions about English are the intuitions of native speakers. Most of what they need to know has already been learned—without teachers. They can swiftly unscramble sentences that the foreign-language student would have to puzzle over. Persuaded that they know nothing about the verb-tense system, they are nonetheless able to follow without difficulty a passage such as the following, in which the tenses shift with almost every verb:

> She *knows* what I mean because I *told* her yesterday. In fact, I *have told* her a million times that if she *refuses* to listen to me now, she *will be* sorry later. I wish I *had listened* to someone when I *was* her age.

What the students are not in the habit of doing is looking long and carefully at sentences in order to understand the way they work rather than what they mean. This involves a shift in perception which is ultimately more important than the mastery of any individual rule of grammar. Thus although it is the nature of grammar books and handbooks to proceed deductively, with the statement of a principle or rule and then the illustrations of that rule, it is important at least at the outset of grammar study to allow time for inductive learning. And throughout instruction, a student should be encouraged not simply to have the right answers but to have grammatical reasons for what he does, for grammar is more a way of thinking, a style of inquiry, than a way of being right.

One of the best ways to promote this view of grammar at the outset is to isolate the grammatical elements of the sentence from the lexical so that the student experiences the difference. This can be done by having the student observe a number of word groups that are punctuated as sentences but that the student can recognize intuitively as falling short, either for lexical or for grammatical reasons, of being acceptable sentences:

Scrambled sentences	Boy the hit man the.
Incomplete sentences	Buses that come late.
Illogical sentences	My old toothbrush is new.
Jabberwocky sentences	His radsom rolters brashed heliently.
Sentences with erroneous forms	He runned the mile in three minutes, fifty-one seconds.

The exercise requires the student first to distinguish by intuition acceptable sentences from unacceptable sentences and then to analyze the reasons behind these judgments. The fact that some of the sentences are unacceptable for semantic reasons (the words themselves don't make sense even though they are cast in grammatically acceptable patterns) and others for grammatical reasons (missing parts, wrong word order, or erroneous forms) sharpens the student's sense of what he has to notice when he is looking at a sentence grammatically.

2. The grammar students study for the purpose of reducing error should accomplish two objectives: introduce them to several key grammatical concepts that underlie many of their difficulties with formal English and equip them with a number of practical strategies for checking on their own writing. That grammar is best which gives the greatest return (i.e. ability to reason about errors) for the least investment of time. The pleasure of presenting complete grammatical descriptions can easily outweigh the wisdom of doing so, but the teacher's purpose in teaching grammar at this level is not to describe the English language but to help the student understand certain features of that language that give him difficulty.

This is not easy advice to follow, however, because grammar itself is a web, not a list, of explanations, and often a seemingly simple feature of instruction will be located at the interstices of several grammatical concepts. For a student to decide whether a subject "agrees" with a verb, for example, he must:

1. Understand what is meant by the term "agreement."
2. Identify the base words of the subject and predicate.
3. Determine whether the subject should be counted as one or more than one according to the conventions of formal English.

4. Know the appropriate form for indicating the number of a particular noun.

5. Know the appropriate form for indicating the number of a particular verb.

Thus an error that appears on the surface of a sentence as a detail of usage may in fact be so interlocked with other grammatical concepts that the teacher is like someone who, seeing only the tip of the elephant's tail, finds upon grasping it that he has the whole bulk of an animal (in this case a language) in tow. Listing the kinds of errors students regularly make is not difficult: what is difficult is to determine how deep the roots of instruction must go in order for students to cope with those errors. Clearly the needs are different for different students, but is there not some common base of understanding they need in order to approach a variety of individual errors? I have found that at least four grammatical concepts underlie most of their misunderstandings about forms and that while these concepts cannot be more than touched upon in a course designed for unpracticed writers, the time spent in introducing them is worthwhile.

Concept 1: The sentence
As we observed in the chapter on punctuation, students who speak in sentences don't necessarily know analytically what they are. Yet being able not only to recognize sentences but to account for their constituent parts is probably the most essential of all the grammatical skills. Unless he can reduce sentences to their basic patterns, the student cannot apply the rules for agreement or even know for certain whether he has a sentence. One of the best ways to develop this sense of the sentence is not merely to reduce sentences to simple subjects and predicates but to practice building them up from basic parts. Given a number of base sentences (e.g., *Students study. The problem will be solved.*), students are asked to expand them in any way they can without adding another base sentence. These are written on the board. Compound sentences or sentences that disqualify for some other reason (faulty syntax, fragmentation, etc.) are crossed out without explanation (a procedure that often stimulates students to scrutinize them), and the rest provide data for classifying the ways in which sentences can be expanded. What usually emerges from such an exercise are the major grammatical devices for expanding sentences—single-word modifiers, prepositional phrases, modifying clauses, etc.

The students are next asked to make more deliberate expansions, first expanding the subject and then the predicate in a variety of sentence patterns and then combining the two expanded parts:

Students			*Study*
College	students		study
College	students	at City College	study
College	students	at City College who major in biology	study

Students			*Study*	
Students		study	late	
Students	always	study	late	

Students   always   study   late   when they get nervous about exams.

College students at City college who major in biology always study late when they get nervous about exams.

Finally, specific kinds of subject and verb expansions are called for, either by their traditional names or by non-grammatical terms (e.g., *who structure* rather than *relative clause*). In subsequent classes, students are asked at the outset to expand a base sentence and list on a separate page the devices they used to do so. Other students, without seeing the list, are asked to return such sentences to their original bases. In time, this constant practice with expanding and reducing their own sentences not only prepares the students to locate subjects and verbs but greatly increases their facility with sentences. Thus one student, a timid writer at the outset of the semester, ventured this sentence when asked in an exam at the end of the semester to add adverbial modifiers to the base "The problem will be solved."

> The problem will be solved with the help of the Almighty, who, except for an occasional thunderstorm, reigns unmolested, high in the heavens above, when all of us, regardless of race or religious difference, can come together and study this severe problem inside out, all day and night if necessary, and are able to come to you on that great gettin' up morning and say, "Mrs. Shaughnessy, we do know our verbs and adverbs."

What becomes clear from such exercises is that the sentence is not simply a subject and verb but rather a base containing a subject and verb to which all other information can be attached, either directly to the base itself or indirectly to words that are attached to that base. The perception of the sentence as a structure rather than a string of words is probably the most important insight a student can gain from the study of grammar, an insight that is likely to influence him not only as a proofreader but as a writer. There are quicker ways to locate subjects and verbs but they may not be more efficient in the long run.

Concept 2: Inflection
For some students the whole idea of inflections, of systematically adding letters to the stems of words in order to affect their meaning, is alien. For other students, only certain forms within the inflectional system are alien. Both groups, for different reasons, have difficulty hearing, seeing, or believing in the importance of the key inflectional letters in formal English——*s* (-*es*) and -*ed*. This suggests that the approach to teaching these inflections ought to be multi-dimensional, attending to the sound and look of these letters as well as to the rules that control their use. It also suggests that the immediate return on even a substantial investment in inflections is likely to be small. The best a teacher can do is make a clear case for the importance of these inflections to the general reader (and therefore to the writer), provide a way of reasoning about the individual inflections, and make certain that, once the student has demonstrated a cognitive grasp of a rule for using an inflection, he applies it systematically in proofreading. And where a student overgeneralizes from a rule—a problem that a teacher cannot always foresee —the rule need not be overturned but rather modified and the irregular pattern rehearsed long enough to be remembered. The damage comes when neither the student nor the teacher sees that it is the student who is being consistent, not the language, or that the student or teacher has missed or forgotten some important part of the rule that makes it inapplicable in a particular instance. Thus the student who uses the -*s* inflection in the sentence "He watches the car moves" probably is unaware that the second verb is non-finite and therefore has no tense so that the rule governing the choice of a finite verb form does not apply. He would benefit most from learning some infinitive patterns with and without *to*:

He wants	Kathy	to walk into the building
		to mix them a drink
		to move the piano
		to win the game
		to join in

He watches	Kathy	walk into the building
		mix them a drink
		move the piano
		win the game
		join in

Before a student begins to work on specific inflections, however, it is often helpful to consider, if only briefly, the function of inflections in other languages and in English at earlier stages. He should be aware of the relatively modest amount of inflection in English as compared, for example, with a language like Greek, or of the differences in inflection among different dialects of English, and of the absence of inflection in certain languages such as Chinese. He should be encouraged to conjecture about the reasons for inflections, their possible role in reducing the number of forms or positions to be learned, or their role in protecting messages from the accidents of speech by providing extra clues.

Aware of the compulsory nature of inflections through years of correction, students are likely to approach them doggedly, like so many other blind tasks of academia. Within the world of language, however, we can see inflection functioning as a form of shorthand in the larger symbolic system (making it possible, for example, to say *books* rather than *more-than-one book*) and as a way of protecting or emphasizing certain kinds of information that a language, for reasons lost in the past, has deemed important. This insight, while it does not remove the work of learning certain troublesome inflections, links that task to a larger concept and thereby not only helps the student notice inflections but makes that task seem less arbitrary or at least makes the arbitrariness of the task more acceptable.[8]

Concept 3: Tense
Probably no part of English grammar is more resistant to explicit in-

8. Chapter 7 of Barron's *How to Prepare for the Law School Admissions Test* (Woodbury, N.Y.: Baron's Educational Series, 1973) contains a number of exercises that require students to analyze an artificial language by using a group of paradigms in the form of cartoons and captions. The material is excellent for introducing the concept of inflection.

struction than the English tense system. A complex system in itself, it is made even more difficult by the efforts of many teachers to equate the grammatical device of tense with the philosophical concept of time itself. Thus students are encouraged to fit all uses of the present-tense form into a concept of present time (a difficult task with sentences like *When he comes, I go* or *Shakespeare uses the name of flowers to suggest stages of mind* or *I'll lock the door after you come in*), and when students have difficulty with tenses, teachers often conclude that they lack "a concept of time," as if the particular way that formal English segments the abstraction we call time were the only way that squared with experience or "real" time. The fact that the tense system uses terms that trigger philosophical notions of time makes this confusion almost inevitable.

In introducing the concept of tense, therefore, the distinction must be made between the closed linguistic network whereby certain kinds of time relationships are built into the verb system (*tense*) and the larger experience of time that seems to begin with infancy and culminate in adult perceptions that are too subtle and various for us to describe or fully explain (*time*). There is no way to "teach" students about time. Indeed, they already know about it. But it is possible to describe in general the way a specific tense system works, to enumerate the parts of that system, to give guidelines for the ways in which these parts can be combined, to point up the irregularities in the system, and even to build, by the careful selection of examples and the assignment of essay topics that elicit particular tenses, dependable intuitions about the use of less familiar tenses—the future perfect, for example, or tense forms that are commonly contracted in speech (*He'd had a good time* for *He had had a good time* or *She'd have done it* for *She would have done it*) and therefore appear "new" to the student.

At least two different kinds of learning are involved in mastering the tense system. One kind requires that the student have a grasp of the formal system for producing tense changes; the other, that he develop an "ear" for tense combinations in a range of situations. The first task can be accomplished by straight instruction; the second, by drills and pattern practice that support analogical learning, and of course by exposure to the wanted forms in reading and conversation. Almost all standard handbooks of English composition devote some space to a description of the tense system. These descriptions need to be adapted to the kinds of problems I am describing: fewer assumptions can be made, for example, about the students' familiarity with grammatical terms; more attention must be given to the distinction made between singular and plural in the present tense (i.e., to the -s form); and the combining patterns for modal auxiliaries must be clarified in relation to the auxiliaries that combine with the perfect form of the verb. So similar in some respects are the verb problems of BW students to those of foreign-born students that teachers often find it easier to adapt second-language handbooks to their students' needs than to work with conventional college handbooks. This requires, however, adaptations of another kind so that the teacher can avoid the discouraging and annoying kind of "over-teach" that results when students already functioning with variant forms of English are taught at the abecedarian level of the student encountering English for the first time.

Concept 4: Agreement
The idea of agreement—that is, of certain words in sentences being formally linked to others so as to reinforce or repeat some kinds of meaning rather than others—is common to many languages. What is arbitrary in each language is what that language chooses to reinforce. Standard English, for example, is laced by forms that reinforce number. The sentence "The students *are* studying *their* lessons" has six words, of which four carry information about number. Conceivably a plural subject (or a pluralizing adjective in front of the subject—a determiner like *many*, for example) could carry the whole burden of number for that sentence, with all the other words being neutral on the matter of number, but formal English doesn't work that way. It also casts all sentences into a time frame that dictates the choice of verb forms not only within sentences but within whole pieces of discourse. And finally, it requires most pronouns to reinforce not only number but gender and person.

As we have seen, all these possibilities for agreement are also possibilities for error. The memory of inexperienced writers is short and agreement requires either a good grammatical memory or an ear so habituated to these conventions of agreement that they are followed unconsciously. Students who make many errors in one or all of these fields of agreement must eventually look at the conventions that govern each of them separately, but before that happens it is often helpful to relate these individual problems to the larger principle of agreement and particularly to demonstrate how the same phenomenon can be found in many other languages. Spanish, for example, extends the agreement principle to the gender and number of adjectives; BEV, along with many other languages, calls for negative concord whereas modern Standard English rejects it; and both Cantonese and Mandarin escape the problem of agreement by depending almost entirely on word order as a way of relating words in sentences.

Applications: A sample lesson

The student who has been introduced to the grammatical concepts of *sentence, inflection, tense,* and *agreement* has a conceptual frame within which to view his own difficulties in those areas. Without such a frame, he has trouble understanding what is wrong or perceiving a pattern in his errors. Just as the person who understands nothing about a motor must tamper blindly with this valve or that screw when the motor breaks down, so the student who is not conscious of the grammatical principles underlying a language must make guesses or find inefficient ways of locating and correcting his errors.

This is not to say that concepts are enough, but only that they help make the correction process intelligible to young adults. In addition to concepts, students need a variety of practical aids and many opportunities to produce the wanted forms. Grammar should be a matter not of memorizing rules or definitions but of thinking through problems as they arise. Since the composition process allows time for correcting and perfecting, there is no need for students to load their memories with information that can be found in a handbook or in charts or guides designed for their use. Lists of the common irregular verbs and their inflected forms, of the common prepositions in phrases, of rules for determining the number of a subject; charts that clarify the system for combining auxiliaries with verbs or that help identify the parts of speech; guides for locating subjects and verbs or for using troublesome verb combinations—these are the tools of the apprentice writer and only by learning to use them in real writing situations will the writer become independent of his teacher.

But often these tools are inaccessible because no one has explained to the writer the nature of the problem they are designed to solve. A list of irregular verbs, for example, is of little value unless the student understands what regularity is in the tense system and how certain irregular verbs function in relation to that system. Once he has grasped this, he needs simply to increase his vocabulary of irregular verbs. Grammar study prepares students to use the materials available in conventional handbooks, but too often, teachers begin grammar instruction at the handbook level instead, unaware of the extent to which traditional explanations belie the complexity of language. As a result, their "lucid" explanations, successful perhaps when applied to controlled situations, collapse under the rush of language, leaving the student even less confident than he was before. Thus if one is going to invest time in this kind of instruction at all, it is best to make as thorough an effort as possible to cover the points that are likely to puzzle the student once he is on his own.

The lesson that follows is an example of the expanded coverage that a seemingly simple point of grammar can demand when a student must acquire it through direct instruction. The lesson is intended to 1. clarify the distinction between the -s (-es) inflection in the noun and the same inflection in the verb and 2. develop a strategy for deciding when to use the -s form of the verb. Preceding lessons would have covered verb recognition, noun recognition, sentence parts, subject-predicate recognition, and the tense-forming system. The lesson itself has four parts, the first three of which are presented here: Diagnostic test,[9] Introduction, Explanations, and Exercises. In the student's version of this lesson, the colors red and green would be used to heighten the distinction between the -s that indicates a third-person singular verb and the -s that indicates a plural noun.

Diagnostic test

(To be administered by a teacher or tutor)

Test 1: *Hearing the* -s (10)

Read aloud the paired phrases listed below and ask the student to mark "S" if the two phrases sound alike and "D" if they sound different:

1. four friends talking together
   four friend talking together
2. seven innings
   seven inning
3. Henry walk to the store.
   Henry walks to the store.

4. wild beasts
   wild beast
5. student's troubles
   student trouble
6. fifty cent
   fifty cents

9. This diagnostic test is adapted from a test that was designed by Patricia Laurence.

7. agricultural crops   9. She like this job.
   agricultural crop   She likes this job.
8. a month vacation   10. He's not here.
   a month's vacation   He not here.

Test 2: *Seeing the -s (20)*

Ask the student to read Passage A below out loud or on tape. Check below whenever the -s is not sounded.

1. man's	6. it's	11. calls	16. brakes
2. blows	7. kids'	12. mass	17. thanks
3. packages	8. bicycles	13. trucks	18. smiles
4. steps	9. toys	14. buses	19. thinks
5. bus	10. flies	15. motorcycles	20. that's

Test 3: *Detecting -s errors (10)*

Ask the student to read Passage B and circle any error he finds. Indicate below the errors he misses. If he corrects items that are already correct, list them below.

1. try_____   6. mean_____
2. contain_____   7. know_____
3. idea_____   8. come_____
4. say_____   9. claim_____
5. want_____   10. begin_____

Test 4: *Producing -s endings in writing (10)*

Ask the student to answer each question with a full sentence.
Example:

Do the girls look as if they are going to laugh?
Yes, the girls look as if they are going to laugh.
1. Do students usually get to class on time?
   Yes, students_____.
2. Does Jerline usually get to class on time?
   Yes, Jerline_____.
3. Does Henry seem unfriendly to you lately?
   Yes, Henry_____.
4. Do other people's problems usually bother you?
   Yes, other_____.
5. Does it ever occur to you that there might be life on another planet?
   Yes, it_____.

Passage A

A man's hat blows off and his packages fall in the gutter as he steps off the bus. The children on the sidewalk laugh. They think it's funny. I try to catch the hat by jumping over the kids' bicycles and toys to the curb, but the hat flies to the middle of the street. The man calls out to tell me not to bother, but I'm already in the midst of a mass of traffic—trucks, cars, buses, and motorcycles. I hear screeching brakes. Then I see the hat a few feet away. It is smashed and striped with tire-tread. I pick it up and take it to the man. He just thanks me and smiles. He probably thinks I'm a fool. A truck driver is yelling at me. That's what I get for my good deed!

Passage B

This book try to help the inexperienced writer. It contain two main idea. First it say that a person writes best when he want to write. Second it says that anyone can write if he is willing to work at it. If someone says he can't write, he probably mean that he either has no experience as a writer or he know of nothing to say at the moment. But once a subject come alive in his mind, the words also begin to come to life and the person who claim he is not a writer suddenly begin to act like one.

Introduction

Word endings

All of the items below are made of letters, but only some of the items are words. Put a check in front of the items that are words.

___s	___ing	___to	___fo	___ly
___I	___ed	___a	___it	___of

Some of the letters below carry some kind of meaning when they get attached to certain words, even though the letters are not words themselves. Others carry no meaning at all. Put a check in front of the letters that have some meaning for you.

___ed	___'s	___ng	___ly	___se
___we	___rb	___ize	___s	___es

All of the items below are words. Some of the words can lose their final letters and still be words; others cannot lose letters without losing their status as words. Check the words that can afford to lose letters at the end.

listening___	questions___	knowledge___
table___	can't___	teller___
wanted___	theory___	regular___
ever___	thirty___	behavioral___
grades___	government___	friendly___
are___	result___	strengthen___
when___	courageous___	breathe___
business___	itemize___	contract___
industry___	continue___	sleepy—
smarter___	friendless___	asks___

As you can see from the list you have just marked, English has not only a vocabulary of words but also a vocabulary of endings, a variety of attachments that multiply the uses and meanings of words. Thus a word like "love" can, with its attachments, have many forms and therefore many different uses and meanings in a sentence (loves, loving, loved, lovely, loveliness, loveless, lovingly). Learning how to make full use of these attachments is important to the mastery of written English.[10]

Note in the following passage from a newspaper article how many words have attachments:

> With the immediate threat of foreign competition, companies that are making big profits are reluctant to tamper with past methods.
> A new breakthrough in technology often dehumanizes a job. Sometimes, for example, by the time a job has become enriched, engineers develop a machine to do the job and do not consider the impact on workers.
> At the American Telephone and Telegraph Company plants, for example, small teams of workers were given the responsibility of producing whole telephone books. Errors went down and morale rose. But the International Business Machines Corporation has developed a new machine that takes care of most of the job.

If you have grown up speaking English, many of the words in the passage above are familiar to you. You do not ask, each time you use them, whether they should have endings attached to them or not because the endings have grown on the words by constant use. You can probably decide which ending is needed in most of the following sentences.

1. He is a _____ man. (courage)
2. They expect vast _____ changes. (technology)
3. We are _____ to a museum. (go)
4. _____ has usually been a woman's job. (teach)
5. _____ is seldom welcome. (critic)
6. She married an _____. (act)
7. He _____ her once, but now he _____ someone else. (love)
8. He grinned _____ at the sergeant. (sly)
9. The children always want to go to my _____ house. (sister)
10. They have begun to _____ their writers. (idol)

For some writers, however, some endings do not slip on as easily as others. They require conscious thinking. This is especially true of the -s ending. Unfortunately, the -s ending is also one of the most frequently required endings in formal English. If you check the newspaper passage again, you will find that over half the endings in that passage are -s endings. And if you look even more closely at those -s endings, you may discover that the -s

10. Some words undergo spelling changes when endings are added to them. Thus *love* loses its e when the -ing ending is added. The changes that words go through in order to get their endings are often a source of difficulty in spelling. See exercise entitled *Spelling: Adding Endings.*

endings do not all carry the same meaning. There are, in fact, two kinds of -s's in that passage.

Type 1	*Type* 2
companies	dehumanizes
profits	takes
methods	
sometimes	
engineers	
workers	
plants	
teams	
books	
errors	
machines	

If the difference between these -s's is not clear to you and if you are not certain when to use the one and when the other, you should go on to the second part of this exercise, which is concerned with the difference between the plural and the singular -s.

Explanations

1: *Distinguishing between the two -s's*

1.1   The following words all end in -s but the -s does not have the same meaning or function in all the words:

this	abacus	cars	has
textbooks	discusses	Paris	kiss
thinks	ideas	bus	does

Five of the words in the list above were in a sense "born" with an -s ending. To put it another way, -s is the final letter in the *stem* of the word.

_____   _____   _____   _____   _____

Three of the words have an -s (or -es) added to them in order to show that more than one of that particular thing is being referred to. In other words, the -s inflection makes the word plural (colored *green* to stand for growth). Which words are they?

_____   _____   _____

Four of the words have an -s (or -es) inflection in order to show that they involve only *one* person or thing (colored *red* because you often have to *stop* to think about this -s). In other words, the -s makes the word singular. Which are they?

_____   _____   _____   _____

1.2 Look closely at the following *green -s* words below. Then indicate in the chart below the part of speech of each of the italicized words. (Be ready to give a grammatical reason for your choice. See earlier units on sentence parts and parts of speech if you have questions.)

1. *Textbooks* cost more this year than last.
2. I sell my used *textbooks* every spring.
3. My bookshelf is crowded with *textbooks*.
4. The best *ideas* come in the morning.
5. He gave me some good *ideas*.
6. He plays with *ideas*.
7. Used *cars* cost more than you expect.
8. I have bought five *cars* from that dealer.
9. The highways are jammed with *cars*.

Sentence	noun	pronoun	verb	adjective	adverb	conjunction	preposition
1							
2							
3							
4							
5							
6							
7							
8							
9							

1.3 Do the same now for the red *-s* words in the sentences below:
1. She *thinks* I believe in astrology.
2. He is the person who *thinks* I was born under the wrong sign.
3. George *thinks* he is so good at thinking that he belongs in a think tank.
4. The teacher who comes to our lab *discusses* the lecture thoroughly.
5. Each person *discusses* the issue from his point of view.
6. My brother *does* what he has to do.
7. Who *does* the cooking in your house?
8. Vermille *has* the best of two worlds.
9. He *has* more luck at cards than we have.

Sentence	noun	pronoun	verb	adjective	adverb	conjunction	preposition
1							
2							
3							

4
_____
5
_____
6
_____
7
_____
8
_____
9
_____

Summary:

1. All the green -s's in the above sentences are attached to _____.

                                                    part of speech

2. All the red -s's are attached to _____.

THE *GREEN -S* IS ADDED TO NOUNS TO SIGNAL PLURALITY.

THE *RED -S* IS ADDED TO VERBS TO SIGNAL SINGULARITY.

1.4   To check your ability to notice the *green* and *red* -s's, try underlining with a green or red pencil the -s words in the paragraph below.[11]

> The *Oxford Dictionary* carries 14,070 different definitions for the 500 most used words in English. This is an average of 28 separate definitions per word. No word ever means exactly the same thing to any two people. What meaning, for example, does the word BAR have? The word means nothing in your mind until it refers your mind to something it already knows. Depending how the word symbols for BAR go to work in your mind, they could mean any one of a dozen or more things—a BAR for drinking, a BAR for prying, a BAR for exercising, a BAR for prisoners, a BAR meaning lawyers, a BAR of soap or candy, a snack BAR, a BAR on a door or a gate, a BAR of silver or gold, a sand BAR, a BAR to health. And even then we have not listed all the possible meanings.
> (Note: there are *eight green* -s's and *seven red* -s's.)

1.5   Compose ten sentences. Each of the first five sentences should contain at least one green -s word. Each of the second five sentences should contain at least one red -s word. Underline the words with the appropriate color.

1.6   In English, when a word shifts from being a noun to being a verb, or vice versa, the form of the word often changes:

I *act* for a living; therefore I am an *actor.*

I *conduct* the orchestra; therefore, I am a _____.

I *bake* cakes; therefore I am a _____.

I will *describe* this room; then I will give you the _____.

11. Adapted from John O'Hayne, *Gobbledy Gook Has Got to Go*, U. S. Government Printing Office.

She needs *food*; please _____ her.

A flag is a *symbol*; it _____ a nation or group.

I need *strength*; what will _____ me?

But many times, the form of the word stays the same and one cannot tell what part of speech it is except by seeing the word in its sentence:

Examples:

The school *buses* stop here.

The school *buses* its students to another borough.

My sister *hopes* to become a singer.

My sister has *hopes* of becoming a singer.

The teacher *looks* to him for an answer.

Her *looks* challenge him.

A good test of your ability to discriminate between the green -*s* and the red -*s* is to be able to do so in sentences where the words themselves look the same but where in one sentence the word may be a *plural noun* and in the other a *singular verb*.

Underline the -*s*(-*es*) words in the following sentences with a red or green pencil, depending on whether they are nouns or verbs.

1. She kisses him.
   Her kisses are sweeter than wine.
2. He bosses her.
   Bosses tend to be unreasonable.
3. She chairs the meeting.
   The committee members sit on leather chairs.
4. Her dresses are old-fashioned.
   She always dresses up for breakfast.
5. He glances at her.
   Her glances annoy him.

1.7   Write sentences of your own using the words below. If a word is underlined in red, then that word should appear in your sentence as a verb. If it is underlined in green, it should appear as a plural subject.

Example:
bosses   The brother *bosses* her because he is older.

1. *questions*	3. *struggles*	5. *hands*	7. *drinks*	9. *walks*
2. *questions*	4. *murders*	6. *hands*	8. *drives*	10. *hints*

1.8   Since the green -*s* makes a noun plural and the red -*s* makes a verb singular, a subject with a plural -*s* (*es*) ending will not match a verb with an -*s* ending. The -*s* will appear on subject or verb but not on both.

| The girl | *likes* food. |
| The *girls* | like food. |

| The lawyer | *wins* all the time. |
| The *lawyers* | win all the time. |

Practice this coordination between the -s's until it becomes familiar:

1. The problem of pollution remains.
   The problems _____.
2. The program appears on Channel 13.
   The programs _____.
3. The rooms need paint.
   The room _____.
4. His ideas seem conservative.
   His idea _____.
5. The girls in my building walk to work.
   The girl _____.
6. The box contains candy.

   _____.
7. The kid jumps rope.

   _____.
8. The classes are too long.

   _____.
9. The lesson is impossible.

   _____.
10. The rules are full of exceptions.

    _____.

2: *Using the -s-form of the verb*

This lesson will concentrate on the -s-form of the verb. So far, we have a rule for using the -s-form that seems simple: THE -S-FORM OF THE VERB IS SINGULAR AND THE -S-FORM OF THE NOUN IS PLURAL. THEREFORE, THE TWO -S (-ES) FORMS CANNOT COMBINE AS SUBJECT AND VERB. The rule sounds quite logical and easy to apply. Unfortunately there are some situations in which it doesn't work, so we must now consider further the conditions under which the -s-form of the verb will NOT work. We will consider five rules for NOT using the -s-form. The rules are worth learning because they cover most of the difficulties with the -s-verb you are likely to come upon in your own proofreading.

Rule 1. DO *NOT* USE THE -S-FORM WHEN A SUBJECT IS PLURAL. You already know from the last lesson that subjects that end in the green

-s (-es) do not AGREE WITH verbs that end in the red -s (-es). We will now extend that rule to include any subject that is plural, whether it forms its plural with an -s (-es) or not.

Most subjects do form their plurals by adding -s (-es), but not all.

a. Some subjects change the letters inside the word rather than adding -s (-es) at the end:

man_____ mouse_____ tooth_____ woman_____ foot_____

b. Some subjects have kept their foreign plural endings:

criterion_____ alumnus_____ analysis_____ fungus_____

c. Some subjects are pronouns that have separate forms for the plural:

he_____ this_____ she_____ that_____ it_____

d. Some subjects are pronouns that can be either singular or plural, depending on the words they refer back to:

The men *who* live in glass houses shouldn't throw strones.
The man *who* lives in a glass house shouldn't throw stones.
The problem *that* troubles him troubles me.
The problems *that* trouble him trouble me.

Cross out the verbs that do not seem appropriate according to

Rule 1.

1. These
   belong   fits   seem   makes
2. The criteria
   are   is   seems   remain
3. He
   believe   hopes   lives   intend
4. Sometimes my teeth
   aches   gleam   hurt   grinds
5. The woman
   listens   speak   is   keeps
6. The person who
   thinks   plan   offers   decide
7. The people who
   vote   register   enlist   sign

Rule 2.   DO NOT USE THE -S-FORM WHEN THE SUBJECT IS *I* OR *YOU*.

There is one exception to this rule (I was). Otherwise, you can depend on it.

Application: Cross out the verbs that are not appropriate.

1. My best friends
   raise   attend   studies   hope

2. You
   have   are   is   does

3. Your intention
   seems   is   was   indicate

4. I
   was   thought   wanted   thinks

5. You
   was   happens   seem   intend
   etc.

Rule 3. DO NOT USE THE -*S*-FORM WHEN YOU ARE WRITING IN THE SIMPLE PAST TENSE.

(Exception: *was* is the only -*s*-verb in the past tense. Like the other -*s*-forms, it is used only with singular subjects.)

1. Yesterday, we
   planned   was   were   does

2. When I was a child I never
   thought   was   wanted   dreams

3. One year he
   tried   struggled   was   forgot

4. Once, after school was over, she
   starts   introduced   happens   happened

5. Whenever my uncle comes to the city, he
   remembers   tried   wants   asked
   etc.

Rule 4. DO NOT USE THE -*S*-FORM OF ANY VERB THAT FOLLOWS AN AUXILIARY VERB.

So far we have been using single verbs, but as you know some verbs are made up of more than one word. These are called *verb phrases* (Examples: *was invited, will ask, had gone, should have gone, might have been called,* etc.). Each of these phrases has a main verb (was *invited*, will *ask*, had *gone*, might have been *called*), which is the final verb of the phrase. The verbs that come in front of the main verb are called helping, or auxiliary, verbs. Our rule here states that the *main* verb in a phrase will not use the -*s*-form.

Below you will find a chart of the main auxiliary verbs and the verb forms they can combine with. Notice that none of the *main* verbs use the -*s*-form.

	Aux. verbs	*Main verbs*
1. Aux. verbs that can be followed by stem or base form of main verb	do, does, did shall will	like want think

Aux. verbs	Main verbs
can	ask
may	go
must	see
should	
would	etc.
could	
might	

	Aux. verbs	Main verbs
2. Aux. verbs that can be followed by the past form of the verb	am, is, are	liked
	was, were	wanted
	have, has, had	thought
	having	asked
	have been, has been, had been	gone
		seen
		etc.

	Aux. verbs	Main verbs
3. Aux. verbs that can be followed by the -ing form of the verb	am, is, are	hoping
	was, were	wanting
	have been, has been, had been	thinking
	will be, might be, could be	asking
		going
		seeing
		etc.

Using the above chart, select the correct verbs:

1. I have to admit that he did

   try   start   begins   listens

2. A student can always

   studies   reviews   learn   begin

3. When the bus comes, she will

   get   waves   remember   stops

4. If my friend had

   tried   listens   saves   considered

5. If he asks her she might

   say   says   consider   does

6. They say that he has

   spoken   seen   listens   wanted

7. In my view, she should have been

   finished   starts   educated   learning

Rule 5. DO NOT USE THE -S-FORM OF THE VERB WITH THE INFINITIVE.

The infinitive form of the verb is not an independent form and cannot serve as the main verb of a sentence. The infinitive can appear in one of three forms:

1. to + verb stem (to move)
2. verb stem (move)
3. to + auxiliary + past form of verb (to have moved)

We will concern ourselves here with the first two forms of the infinitive. The third form is governed by Rule 4, which states that no -s-form will follow an auxiliary verb.

Rule 5 is simple to carry out provided you see a *to* in front of the verb and know the stem form of the verb (something you can check in the dictionary, which lists verbs under their stem forms).

1. He wants her to

   helps   help   forget   remembers

2. We stopped to

   hear   listened   seen   have

3. I woke up to

   discovered   discovers   discover   find

4. My class wants to

   informs   ask   petition   requests

5. I want her to be

   notifies   notify   notified

6. She ought to have been

   register   registers   registering   registered

In some sentences, the *to* that signals the infinitive phrase goes underground and it is difficult to know whether you are in a situation that requires a *stem* form or an -s-form, or some other form. It happens in sentences like this:

She feels	the ground	(to) tremble.
He watched	the hands of the clock	(to) move.
She lets	the girl	(to) leave.
I will help	Mary	(to) carry the bag.

Often your own sense of the way things ought to sound will help you. Otherwise, the following test works for *most* sentences:

Test for the missing To:

Can you substitute *them, him, her* for the subject of the verb in question? If so, the verb is a hidden infinitive.

them

He watched (the hands of the clock) move.

her

She lets (the girl) leave.

her

I will help (Mary) carry the bag.

Note:

So far, we have limited our discussion to the -s-form of the main verbs, but it should be remembered that a few of the helping (auxiliary) verbs have -s-forms. The others cause no problems—they work with any subject. The following chart of the helping verbs indicates the few verbs that have -s-forms.

Present	*Past*
am, (is,) are	(was,) were
have, (has)	had
do, (does)	did
shall	should
will	would
can	could
may	might
must	

When you are uncertain about the correct form to use, check first to see whether you have an -s-form to choose from. For example, there is a choice in the sentence

The students (have, has) finished their essays.

But there is no choice in the sentence

The students (had) finished their essays.

If you find that there is an -s-form, then apply Rules 1 and 2, which state that you should NOT use the -s-form if the subject is *plural* or if it is *I* or *you*.

1. People around here (have, has) always read the paper on the subway.

2. She may (have, has) let the whole story out.

3. You (was, were) taught never to answer back in the classroom.

4. They (do, does) think about leaving the city.

5. He (do, does) want the company to stay in Manhattan.

etc.

(End of lesson on -s-form.)

The exercises that follow these explanations include:

1. Verb selection exercises that require the student to justify each selection.

2. Substitution exercises that develop skill in shifting from plural to singular and vice versa.

3. Analysis of verb forms in passages of increasing complexity.

4. Proofreading for erroneous forms in prepared passages (as in diagnostic test).

5. Proofreading of passages written by the student on topics designed to elicit the -s-form. Typical topics: (1) Write a paragraph that begins, "My best friend differs from me in several ways." Go on to demonstrate the ways in which you differ. (2) Write a paragraph that begins, "This is a typical day in the life of a relative (friend, etc.).

6. Continuing attention during the proofreading stage to -s-forms. At the outset, the student should proofread for one type of error at a time, concentrating, for example, in one reading on -s-forms, then re-reading for some other type of error. In reading for agreement, it is useful to number subjects and their verbs in the following way:

>   1   2   2   1   3
> The woman who lives next door has five children, but only one of them
> 3
> lives at home.

When -s-form errors survive the proofreading process, the teacher should not identify them for the student but merely alert him to the fact that an -s-form error has escaped the net and needs to be corrected.

This lesson, lengthy and involved as it must seem to anyone who has taught this inflection the conventional way—with a definition of *person* and *present tense* and a few exercises—is nonetheless but an introduction to the -s-form. No attempt has been made to introduce the subjunctive, which raises special problems not only because it requires a plural verb with a singular subject (If he *were* . . .) but because it uses *be* as a finite form (I move that he *be* . . .), as BEV does, though with a different meaning (*I move that he be* . . . recommends something that has not happened, whereas *He be sick* speaks of a condition that is constant or continuing). The use of relatively simple subjects is an even more important limitation of the lesson, requiring a subsequent lesson on the location of complex subjects (inverted subjects in questions and in *there is, are* patterns; noun clauses and infinitive-phrase subjects; subjects separated from verbs by long modifiers, etc.) and on the conventions for counting subjects (compound subjects, *either-or* subjects, *each-every-*

one-everybody subjects, units of measure subjects, collective-noun subjects, and several others).

Behind a lesson of this kind lie at least two assumptions: first, that young adults do not learn formal English in the same way they learned their mother tongues, whether these were foreign languages or variant dialects of English; second, that although speech comes before writing, writing need not be bounded by the competencies of speech, that certain forms or conventions, in other words, can become part of a person's writing competence without necessarily being incorporated into his speech.

A child internalizes the rules of his language without noticing them. Something akin to a language-learning instinct acting over a period of five to ten years upon an environment of talk "teaches" him to talk. When, as a young adult, he once again faces a language-learning challenge, however, his situation as a learner has altered significantly. There are practical problems that did not press upon him as a child—the sense of a deadline (a semester or two) for mastering certain features of written English; a much more limited exposure to the language and much less opportunity for practice; a less trusted environment in which to learn; and often, ambivalent attitudes about learning the new language. Beyond this, and much more in his favor, he has developed cognitive abilities that far exceed those of children: he can shorten the learning period by studying rules and principles; he has greater autonomy as a learner and can direct his energies toward specific goals; and most important, he knows a language, which, however it differs from the language he is learning, provides the base from which to study another language or dialect. In other words, there are both practical and cognitive reasons for his approaching formal English analytically.

Fortunately, writing (particularly those stages of writing we call editing and proofreading) is congenial to analysis. It allows time for the deliberate application of principles or rules, for the introduction of unfamiliar patterns that would be washed over in the flow of speech. It does not require that the student first incorporate into speech the forms that he must use in writing. (The forms he acquires as a writer are more likely, over time, to work their way into his speech.) It requires instead that he be able to notice details he would ordinarily ignore and have ways of figuring out whether what he has written is right or wrong according to the conventions of formal English. This is a deliberate, even laborious, task at first, but it gets easier with each assignment. In time, the rules and tests themselves are swiftly applied even as the student is composing. But, as I have tried to demonstrate, unless the rules we ask students to learn are applicable to the range of situations they are likely to encounter when they write, the student is almost worse off than he was before.

Applications: choosing the appropriate method

The reasons for grammatical errors are various and must be considered in the design of grammatical instruction. Most teachers assume they are starting from "scratch," but they do not necessarily agree on where "scratch" is. Yet it is in the definition of "scratch" with each lesson and each student and in a sensitivity to the ways in which grammatical information goes awry that effective teaching lies. Students make the same mistakes for different reasons. Some errors may be accidents of transcription whereas others reflect variant or unstable grammatical habits. The former require a closer scrutiny of the written sentence so that the criteria for correctness the student already has can be applied consistently; the latter require grammatical explanations and exercises. The teacher can try to distinguish between these at the outset in several ways. Writing samples and taped segments of speech can be compared to determine the extent to which a student is producing the wanted forms in spontaneous speech but missing them in writing. Since students write more easily in some modes than in others (usually narrative writing has fewer errors than analytical writing), an estimate of grammatically caused errors can be made from a range of modes. Or the student can be given several chances to correct his writing before anyone notes his errors. The teacher can arrange to have the student's essay typed or projected on a screen so as to produce for him a new visual perspective and ask that he make whatever corrections seem necessary on the new copy. Or the student can be asked to proofread his paper, reading out loud exactly what he has written and correcting whatever sounds wrong. (This is best done with a tutor or teacher since the student will often read what he has not written.)

Once the grammatically based errors have been distinguished from the performance-based errors, it is possible to plan a sequence of lessons based on a number of considerations: which errors occur most frequently, which errors seem most serious, which errors trouble the student most, and which errors ought to come first in a grammatical description. If, for example, most of a student's errors are found to be problems in transcription from speech to writing, then the student needs to learn how to proofread. The teacher must try to determine first *why* he doesn't see his errors. Does he need glasses (an obvious but not uncommon problem among students)? Is he imposing certain schemata on the written page without seeing what is actually there? Is he able to read for individual letters or parts of words rather than for general meaning? Is he, in short, perceptually prepared to see not simply the rough contours of whole words and phrases as they speed by during passive (and frequently reckless) reading but also to make the discriminations among letters and syllables that must be made in writing and noted in proofreading? If he is not ready to make these discriminations, he must be trained to do so. This involves a number of steps in perceptual development, from the perception of specific letters in general settings (words, phrases, clauses, paragraphs, essays) and then in particular settings (where a letter might function in one place as part of a stem and in another as an inflection), through the recognition of errors in controlled sentences or passages (by others and then by the student himself), and finally to the initiation of correct forms in a piece of writing.[12]

The perceptual difficulties that keep students from seeing what they already know to be erroneous will also keep them from incorporating new forms into their writing. Thus proofreading becomes an indispensable aid to the mastery of grammar. It may well be that traditional grammar-teaching has failed to improve writing not because rules and concepts do not connect with the act of writing but because grammar lessons have traditionally ended up with exercises in workbooks, which by highlighting the feature being studied rob the student of any practice in seeing that feature in more natural places.

Where a student's errors cannot be explained as slips of performance but reflect genuine grammatical differences or confusions, the teacher must still choose appropriate strategies for the problem and student. Although many teachers become discipled to particular schools of grammar, there is no evidence as yet that any particular system of analysis is pedagogically superior to all the others. Most teachers will agree, for example, that subject-verb recognition is fundamental to several grammatically based problems in writing, but they will often disagree about

12. For a fuller discussion of perceptual training, see Patricia Laurence, "Error's Endless Train," *Journal of Basic Writing*, Spring, 1975.

the best way of bringing about this recognition, even though it is easy enough to find teachers using very different grammatical approaches who are equally successful (or unsuccessful) in doing it. What is most useful is a repertoire of approaches to a relatively small number of problems rather than an allegiance to a school of grammar. While always the beneficiaries of linguistic theory, teachers have their own data to observe, namely the responsiveness of students to particular strategies, and often this places teachers in seemingly untenable positions *vis-à-vis* current linguistic scholarship, producing what sometimes feels like a Rube Goldberg grammar, full of borrowed and makeshift parts, unsupported by any overarching theory, untransferable to any book or even another classroom, but for reasons never researchable somehow able to do the job at the particular moment.

To make the kinds of grammatical discriminations that lead to the identification of a subject and verb, and from there to the agreement of subject and verb, a student needs to be able to account for most of the words in a sentence or he needs some formula that will isolate the complete subject from other parts of the sentence and thereby reduce the number of words he must account for. How he learns to do this ought to be determined by the amount and kind of grammar he already knows and by the types of explanations and exercises that work best for him, but not by the accident of getting into a particular class where the teacher happens to be committed to teaching grammar one way.

The problem of applicability is especially important where a teacher is considering an over-all method such as contrastive analysis, a technique developed in foreign-language teaching that uses a common analytical frame to describe the mother tongue and the target language at those points where differences between the two languages produce interference errors. The method has the advantage of demonstrating the systematic nature of the learner's first language or dialect, thereby revealing the logic of his ways with formal English and raising his estimate both of himself as a learner and of his native tongue. Questions of pedagogical cost arise, however, over the issue of whether there is among native-born students who speak in other dialects a sufficient range of interference-based errors, at this age and academic level, to warrant the elaborate pedagogical apparatus involved in teaching two grammars instead of one.

We have stressed in this chapter the frequency of certain errors among linguistically divergent groups of students. This is not to say, however, that other errors, distinctive to specific language groups, did not also appear. Such errors, however, were noted less often, sometimes only once or twice in the entire corpus of writing samples consulted for this study. In a city such as New York, the incidence of cross-association among non-prestigious dialects as well as between those dialects and standard English further complicates the picture. Puerto Rican children, for example, often learn English in black neighborhoods with the result that their English contains a mixture of Spanish and BEV forms. Usually a wide range of such errors in a student's spoken and written English suggests a degree of resistance to (or isolation from) the academic world and from other dialect groups that makes his very presence in college (or his graduation from high school) atypical, even in an open-admissions setting.[13]

Most students, whether they started out speaking Chinese or BEV or Navajo, seem to end up in freshman English with a common stock of errors that appear most often to arise directly from interference from other languages and dialects, from problems of predictability within the system called formal English, or from the difficulties associated with writing rather than speaking English. To be sure, the Puerto Rican student who omits the pluralizing -s has a different experience with it from the Chinese student, whose language offers no model for plural inflections, and the Navajo student who writes "three friend" or "my sister husband" is not doing that because he grew up speaking BEV, but because he speaks Navajo and because some parts of formal English appear to be difficult for everyone to learn, including children who are learning it as their first language.

In recent years, contrastive analysis has been recommended by some as a method for teaching formal English to adult students with BEV backgrounds, and at least one fully developed course using that method has been designed by the Language Curriculum Research Group at Brooklyn College.[14] As I have suggested in many ways so far, the dialects of the economically poor are rarely credited with the same

13. I am indebted to Barbara Quint Gray for her analysis of 100 papers by dialect speakers from the City College population. Her findings reaffirmed the impressions of teachers generally that among young adults who have chosen to attend college the number of errors caused by dialect interference may be large, but the range of these errors is narrow.

14. Carol Reed, Milton Baxter, et al., *Standard English for Speakers of Black English Vernacular*, unpublished manuscript, © 1973 by The Language Curriculum Research Group, Brooklyn College of the City University of New York.

complexity and resourcefulness as the dialects of the middle and upper classes, and the young, no matter how hard they try to resist the interpretations that the world imposes on them, tend eventually to absorb negative views of their language that in turn make it even more difficult to learn formal English. The black student has probably felt the bite of this prejudice more persistently and deeply than anyone else, which may in itself be justification enough for introducing him to the dialect he speaks, pointing out its validity as a language in certain contexts, and contrasting it in systematic ways with the dialect he has not yet mastered. Where many features of the dialect appear regularly in the student's writing, a contrastive approach may well be an efficient way of teaching formal English, but the debate about its usefulness as a teaching method will doubtless continue until more evidence has been gathered in its favor.

Conclusion

I have tried in this chapter to document the incidence of certain kinds of errors among BW students, to suggest some of the reasons behind these errors, and finally to consider ways of bringing them under control. Taken individually, most of these errors do not seriously alter a writer's meaning; often, as we have seen, they merely diminish the amount of redundancy in a message. Yet they have the power, when they occur frequently, to hinder or even halt the average reader. From the student writer's point of view, the task of learning to correct common errors is the least rewarding part of writing. Repair work at best, it carries none of the satisfaction that comes with composing. To make matters worse, the errors themselves often raise grammatically complex problems that students are not prepared to consider analytically without some understanding of English grammar.

No wonder then that teachers debate the wisdom of intervening in the cause of correctness. It is heavy work for modest rewards. Still, this teacher at least is convinced that the work is worth doing and that it does not inhibit the student as a writer provided the distinction between composing and proofreading is respected. Correctness is by no means all the work of a composition course, but it must be part of the work so long as readers continue to show but limited tolerance for errors, especially the errors we have been considering in this chapter.

We know very little about the rate at which errors can be expected to disappear from adult writing. Judging from the writing samples of 100 students whose errors were counted at intervals during a semester of instruction, it seems reasonable to expect a student who is making between fifteen and thirty errors in a 300-word essay to reduce that number to eight; some do much better than this. But at this stage of the student's development as a writer, the rate of error reduction, while useful to know, is not as important as other less measurable kinds of behavior—for example, a growing inclination to scrutinize sentences in order to observe the forms of words or increased confidence in one's ability to make deliberate choices of word forms based on grammatical reasoning. A vigorous argument with a teacher or a classmate over a point of grammar may be a surer mark of progress than a perfect score on an objective test or even an error-free composition, for it suggests that the student has invested the best energies of his mind in a problem he would once have been unable to notice or define, let alone solve. Whenever the effort to correct common errors can thus engage the adult intelligence of students, the teacher should feel that he has prepared his student to cope with common errors, even though some of those errors still cling to the student's writing.

5
Spelling

Most of the writing problems we have considered so far—punctuation, syntax, and common errors—are grammatical. That is, they have been defined in relation to the rules and conventions that govern sentence-making in formal English. A particular mark of punctuation or an inflection, for example, is neither right nor wrong until it appears in the context of a sentence. Until then, such units are grammatically neutral, like pieces of colored glass that have not yet been set in a mosaic. A number of the difficulties students have as beginning writers, however, lie outside the context of grammar and within other contexts or systems that can figure as importantly as grammaticality in the assessment of writing skill. In the next three chapters we will be considering three of those systems and the difficulties students have with them. Anyone who has been reading the student sentences used in earlier chapters to illustrate grammatical problems is surely aware of the problems we will be considering in this chapter and the next: misspelling and imprecise, inappropriate, and erroneous word choices. The third problem concerns organization and development and will be discussed in Chapter 7.

When we move from the grammatical context to the orthographic (spelling) and semantic (vocabulary) contexts, we move in two opposite directions from grammaticality. Orthography moves us toward even greater strictness and arbitrariness than we encountered in grammar; semantics, toward a seeming luxuriance of options that is itself both a challenge and a bewilderment to the inexperienced writer. Still, the problems we have noted in the grammatically governed skills reappear in spelling and vocabulary in new guises, reminding us that in teaching inexperienced writers to write we are usually contending not with a number of discrete difficulties (as can sometimes happen with an advanced writer who may be weak in spelling, for example, or punctuation but nonetheless seems competent except for those flaws) but with a central condition of ill-preparedness with formal written language. This condition pervades all the sub-systems of that skill, producing errors that may be classified under different headings in a composition handbook but that nonetheless rise from common ground: from the student's rootedness in spoken rather than written language and his habitual preference for forms of English that diverge in a variety of ways from formal English; from a general lack of visual acuity and memory in relation to written letter and word patterns; from the student's efforts to simulate a register or code he is not sure of; and finally from an urge to move into deep grammatical and lexical waters in the effort to communicate complex thoughts.

The ability to spell grows slowly out of a number of different kinds of encounters with words—with the sounds of words (phonological encounters), the looks of words on paper (visual encounters), the feel of words as the hand moves to form them in writing (kinesthetic encounters), and the meanings of words as they take their places in the contexts of sentences (semantic encounters). Students differ greatly not only in the amount and variety of experience they have had with words but also in their abilities to perceive words through these different avenues of response. So tangled are the roots of misspellings, in fact, and so inconclusive the research on how students—especially adult students—can learn to spell, that often students with average or better-than-average academic preparation in other subjects are allowed to slip through their courses and out of college without ever having to come to terms with their incompetence as spellers. Of all the encoding skills, spelling tends to be viewed by teachers and students alike as the most arbitrary, the most resistant to instruction, and the least related to intelligence (a myth that has comforted many bad spellers). It is the one area of writing where English teachers themselves will admit ineptness. Outside the academy, however, the response to misspelling is less obliging. Indeed, the ability to spell is viewed by many as one of the marks of the educated person, and the failure of a college graduate to meet that minimal standard of advanced literacy is cause to question the quality of his education or even his intelligence.

Perhaps the best measure of the seriousness of the spelling problem among BW students, however, is the fact that teachers themselves are alarmed by both the number and kinds of errors they find in BW essays. For here, in addition to the errors they have often seen in the work of more advanced writers, they find errors of a very elementary sort, misspellings of such basic words as *still* (*stil*), *which* (*wich*), *maybe* (*maby*), *often* (*offen*), *are* (*our*), *with* (*whith*), *goes* (*gose*), *modern* (*morden*), along with approximations of less common words that reflect but a blurred sense of how the sound system of spoken English relates to the letter system of written English (e.g. *assumion* for *assumption*, *availiable* for *available*, *duagter* for *daughter*, *dinning* for *dining*, *graduedet* for *graduate*).

Over a third of the errors BW students make at the first level of instruction are spelling errors, and as the students move into more advanced vocabulary and begin to take greater risks with words, the proportion of errors may grow to almost half. To be sure, there are many more "opportunities" for misspelling than for grammatical errors. Every word is a potential misspelling, whereas only certain words in each sentence figure in grammatical errors. Readers tend also to tolerate more misspellings than grammatical errors such as subject-verb agreement. Even so, the misspellings of BW students remain a major hindrance both to their readers and to themselves. (We cannot tell how many needless circumlocutions or imprecise phrasings result from the fear of misspellings, but the number is undoubtedly high. "Sometime, I know the word I want to put down," writes a student, "but then I know I can't spell it so I get an easier one instead.") Meanwhile, the teacher, reluctant to turn his writing course into a spelling course and skeptical about whether a skill that grows so silently over years of exposure to writing and reading can be acquired at this late stage, hesitates to do more than make his marginal "sp" and urge the student to "look up words you are uncertain of" or "proofread!"

For many students, unfortunately, this is lost counsel. Their difficulties with words lie below these surface remedies and nothing but the observation of misspelling patterns, the exploration of causes, and the nurturing of new spelling habits will finally make much difference in the way they spell. And while the adult bad speller is probably never going to become an exceptionally good speller, the discovery that intelligent effort can reduce spelling errors significantly and that the domain of spelling is not quite as "unruly" as it once appeared can generate a will to work on the problem.

It is beyond the resources of this study—and of most English teachers—to carry on the kind of research that needs to be done on the spelling difficulties of BW students. This would call for more extensive and refined data than have been gathered for this chapter, including an analysis of the spoken as well as the written repertory of BW students and ultimately a fully developed typology of errors that would correspond, as our present typologies do not, to the kinds of misspellings we find in BW papers. What follows here, therefore, is but a rough-and-ready classification of the kinds of difficulties one teacher has observed in the essays of over a thousand BW students and some recommendations for working on these errors "Monday morning."

Identifying misspelled words

One must distinguish at the outset between words that are misspelled and words that are miswritten or incorrectly inflected. Just as those accidental word skips and misses we encountered in the chapter on syntax may reflect less upon the grammatical competence of a writer than upon his manual difficulty with writing, so a number of "misspellings" may be caused by accident, a slip of the pen or an ambiguity in the formation of a letter—the habitual omission, for example, of a dot over the *i*. To complicate matters, uncertain spellers often deliberately camouflage their uncertainty by writing illegibly so that it becomes difficult to separate genuine misspellings from illegibilities. Or the "misspellings" may reflect difficulties with the grammar of English rather than the spelling of a word. The student, for example, who writes *assistancs* for *assistance* has not learned the correct orthographic representation of this sound when it occurs in this particular suffix; however, the student who writes *ten assistant* for *ten assistants* has probably not learned (or remembered) the grammatical convention for marking plural nouns in formal writing. He has, it is true, failed to add a letter where formal usage demands it, but the omitted letter, if it lacks grammatical significance to him, is not likely to get added in response to lessons on the correspondence between the sound of *s* (which for grammatical reasons he is not sounding) and the look of *s*. The isolation of these wrong-lettered but not necessarily misspelled words from the body of words to be worked on in spelling is an important first step for both teacher and student. It reduces and clarifies the work to be done. The following passage, for example, might seem at first glance to reflect a serious spelling problem. Yet a closer look should reveal that the spelling, by BW standards, is advanced and that the more serious difficulty lies with inflections and word-class forms:

> Yesterday in a busy town of the capital, a fatal incidented took place. This incident, involved a child and a vehicle. as a results, there were a big conjection involved vehicle and padistrians. People running from all direction to the particular place where the incident occurred. The child was knocked to the opposite side of the Road.
> Although the driver of the vehicle was considers wrong, he did not stopped. This caused a confusion, Since most of the Padistrians where trying to get the car license number, other ran toward the aid of the child. A few minutes latter the Ambulance and Police vehicles were on the spot. The child's condition was considered serious.

Among the erroneous words in this passage, a number reflect grammatical problems (*incidented, results, involved, direction, considers, stopped, other*). Of the misspellings, one (*where* for *were*) appears to be an oversight since the writer correctly distinguishes the forms elsewhere in the passage. One (*conjection*) may be an accurate orthographic representation of the writer's pronunciation of *congestion*. Only two are straightforward misspellings (*padistrian* and *latter*). Meanwhile, the student has managed to spell correctly a number of difficult words (*capital, vehicle, license, occurred*). With more practice and better habits of proofreading, his spelling errors would probably clear up by themselves.

Misspellings caused by unpredictabilities within English spelling

Although the spelling of English words is doubtless more difficult than the spelling of, let us say, Spanish words, where the correspondence between letter and sound approaches the ideal ratio of one to one, the fact remains that millions of students have learned and do still learn to spell English words with a high degree of correctness. Just what is involved in this feat of literacy is not totally understood, but recent research in English spelling suggests that the orthographic system is far more alphabetical than we have realized—that is, the letters we use to spell words represent sounds far more systematically than a superficial look would suggest. To be sure, the system is complex, involving a larger alphabet than the twenty-six letters we call the alphabet and more complex rules for combining these letters than any we can consciously acquire by memorizing rules.[1] But the fact remains that an average speller, in addition to having found ways of remembering the correct spelling of the so-called "demons" and of keeping homophones straight, has acquired unconsciously a large number of spelling rules that enable him to make his way through a bewildering array of graphemic options. This is true, in fact, even of poor spellers whose errors generally represent but a small fraction of the words they write. What is distracting, however, about their misspellings (what makes them "glaring") is that they are the kinds of errors better spellers cannot imagine making. It is one thing, for example, to spell the suffix in *appearance* with an *e* (*appearence*). This is an easy mistake to make because of the phonetic similarity between *-ance* and *-ence* (as in *difference*). But it is another thing to write *appearencs* (for *appearance*), which would not occur to the average speller as a real option. And even where the spelling can be seen to make some "sense" in relation to the letter-sound correspondences of English orthography, the reader has the impression of a vastly simplified system of correspondences, perhaps not a system at all but a confused stock of graphemic options with which the writer invents spelling as he goes along. Thus the familiar *-ion* suffix will often be spelled in a variety of ways within an essay:

explo*sun*	condit*ing* (condition)	educat*an*al
deci*sien*	direct*en*	

Or a writer will produce the same word anew with each effort:

benefitial	benefical	benefishal

The BW speller has learned one important fact about English spelling, namely, that there are more ways than one to spell many of the sounds in English. The *sh* sound, for example, which is represented

---

1. For a full discussion and classification of phoneme-grapheme correspondences, see Paul R. Hanna et al., *Phoneme-Grapheme Correspondences as Cued to Spelling Improvement*, OE-32008. (Washington, D.C.: U.S. Department of Health, Education, and Welfare, 1966).

in *beneficial* as *ci*, can also be represented in other words in the following ways:[2]

Grapheme	Position in Syllable		
	Initial	*Medial*	*Final*
C	o Ce an ic		de fiC ient
CE	o CEan		
CH	CHef		eCH e lon
S	Sug ar		
SC	cre SCen do		faSC ism
SCH	SCHwa		
SCI	con SCIous		luSCI ous
SH	SHip	fin iSHed	wiSH
SI	pen SIon		
SS			preSS ure
SSI			miSSI on
T	ne go Ti ate		i niT i ate
TI	ac TIon		i niTI al

The $\bar{e}$ sound, to use another example, has sixteen graphemic options, most of which the average speller has learned, by look and feel and rule, to use correctly. But the student who has had less experience with written words is likely to reduce the number of $\bar{e}$ graphemes he has to select from and then to use these in seemingly unpredictable ways. The following words, for example, from the essay of a poor speller, show a familiarity with three graphemes for $\bar{e}$ (*e*, *i*, and *ea*). Correctly spelled, the words call for five different graphemes for the sound $\bar{e}$. In two of the words (*ea*ser, *deciving*), the correspondences are correct for at least part of the word, but all the words contain erroneous choices:

delicac*es*	(*e* replaces *ie*)
*ea*ser	(*i* is omitted)

2. Adapted from Hanna et al., p. 29. Although the language appears at the outset to have a distressing oversupply of letters and letter combinations for sounds (Hanna mentions 170 graphemic options for 52 phonemes), the Hanna study reports that the ratio of graphemes to phonemes can be reduced for 90 per cent of the phonemes in the language to 77:52 by eliminating once-only correspondences and by taking into consideration such environmental influences as stress and position in the syllable. The *sh* phoneme, a difficult phoneme to spell because of the many variant forms, is thus not as unpredictable as the list of options would suggest. The sound is quite consistently spelled *sh* at the beginnings and **ends of words, for example,** except in special terms like *schwa* (German) or *chef* (French). The unpredictability is highest where the *sh* phoneme initiates an interior syllable.

dec*i*ving	(*i* replaces *ei*)
*ea*ther	(*ea* replaces *ei*)
extr*ea*m	(*ea* replaces *e*)
unr*e*sonable	(*e* replaces *ea*)

Wherever the orthographic system is highly unpredictable (as it is with the long vowels and such phonemes as *sh, er, f, j*, and the treacherous *schwa* sound with its twenty-two variant spellings) the BW speller is almost inevitably in for trouble, for he has not *seen* the words often enough as a reader nor felt the spelling of them as a writer to be able to make the right choices. Where the rules give out, experience is essential. Otherwise, the writer must simply sound his way through words, using the graphemic options he trusts most to transcribe the sounds he intends. The result is an idiosyncratic form of "basic" spelling which the average reader is not likely to accept:

biggut (bigot)	hier (hire)	traned (trained)
bott (bought)	honist (honest)	taks (takes)
broden (broaden)	marrage (marriage)	truble (trouble)
buget (budget)	mgiority (majority)	waching (watching)
consearn (concern)	offen (often)	wich (which)
delt (dealt)	romed (roamed)	wot (what)
discrace (disgrace)	sholder (shoulder)	wreckonession (recognition)
doughtfully (doubtfully)	scedualdes (schedules)	
falts (faults)	swich (switch)	

Misspellings caused by pronunciation

No one speaks "spelled" English. We glide and blur and skip our way through words when we run them together in spoken sentences. Only when we must put our words down on paper, separating each one from the other by a space and getting down every letter that convention has assigned to each word, do we experience the sharp literalism of literacy, the letter-by-letter accountability that suddenly checks our pace and turns our attention to the smallest units of the language.

Even if a speaker were to speak English in such a way as to voice every vowel and consonant and then to transcribe every sound with a letter that represented that sound, not only would his speech be tediously exact but he would still have problems with spelling, because of the unpredictabilities within the orthographic system itself. But of course the reality is that no one pronounces words this way. Not only do speakers blend and slight and rush the sounds in words but they often diverge widely from the model of spoken English that is called standard, and although far from perfect, the "fit" between standard pronunciation, or a close approximation of that model, and spelling is much closer than the fit between non-standard English speech and spelling. Thus where a student is both an inexperienced writer-reader and a speaker of a variant form of English, he is in a sense at a double disadvantage as a speller: not only must he deal with the unpredictabilities that inhere in the orthographic system without the advantage of a large vocabulary of visually remembered words but he must translate *his* spoken form of English into the standard form before the alphabetical system will make sense. If he says *tole* for *told*, he cannot depend upon his ear to guide him in spelling that word. Yet if he lacks experience seeing words, his pronunciation must often be decisive in spelling. This helps to explain the large number of misspellings that occur at the ends of words, where there is often strong phonological support in the student's vernacular for omitting sounds. This is true of the *er* sound, for example, which may be added where, in standard pronunciation, it is not needed and omitted where it is (as in *diplomer* for *diploma*). More often it is absent in the speech of the students we are describing here. Thus we find misspellings of this kind in very common words:

> anothe (r)   daught (er)   moth (er)   wheneve (r)

Or we find the common consonant clusters that terminate many English words reduced to one consonant, as in:

> attrac (t)   complain (t)   contac (t)   curren (t)   dept (h)
>
> fine (d)   migrat (n)   mine (d)   perhap (s)   statistis (c)

In addition to the sounds the student may rarely produce (such as terminal consonant clusters) there are the sounds that he easily confuses. And while these confusions may be difficult to hear in the hubbub of speech, they stand out on the page, often creating a different word from the one the writer intends. The sounds *d-t, m-n, f-v,* and *b-d* are among the most common confusions:

> *d-t*
>
> altitute (altitude)   attendand (attendant)   bandid (bandit)
>
> badle (battle)   medal (metal)   presidend (president)

thread (threat)

m-n[3]

abandoming (abandoning)   blaned (blamed)

conparing (comparing)   comtrol (control)

disconfort (discomfort)

f-v

believes (beliefs)   releave (relief)

strive (strife)   savely (safely)

b-d[3]

decome (become)   biploma (diploma)

goob (good)   buring (during)

If we add to these the prefixes that are often difficult to distinguish in spoken English (*en-in* as in *entelect* for *intellect,* and *inter* for *enter,* or *pre-pro-per* as in *proform* for *perform, presist* for *persist,* and *prehap* for *perhaps*) and the suffixes (especially *-s, -ed, -ly,* and *-ing*) that are often left off in the rush of speech, even where the speaker's grammar supports the inflection, we have a large collection of misspellings that may represent fairly accurately the writer's spoken English but not the English on which the spelling system is based.

Homophones

Homophones are words that sound the same but have different meanings and spellings (thus the *e* sounds in *here* and *hear* are aurally indistinguishable but semantically and orthographically different). For BW students, they are a source of many errors—errors that experienced writers have generally learned to avoid early in their training, but that BW students have difficulty noticing and readers have difficulty overlooking. Unfortunately, they often involve words that are needed in sentences all the time:

do-due   two-to-too
for-four-fore   through—threw
here-hear   won-one
know-no   whether-weather
there-their-they're   you're-your

3. Can also reflect graphic confusions rather than pronunciation.

Predictable only by context, such words seem to slip off the pen and past the eyes of the writer so easily that even in proofreading he is likely to miss them unless he is in the habit of methodically checking all incidences of words like *too-to-two* or *by-buy*. The differences in meaning can generally be learned by various mnemonic tricks (e.g., the *there* that points to a location has a *here* in it but the *their* of possession has an *I*, or the student can memorize a model sentence such as *Put their money there*), but like the simple *-s* inflections, the habit of using the unwanted forms is deep and students generally have to work steadily and systematically at noticing the errors before such methods are of much use.

Misspellings caused by unfamiliarity with the structure of words

Just as BW students have not learned to see the parts of sentences and therefore have difficulty marking them off, revising them, or holding them together when sentences get complex, so they have difficulty discriminating (both visually and aurally) among the syllables of words or carrying out instructions that require an understanding of the system of affixation whereby words are made to change their class (*courage-courageous*), their tense, number, or degree (*walk-walked, walk-walks, slow-slower*), or their meaning (*view-review, help-helpless*).

The absence of this kind of information about words is not difficult to document. First, we find that students add syllables to words without seeming to realize that they have done so, creating words that they themselves would probably reject if they were to pronounce what they spelled. Sometimes a superfluous syllable is created:

availiable (available)	**answewer** (answer)	diplomia (diploma)
emphesises (emphasis)	**fashison** (fashion)	simiple (simple)
graduedet (graduate)	**jellious** (jealous)	

More often a syllable is omitted, especially in the middle of a word:

crated (created)	clerial (clerical)	consired (considered)
finncal (financial)	imblance (imbalance)	inaccute (inaccurate)
motvation (motivation)	parell (parallel)	strugged (struggled)
surban (suburban)		

What is usually revealed when the student is asked to pronounce what he has written or to work out the pronunciation of a word he doesn't know is that he has had no practice in sounding words out syllable by syllable. Like someone driving in a rainstorm without a windshield wiper, he moves uncertainly into the blur of sounds, doing his best to find his way but wandering often very far from his destination. The various approximations of *prejudiced* that appear below suggest just how far off course this inefficient approach to spelling can take a writer:

> prejudeicced   prejeduce   prejudgiced   prejusticed

A similar kind of confusion dominates students' approaches to affixation. Aware that things often have to change when letters are added at the beginnings or ends of words, students are not prepared to make these changes deliberately. Here again their unfamiliarity with the "carpentry" of words keeps them from being able to apply some of the useful rules for affixation, which requires the perception of syllables and stress and an understanding of the way certain letters such as the diacritic, or silent, *e* and doubled consonants affect the pronunciation of vowels (*write-written, cope-coped, cop-copped,* etc.). Thus even in areas where English spelling is, for the most part, unambiguous and where the student could dramatically reduce his misspellings by learning to apply those rules, we find that little or no effort has been made to teach them. Thus we have misspellings such as these:

1. The elimination of the diacritic *e* between two consonants:
   advancment   densly   excitment   precisly   taks

2. The retention of the diacritic *e* with a suffix that begins with a vowel (mainly with *-ing*):
   haveing   houseing   liveing   useing

3. The addition of an *e* where the root itself does not require it:
   considereing   departement   limiteing   murderes (murders)

4. Failure to double the final consonant when a suffix beginning with a vowel is added to a word and the word itself has a final syllable that contains a short vowel and is accented:
   begining   draging   geting   ploted   puting   quiting
   robed (robbed)   stabing   writen

5. The doubling of a final consonant when the final vowel is long or unaccented:
   cleanning   dinning   keepping   listenning   limitted
   scrapped (scraped)   writting

Once aware of the phonemic principles underlying the doubling of consonants at the ends of words, the student can be aided by his *own* use of the language, that is, by the contrasts that he himself produces when he pronounces words like *writing* or *written, scraped* or *scrapped*. It may also be that a student is more likely to err in doubling a consonant when the resulting word is not part of his active vocabulary and therefore suggests no alternative meaning. Thus *bated* might be correctly spelled and *dining* incorrectly spelled (as *dinning*) because the student recognizes another meaning for *batted* but not for *dinning*.[4]

Misspellings caused by failure to remember or see words

People who read and write a great deal are occasionally bad spellers, but people who do little reading and writing are inevitably bad spellers, for without constant experience with written words, it is impossible to absorb the sound-letter correspondences that govern English spelling, to build a memory for the looks and haptical feel of words, or to become a close observer of letters. The misspelled words of BW students reflect in a variety of ways their inexperience with letters. Dependent mainly on their ability to remember the sounds in words, they are hindered, as we have seen, from representing these sounds by an uncertain knowledge of the complete range of sound-letter correspondences.

Given the unpredictabilities in the spelling system, almost all writers must at times make guesses or back off from what they have written to see whether it "looks" right, but the BW student, because of his limited exposure to written words, has less well-developed hunches about words and will often produce spellings that no experienced eye would accept, so far do they wander from the model. We have already seen examples of such misspelling (*duagter, finncal, thrgh-thur-throuh,* etc.). The splitting or joining of common words in unconventional ways also suggests a lack of exposure to such words in print:

atleast	in stead	suchas	with out
house whold	mean time	to gether	whatso ever

Unprepared to recognize the way certain words are supposed to "look" when they are written down, the student is at the same time prevented, by his inexperienced eye, from noting accurately what he

4. Oscar Chavarria-Aguilar makes this suggestion in "Proposal for a Study of Spelling Problems and Possible Remedies," City College, 1973 (unpublished).

actually has written down. In other words, he has trouble remembering what he has seen and seeing what he has written. For the spelling of English words, this means trouble—not only with unfamiliar or orthographically unpredictable words but even with the words a person knows how to spell. And here we come upon what is probably the single largest cause of misspellings among BW students—the lack of visual acuity with words and letters, a habit of seeing which swiftly transforms what is on the page to what is in the mind of the writer, even where the divergence between the written and intended form is great, producing not simply a misspelling but a completely different word from the one the writer has in mind:

Intended Word	Written Word	Intended Word	Written Word
about	out	most	must
bring	being	never	nerve
by	my	open	oven
car	care	place	play
chance	change	quiet	quite
class	glass	quite	quit
country	county	roof	root
community	committee	series	serious
defending	defining	sink	sick
except	expect	sense	since
follow	fellow	taught	tough
farther	father	turn	term
fight	flight	trial	trail
intend	indent	think	thing
instant	instead	very	every
job	joy	wish	which
left	lift	went	when
much	mush	where	were
many	may		

Letter reversals or scrambles can also be blamed on the difficulty of seeing what has been written. Letter or even word reversals, whether in typing or handwriting, are common to all writers. The difference is in the number of such reversals in BW papers and the writers' failure to see them once they have occurred. With some words, it seems, the writer remembers that a certain letter belongs in the word, but he is not certain where it goes (as with the r in *modern*, which ends up *morden*); with other words, he simply fails to see what he has written (as with *flims* for *films*):

Intended Word	Written Word	Intended Word	Written Word
afraid	afriad	modern	morden
affluence	affulence	material	materail
catch	cacht	never	nerve
children	childern	obtain	obtian
destroy	destory	preachers	pearchers
detailed	detialed	paradise	paraside
exciting	exicting	sloppy	sopply
else	esle	secrets	secerts
films	flims	soldier	soilder
field	flied	system	stysem
family	faimly	situation	stiuation
graduate	graudate	true	ture
goes	gose	trial	trail
impulses	impluses	ugly	ulgy
judge	jugde	who	how
liars	lairs	worst	worts

What one senses in these and other misspellings that surprise the reader by the degree of their inaccuracy is a general inattentiveness to words on the page, a visual slurring of configurations so extreme at times as to suggest to the teacher a perceptual disorder rather than mere inexperience. Certainly were such errors to appear in the papers of academically advantaged students (i.e., students from schools where there was opportunity to learn to read or write), there would be good reason to explore the possibility of an underlying disorder. But where students have had limited practice in reading and writing, they cannot be expected to be able to make visual discriminations of the sort most people learn to make only after years of practice and instruction.

Nonetheless, the errors students would themselves recognize if they could see them are among the most difficult to get at by direct intervention. Accustomed to seeing whole words rather than word parts and to seeing the beginnings of those configurations more clearly than the middles, where letters tend to coagulate, the student must re-train his eyes to see in terms of schemas he is only beginning to acquire. Spelling, the "leveler" of letters, demands equal attention to all letters whereas speech and reading demand selective attention to words and syllables. Thus the student must have new strategies for breaking into words that allow him to give attention to all letters. At the same time, spelling is not independent of semantic context. Not only do we have homophones, with their total dependence upon context, but the large number of correctly spelled words that are simply wrong for the sentences or phrases they are in (e.g., *What I thing about school* or *We do this instant of drinking*). Such errors may point up the need for perceptual training that goes beyond rules or orthographic principles (although these are also eye-sharpening) and requires the student to exercise his eyes, first with non-verbal configurations and then with increasingly complex verbal configurations that eventually lead him to recognize differences among paired words that have been confused in his own writing.[5]

Suggestions for improving spelling

We have described four main causes of misspelling among BW students: the spelling system itself, differences between spoken and spelled English, ignorance of the rules that work, and the inexperienced eye. We will now consider ways of helping students who misspell for these reasons.

1. *Assume at the outset that the misspellings of young adults can be brought under control.* Nothing inhibits growth among BW students more than the conviction that their errors are both infinite and unpredictable. Where spelling is concerned, teachers too often communicate this message themselves, and since students take their cues about educability from their teachers, it is almost inevitable that the teacher who thinks spelling cannot be taught and merely notes misspellings in the margin without giving the student a strategy for reducing them is confirming the student's impression that he is a "born" misspeller. Once, however, the student senses a teacher's confidence in the face of a problem the student has despaired of solving, he begins to redefine his situation as a poor speller. And if, at this early stage of re-definition, he can succeed in controlling even one kind of misspelling, he is usually willing to move to the next.

2. *Begin by teaching the student to observe himself as a speller.* Most students have become accustomed over the years to being corrected for their misspellings. Rarely, however, have they been encouraged to explore the reasons behind these misspellings. As a result, they tend to see each misspelling as a discrete error and the work of improving spelling as an overwhelming task in memorization. If, however, instead of

5. For more detailed suggestions on perceptual development in spelling and grammar, see Patricia Laurence, "Error's Endless Train," *Journal of Basic Writing,* Spring, 1975.

merely correcting errors as they are pointed out, students collect them for a time, entering each misspelled word on a chart that classifies types of errors, they will begin to see the outlines of their own spelling problems. The writer who filled out the following chart, for example, had fourteen errors in a 200-word essay, but the chart served to group these errors under three main headings: long vowel sounds (mainly $\bar{e}$), homophones, and suffixes. Of the two words that fall outside these categories, *magement* could be an oversight and the *of/off* confusion might be listed under the homophone heading. The beginning writer is rarely prepared to work with such a chart without help, but with a short introduction to the terms and several sessions with a teacher or tutor, he can usually classify his misspellings independently. And once these misspellings are seen to pile up under certain headings, the student himself begins to wonder why he has made those errors rather than others. Having begun to describe himself as a misspeller, he is usually ready to look more deeply into his reasons for being wrong in particular ways.

Spelling chart

Word	Misspelling	Letters or syllables involved	Type of misspelling
1. deceiving	deciving	ei/i	1
2. buy	by	uy/y	5
3. do	due	o/ue	5
4. either	eather	ei/ea	1
5. they	thay	ey/ay	1
6. management	magement	na	9
7. capable	capible	able/ible	6
8. easiest	easyest	i/y	6
9. unreasonable	unresonable	ea/e	1
10. experience	experiance	ence/ance	6
11. extreme	extream	e/ea	1
12. wear	ware	ear/are	5
13. of	off	f/ff	10
14. assistance	assistancs	ance/ancs	6
15.			
16.			

Types of misspellings

1. Long vowel sound	6. Suffix	11. Letter reversal
2. Short vowel sound	7. Prefix	12. [others]
3. Final consonant or consonant cluster	8. Double consonant	13.
	9. Missing letter or syllable	14.
4. Diacritic *e*		
5. Homophone	10. Word confusion	

---

3. *Before attempting to work on individual errors, make certain that the student understands certain terms and operations.* From his work on the chart, he will already have acquired some of the words he needs in order to talk and think about spelling. The terms should include:

accent	consonant cluster	prefix	syllable
compound	diacritic *e*[6]	*schwa*	vowel
consonant	homophone	suffix	

The student should also be able to:[7]

1. Sound out written words
2. Understand the three main diacritic marks (—, ∪, /)
3. Divide words into syllables.[8]

4. *If possible start to work on misspellings that can be controlled by the application of rules.* There are problems with rules, as everyone knows. Some of them are too complicated to work with and almost all of them have exceptions. Furthermore, some students have difficulty using rules. Nonetheless, some rules, mainly those pertaining to affixation, work much of the time for most students, provided the rules are formulated clearly. It is, for example, much more difficult to apply a rule that combines in one sentence all the conditions for application than it is to follow a sequence of instructions. Thus the rule for doubling the final consonant is simpler to apply in the second formulation than in the first:

6. The term *silent e* may also be used, although it is somewhat misleading in that its effect phonetically is to strengthen rather than silence a sound.

7. To test the student's understanding of these operations, it is useful to practice with nonsense words at first.

8. Hanna and Hodges recommend that the rules of syllabication be arrived at inductively, by the examination of word lists that illustrate the most useful principles of syllabication. Paul R. Hanna, Richard E. Hodges, and Jean S. Hanna, *Spelling: Structure and Strategies* (Boston: Houghton Mifflin, 1971), p. 229.

1. Words ending in a single consonant immediately preceded by a single vowel bearing primary stress double the consonant before a suffixal vowel but not before a suffixal consonant.

2. Does the word end in one vowel plus one consonant?
   Is the accent on the final syllable?
   Does the suffix begin with a vowel?
   If YES to all three, double the consonant.

Of the many rules that govern English spelling, at least four are worth learning, provided, of course, the student's misspellings reflect no understanding (conscious or unconscious) of these rules:

1. *i* before *e*
   except after *c*
   or when sounded like *a*
   as in *neighbor* and *weigh*
   This rule works only where the student's confusion is between *ie* and *ei*. For other spellings of the *e* sound, the rule is not useful (*reach*, *extreme*, etc.). Also, the rule does not apply to nouns that form their plurals by changing the *y* to *i* and adding *-es* (*democracies*).

2. Is there an unpronounced *e* at the end of the word?
   Does the suffix begin with a vowel?
   If YES to both questions, drop the *e*.
   Another rule can be attached to this that covers the main exceptions, namely that when the "silent" *e* is preceded by *c* or *g* and the suffix begins with *a*, *o*, or *u*, the *e* remains. However, the student can usually discover the phonemic principle that underlies the rule simply by seeing lists of words that retain the diacritic *e*—*manageable, peaceable*, etc.

3. Does the word end in a consonant + *y*?
   Change the *y* to *i* and add the suffix.
   Exception: Keep the *y* when suffix is *-ing*, possessive *'s*, or a proper name.

4. Rule for doubling final consonant (given above).

Rules such as these tend to distort the student's sense of the larger patterns in English spelling unless they are applied during practice to a broad range of words. That is, the student who works exclusively on the words that require a doubling of consonants or a change of *y* to *i* is in danger of missing the point that most words in English are unchanged by suffixes. Of the seventeen leading rules listed in *Webster's Seventh New Collegiate Dictionary* for adding suffixes to words (1.1-1.13.2), twelve state that the words being described remain the same. To be sure, most of these rules have exceptions, but the unmistakable pattern in the language is not toward doubling nor dropping but simply adding. Ideally, exercises designed to give students practice in applying the rules will reflect this reality.

5. *Develop an awareness of the main discrepancies between the student's pronunciation of words and the models of pronunciation upon which the spelling system is based.* As we have seen, the student is led by his pronunciation to misspell many words. Most commonly, he is likely to 1. drop letters on the endings of words where consonants combine (*ct, cs, nd, nt, fs,* etc.); 2. drop syllables that are easily blurred in speech (*intlect* for *intellect, plusion* for *pollution, facsnate* for *fascinate, libral* for *liberal,* etc.); or 3. miss the distinctions between certain sounds (*discrace* for *disgrace, baddle* for *battle, sucurity* for *security,* etc.). While it would be unrealistic and unacceptable to set about changing a student's speech in order to improve his spelling, it is essential to alert him to the features of pronunciation that are likely to mislead him as a speller. Such awareness is built up through exercises that allow him to hear and see the contrasts between spoken and written words. Dictation exercises that incorporate the kinds of pronunciation errors the student has already produced, paired word lists of pronounced versus spelled forms, taped exercises that require the student to transcribe his own speech into standard written English—all such exercises serve to impress the student with the need not to change his speech but to *translate* spoken words into spelled words. And where such lessons are tailored to the student's individual pattern of misspellings, he is certain to develop that most useful of spelling skills—the sense of doubt in the right places, which prompts the writer to stop and reason spellings out or look them up.

6. *Develop an awareness of the ways in which pronunciation helps the speller.* While it is true that a student's pronunciation will often cause him to misspell, it is also true that the way he pronounces a word —whether, for example, he stresses a syllable or not (as in *sick/classic*) or whether he uses a short vowel or a long vowel (as in *bit/bite*)—will often give him a clue to its spelling. Through the study of word lists that demonstrate certain phonemic-graphemic principles a student can discover a number of fairly dependable spelling patterns that will give him greater security with whole groups of words rather than merely with the specific words that happen to show up in his papers.

Probably the most useful of these phonemic principles is the one that enables the student to see the relationship between certain vowel-consonant sequences and pronunciation, a principle that, once understood, can greatly reduce the confusion over when to double consonants and when to omit or use the silent *e*. The principle is that in a sequence with the pattern

accented vowel-consonant-vowel (V-C-V)

the first vowel is long. And in a sequence with the pattern V-C-C or V-C (at end of word), the first vowel is short. Thus:

V-C-V	V-C-C	V-C
b i t e	b i t t en	b i t
h o p ing	h o pp ed	h o p

Once this principle is discovered, the student can test his spelling of a word by pronouncing it and thereby avoid such common misspellings as these:

baned (banned)	clasic (classic)	draging (dragging)
diner (dinner)	dismising (dismissing)	ploted (plotted)
quit (quite)	stabing (stabbing)	steping (stepping)
writen (written)	tottally (totally)	

As usual, there are exceptions (the verb *coming*, for example, which is often given a double *m*, perhaps in unconscious response to the principle), but the principle is so widely applicable that it is easier to deal with the exceptions than to ignore the principle.

Other patterns of more limited scope are also worth discovering through the study of word lists that highlight the operative principle and incorporate words from the student's own error list.

1. The final *ch* sound is usually spelled *tch* in one-syllable words preceded by a short vowel. The rule also holds when a prefix is added to such words (*mismatch*). (Exceptions like *such, much,* or *kitchen* are usually stabilized spellings and therefore not threatened by this principle.) In polysyllabic words (*sandwich*) or words with a long vowel (*reach*), the spelling is *ch*.
2. The final *k* is usually spelled *ck* in stressed syllables (*sick*) and *c* in unstressed syllables (*classic*).
3. The initial *k* is usually spelled *k* when followed by *i, e* and *c* when followed by *a, o, u* (*kitchen kettle/catching cold*).

4. The final *f* is usually spelled *ff* when preceded by a short vowel (*stuff, staff*) unless the short vowel sound is formed by *au* or *ou*, in which case the spelling is *gh* (*enough, laugh*).
5. The final *j* sound is usually spelled *dge* when preceded by a short vowel (*bridge, edge*) and *ge* when preceded by a long vowel (*age, siege*).
6. The *oi/oy* sound is usually spelled *oi* in the middle of a word (*point*) and *oy* at the end (*joy*).
7. The *sion* syllable is usually used where the pronunciation is *zyun* (*explosion*) or where the *shun* sound is preceded by *l* or *s* (*passion*). Otherwise, the *tion* syllable is used (*motion, reaction*).

7. *Develop the student's ability to discriminate among graphemic options.* Even poor spellers are aware that similar sounds may be represented by different letters, and we have seen that many of these options can be linked to certain conditions such as the environment of a letter (thus the *f* sound following *s* will always be spelled *ph*), stress (thus the *k* sound will be represented as *c* in *classic* and *ck* in *sick*), position (thus we have *oi* in the middle of a word and *oy* at the end), or the origin of a word (thus the troublesome *ant/ent* endings, which are pronounced the same, usually stem from words of Latin origin that belonged to different conjugations, or the atypical spellings of the *sh* sound in *chef* and *echelon* are taken over from French).

These are patterns that seasoned spellers have reduced to reflexes, but the student with widespread difficulties in spelling cannot be expected to memorize all the conditions and patterns relevant to his misspellings. Where many errors are linked to one or two such patterns, it may be useful to lead a student, by the observations of word sets, into a discovery of those patterns. When, however, we search for useful generalizations that will help the student select the correct options for most of the long vowels (or for a consonant sound such as *sh*), we are in trouble, for here, despite some regularities, the spellings are either highly unpredictable or predictable through formulations so complex as to be pedagogically useless.

Then it becomes necessary to deal first with the general idea of graphemic options, demonstrating the variant spellings of each of the long vowels so that the student will begin to observe his spelling of those sounds in particular words.[9] Next the student needs to work from

9. The *Words in Color* charts developed by Caleb Gattegno for beginning readers are useful for this purpose as well (Educational Solutions, New York).

his own list of misspellings, noting his preferences for certain graphemic options over others (the preference for *i* or *ie* over *ea* or *ei*, for example) and enlarging his stock of word sets that represent the less familiar spellings. Audio-visual instruction, by concentrating the aural and visual experience of words and by enabling the student to move at his own pace, serves to accelerate this kind of learning for most students.

8. *Develop precision in viewing written words.* All writers have difficulty seeing what they have written with objective eyes. They need friends and enemies and editors to reveal to them what they have communicated. Among advanced writers, subjectivity most often hinders the writer from following through with a line of reasoning or filling out a point he is himself persuaded of or seeing that something he has written is ambiguous or murky. For the inexperienced writer, as we have already seen, the problem of subjectivity appears at even more basic levels—with the so-called "mechanics" of expression, where writers tend not to see flaws in the way they have punctuated or spelled or cast their sentences, although they can often see the same flaws in what others have written. Moved along by the flow of their own intent, they somehow miss seeing what they have in fact written and no matter how well they may do on exercises that mark in obvious ways the features to be noticed, they still have difficulty transferring the same disinterested watchfulness to their own words and sentences.

So we are back to the problem of proofreading—to the perception of letters and fine differences among letters. Such differences are of course made more evident by the kinds of instruction we have recommended so far; learning to look for certain spelling patterns is, after all, learning to look. But in addition to being able to spell words in lists, the student needs to learn how to fend for himself in the melee of sentences he produces on his own. Spelling drills and exercises may give him strategies for working out the spellings of selected words, but finally the words must return to contexts and vie for recognition even as other claims—semantic and grammatical—are being made on the writer's attention. One way of developing this kind of precision-in-context is to immerse the student in passages dense, even grotesque, with misspellings that are phonetically close to the intended words but semantically way off course. Here, for example, is a sentence of "double-spell" built from a list of student misspellings:

> When I travail I prefur a plain to a care: I tak a first glass flight, have a good diner, and relax my mine wile I watch the clouds go buy

and here the quite hum of the plain, witch hasn't stoped yet wile I've been abored.[10]

The following passage, a tour de force in double-spell, is certain to sharpen the eyes of anyone who stays with it until it is letter-perfect.

Ladle Rat Rotten Hut

Wants pawn term, dare worsted ladle gull hoe lift wetter mutter inner ladle cordage honor itch offer lodge, dock florist. Disc ladle gull orphan worry ladle cluck wetter putty ladle rat hut, and fur disc raisin, pimple caulder Ladle Rat Rotten Hut. Wan moaning Ladle Rat Rotten Hut's mutter set, "Heresy ladle basking winsome burden barter end shock her kook keys. Tick disc ladle basking tudor cordage offer groin mutter hoe lifts honor udder site offer florist. Shaker lake, dun stopper laundry wroter, and yonder nor sorghum stenches shooed jew stopper torque wet strainers."

"Hoe-cake, murder," resplendent Ladle Rat Rotten Hut, end ticking ladle basking, stuttered oft.

Honor wrote tudor cordage offer groin murder, Ladle Rat Rotten Hut mitten anomalous woof. "Wail, wail, wail," set disc wicket woof. "Evanescent Ladle Rat Rotten Hut. Wares or putty ladle gull goring wetter ladle basking?"

"Armor goring tumor groin murder's," reprisal ladle gull. "Grammar's seeking bet. Armor ticking arson burden barter and shirker cockles."

"O hoe. Heifer present woke," setter wicket woof toe Ladle Rat Rotten Hut. Buddy taught tomb shelf, "Oil ticker shirt court tudor cordage offer groin murder. Oil ketchup wetter letter, end den—Oar bore!!!"

Soda wicket woof tucker shirt court end whinny retched a cordage offer groin murder, picket inner winner and sore debtor pore oil worming worse lion inner bet. Inner flask disc abdominal woof lipped inner betting adder rope. Zany pool darner nut cup and gnat gun, any curdle inner bet, any wafer Ladle Rat Rotten Hut.

Inner ladle wile, Ladle Rat Rotten Hut a raft attar cordage and ranker dough ball. "Comb ink, sweat hard," setter wicket woof, disgracing hiss verse. Ladle Rat Rotten Hut entity bet rum and stud buyer groin mutter's bet.

"O Grammar," crater ladle gull; "Watt bag icer gut! Ah nervous sausage bag ice!"

10. If passages of this kind can be prepared in script rather than typescript, the exercise is even more effective since spelling errors are more difficult to notice in handwriting.

"Buttered luck a chew whiff, doiling," whiskered disc rachet woof, woof, wetter wicket small a pawns faze.

"O Grammar, water bag noise! A nervous sore suture anomalous prognosis!" eggs blamed ladle gull.

"Buttered small your whiff," inserter woof, ants noise worse twisting ants mouse worse waddling.

"O Grammar, water bag mousey gut! A nervous sausage bag mouse!"

Doze wordy gull's lest warts. Oil offer sodden, throne offer carvers an sprinkling otter bet, disc curl end bloat Thursday woof ceased pore Ladle Rat Rotten Hut end garbled erupt. Indite worse therein offer pore ladle gull.

Mural: Yonder nor sorghum stenches shut ladle gulls stopper torque wet strainers.[11]

The difference between double-spell exercises of this sort and real proofreading is that the student is not the author of the passages and must look closely at the words to puzzle out the meaning. With his own passages, the words are transparent; he sees through them to his meaning. Proofreading, however, should impede reading by calling attention to words as words. Some teachers even recommend that when proofreading a paper for misspellings the writer should read from right to left or from the last word in the paper through the first. Such a complete reversal of the normal reading pattern, however, removes context as a clue to spelling and thereby gives the writer no protection against homophones or misspellings that produce other words (as with *quit, quite,* and *quiet*). What the student seems to need most is some limit on what he is looking for when he proofreads; otherwise his search is no more than a loose scanning that inevitably falls into old rhythms. When, however, he has preciser purposes—to check *ie-ei* words, for example, to note the spellings of words with the $\bar{e}$ sound, or to question certain troublesome homophones wherever they occur (*there-their, to-too,* etc.), he is more likely to see, rather than see through, words. Such an approach to proofreading requires the student to know in advance what his spelling problems are. It also assumes that the ability to see misspellings will develop no faster than his awareness of what and why he as an individual writer tends to misspell. In the first stages of spelling instruction it is necessary therefore for the teacher to help the student identify misspelled words, but there should be no expectation that the "sp" strategy will do any more than accelerate the collection of mis-

11. I have not been able to identify the author of this passage. It was passed on to me by Sarah D'Eloia, who recalls that it circulated in the Atlanta high schools during the spring of 1959 or 1960.

spellings which the student must eventually analyze (preferably by using the kind of chart described earlier in this chapter). Once the student begins to know what he is looking for, however, the teacher can begin simply to note at the end of an essay the number of spelling errors, with possibly some hints about the types of errors involved. This method, sustained over the work of a semester, will reduce significantly the number of misspelled words. Slowly, the student begins to assume the work of the teacher in identifying his own errors—and in time the correct forms begin to appear in the first stages of composition rather than the last.

9. *Teach the use of the dictionary.* Doubt is the most useful spelling aid—not, of course, the generalized debilitating doubt that convinces students they can't spell anything but rather an informed doubt that prods them to question the way they have spelled particular words or sounds. Experienced writers have been trained to doubt at the right places and then to turn to the dictionary; inexperienced writers not only doubt in unproductive ways but are intimidated by the dictionary. Like the other "simple" skills that many students acquire early in school, the skill of dictionary-using is not as simple as it seems. It requires, for one thing, a nimbleness with the alphabet and an awarenes of spelling options that BW students often lack at the outset.[12] Then there are the various codes (for pronunciation, etymology, grammatical class, inflection, and levels of usage) that worry the reader until he learns how to read them. Once understood, however, the dictionary can become a continuing source of insight into spelling, not only because it lists correct forms but because it presents words in ways that illuminate spelling rules and patterns, breaking them into syllables, indicating stress, and marking the pronunciation of vowels. The dictionary remains, in short, the most useful single book the apprentice speller can own, and the habit of using it, the most important aid to spelling—more portable, lasting, and quiet than teachers.

Concluding comments

Two common beliefs undermine the teaching of spelling—the belief that spelling cannot be taught, perhaps not at all but certainly not by the time people are young adults, and the belief that spelling can be

12. One relatively painless way of fostering this kind of flexibility is to have "anti-spelling bees" that require students to look up words they have never heard before (e.g., *arachnid, duniewassal, sockdolager, lagniappe*), with points going to the team that finds them fastest.

taught only one way. The first belief keeps both teachers and students from trying at all and the second keeps the teacher from trying something else when The Method doesn't work. To teach spelling, a teacher must be prepared to move, with the student, straight into the tangle, systematically scrutinizing and classifying misspellings until patterns of difficulty begin to emerge. From there they may choose from a number of methods, depending on the problem and the student's way of learning. At one point, perhaps, a lecture on the roots of words may seem called for; at another, some exercises in the perception of letters; at another a spelling rule, or simply the cultivation of doubt. And the aim in all this is not to replicate the child's way of learning spelling but rather to find alternatives to that slow, unconscious process whereby the underlying principles of spelling seep into behavior. To be sure, the BW student, as he reads and writes more, will probably improve as a speller, but if he is a very poor speller he will need, in addition, a more efficient form of instruction, one that will allow him to use his adult powers of awareness and self-direction for the time he cannot regain.

As for the time the student must now spend on spelling, it is not as formidable as it must seem, following this description of spelling problems. Most students, however bad they seem as spellers, are nonetheless spelling most of their words correctly. Furthermore, analysis of their misspellings will usually reveal that while they may have, let us say, fifteen errors in a paper of 300 words, their errors reflect perhaps four or five problems, if that many, which tend to generate errors paper after paper. To get at these problems, the student must first spend time discovering them, but once he has learned how to use a diagnostic chart, the analysis of errors becomes a habitual part of the proofreading stage of composition. He will need, in addition, introductory class sessions or films that demonstrate basic spelling operations such as syllabication or affixation and that describe the spelling system in general. And he will need to work from time to time on prepared exercises that isolate those features of spelling that trouble him. But like the money we spend on pay-as-you-go taxes, the time for spelling is spent mainly in small amounts—short explanations at the beginning or end of class, moments during the conference or tutoring hour or at the proofreading stage of composition. Yet the sum of these expenditures is considerable, namely, the habit of noticing, doubting, and thinking about the spelling of words and the awareness that even misspellings yield to thought.

6
Vocabulary

The language the BW student inherits when he enters college is a language that has been developed over several centuries by writers who were discovering and exploiting the analytical powers of written English. It is not the purpose of this study to describe the ways in which that language has been and can be misused—how it has served to sharpen class divisions or dull the wits of captive readers or camouflage the mediocrity of people's thoughts—but rather to view it as the common language not only of the university but of the public and professional world outside, in short as a language BW students need to learn if they are to cope with the books and lectures and papers that constitute the work of college.

For many reasons, the mastery of this language, even for the student who speaks English natively, is a slow and demanding task. Not only are there new words and routines to learn but the very situation out of which the language has grown is unfamiliar to the student. It is, first, a situation that requires him to communicate with an anonymous reader (for whom the teacher might be said to act as surrogate), generally on an impersonal subject and in a formal register. It is, second, a politely polemical situation in which the reader is assumed to be, if not hostile to the writer's view, at least obliged to consider it carefully, according to criteria for evidence and sound reasoning that are themselves part of the legacy of the academic language. It is, finally, a situation that is locked peculiarly into time—distanced from the present by the absence of a listener and linked to the past by a tradition of discourse that has in large measure determined what topics and terms and styles of thought are appropriate to the subject.

The BW student is sensitive to the differences between the language he speaks and listens to in his daily life and the language he reads in textbooks or hears in lectures. He senses, too, a pressure to acquire facility with academic language speedily. He is less likely, however, to see this contrast between languages as a function of different social and linguistic situations. Instead, he views it as a problem in vocabulary, the solution to which lies in the swift acquisition of the prestigious words of academia and the substitution of these words for the plain words of daily life. Just as abstract grammar study seems to hold out the answer to all his difficulties with inflections and syntax, so vocabulary drill seems to lead the way to an academic style. (To speed up the process, students will often buy self-help vocabulary books which tend to reinforce this simplistic view of vocabulary growth.)

But the approach is ineffective. The student cannot learn the new words well enough by this method to manage the lexical transplants he intends without producing a range of semantic dissonances and outright errors. The academic lexicon is in itself formidable: there are too many new words to learn all at once in every subject; the words refer to situations or relationships that are difficult to picture in the mind; and many of the words are rooted in Latin and Greek, which means that the semantic motivation (the extent to which a word or part of a word already carries some meaning) is low unless a student has studied classical roots or absorbed a number of such words into his working vocabulary. The words, as Jesperson said, "have . . . none of those invisible threads that knit words together in the human mind."[1]

But even more important than remembering the forms and definitions of words is having the judgment to use them in appropriate ways, a judgment that comes not from the study of vocabulary lists but from having been a steady reader of the kind of writing people do in college. And here, of course, the BW student is at a disadvantage and must make guesses about acceptable contexts and appropriate tones that are often so far from the mark as to make him appear completely inept. Furthermore, in his straining to approximate a style he knows but

1. Otto Jesperson, *Growth and Structure of the English Language* (Garden City, N.Y.: Doubleday, 1955), p. 150.

slightly, he is likely to miss the point that the availability of certain words within the academic lexicon opens up the possibility of changing the thought-style as well as the word-style of his writing. For although words that are half-learned or exploited for the wrong reasons can obfuscate meaning, as we will presently see, words learned well clarify and extend meaning. Like tools in a craft, words prompt the writer to do more—elaborate, compare, condense, define, allude, etc.—than he would have done without them. "The birth of a new concept," writes Sapir, "is inevitably foreshadowed by a more or less strained or extended use of old linguistic material; the concept does not attain to individual and independent life until it has found a distinctive linguistic embodiment."[2] So too, words, well learned, enter into the conceptual life of the student, almost as inventions created by the necessities of the writer's peculiar audience, which is present only in his imagination.

Let us look briefly at the kinds of difficulties BW students encounter in their efforts to use the academic vocabulary—or what they perceive to be that vocabulary. Then we can consider the ways in which the absence (or near-absence) of certain classes of words in a student's vocabulary affects what he has to say about a subject. First, then, the words that, for one reason or another, go wrong.

Vocabulary errors

When we say that a student does not know a word, we generally do not mean that he has never heard or seen it. In fact, we usually discover that he doesn't know a word by observing the way he uses it. At the deepest level of "not knowing," a student would not know of a word's existence or even perhaps of the existence of what it names. But errors in vocabulary already attest to the student's knowledge, at some level, of the words he is using (or misusing). He may have learned to say the word without learning what it stands for; or he may have learned what a word stands for without having learned the exact written or spoken form of it; he may have but a blurred sense of both the meaning and form of a word; he may know the word well enough to move past it as he reads but not well enough to initiate its use in his speaking or writing; or he may know one meaning of a word that has multiple meanings—a figurative meaning as well as a literal meaning, perhaps, a technical meaning as well as an everyday meaning, a connotative as

2. Edward Sapir, *Language* (New York: Harcourt Brace, 1949), p. 17.

well as a denotative meaning. Or finally, he may know a word and what it stands for without having a sense of how the word is affected, semantically or syntactically, by the words around it.

Getting the form of a word wrong is probably the most rudimentary of vocabulary errors, particularly when the erroneous form produces a word that doesn't exist in the language:[3]

- ☐ I wish my life to be *forfilling* with happiness.
- ☐ I would like to *coulternate* childrens mind.
- ☐ With my capacities of learning brought forth by my education, I can be *subcepticle* to learn a variety of things.
- ☐ Junkies are often seen on the sidewalk, in cars, or in some old houses with their bottles of whisky siping and passing it around to each other which *prescible* laziness.

Errors of this kind, while they do occur in BW papers, are, however, far less common than errors with derivational suffixes, which disorient the reader syntactically more than semantically. We have mentioned such errors elsewhere, but let us illustrate them again here for they are among the most troublesome of vocabulary errors for BW students:

- ☐ He is headed in a *destructional* way.
- ☐ People are judged by what they *product* on the job.
- ☐ There should always be *preparance* in any occupation wether big or small.
- ☐ He works without *supervise*.
- ☐ They only feel a sense of *secure* for their own people.
- ☐ The loser would be the Chinese people, who *resemblance* the God-father.

Another type of vocabulary error reflects the student's effort to bring meaning to a word that otherwise seems semantically arbitrary. Usually he does this by substituting for the appropriate word a more familiar word that is phonetically similar but semantically unrelated to the word the reader expects. This satisfies the writer's need for a word that carries meaning and, where the confusion among language users is

3. Where a student's pronunciation of a word does not bear out his spelling but instead attests to his knowledge of the word, then of course one is dealing with a spelling rather than a vocabulary problem. Sometimes the borders are blurred, however.

widespread, may even produce a change in the language. More often, unfortunately, it surprises the reader by carrying its meaning into an alien context:

☐ The program uses a new *floormat*. (format)

☐ I want work in a *pacific* field. (specific)

☐ They used him as an *escape goat*. (scapegoat)

At times, the meanings brought on by such substitutions make uncanny connections within the context, but in a direction quite different from what the student seems to intend:[5]

☐ Coming to writing class *stifle* not only our will to write but your drive to think. This opportunity is a unique one which every student should avail himself.

☐ Because the requirements to find a place in our academic fields of study have changed; our students must also make an effort to make the necessary *transgressions* to fulfill their needs.

☐ School increase the childrens ability to *withhold* meaning.
Context suggests student intended to *hold* or to *assimilate*.

Errors that cut so sharply across the reader's expectations are relatively easy to correct. The differences between *floormats* and *formats* or *transgressions* and *transformations* are memorable once they have been pointed out. But many of the words BW students use incorrectly carry meanings that are semantically close to the meanings they intend. Yet the words are unacceptable, even though the teacher is not always prepared to explain precisely why. (In fact, he often discovers the contextual constraints upon certain words only after a student has unwittingly ignored them.) The intuitions that alert the teacher to a dissonant word are not yet working for the student, as we see in passages such as the following:

4. See Stephen Ullmann's *Semantics: An Introduction to the Science of Meaning* (New York: Oxford University Press, 1970), Chapter 4, for a helpful discussion on the effects of "transparent" and "opaque" words upon semantic motivation.

5. "Errors" of this kind raise the question of whether the student is not creatively remodeling the formal vocabulary so as to carry his real meaning. Linguists have described such behavior in other culturally dual settings. See, for example, Karl Reisman, "Cultural and Linguistic Ambiguity in a West Indian Village," in *Afro-American Anthropology*, ed. Norman E. Whitten, Jr., and John Szwed (New York: Free Press, 1970).

☐ I will try to *perpetuate* my children in the same track as I am.

☐ They are *eliminating* waste and gas from combining with air.

☐ Once his father *demonstrates* between the two birds this little boy won't have any problems.

☐ I think psychology has *increased* my mind.

☐ Teenagers are more openly *expressed* and more noticed in our society.

☐ The demand for jobs has *prolifically* declined. The college student that is *coercively* taking courses is *affluently* wasting his mind.

☐ That's why it is best to teach and *construct* a childs mind before it gets set.

☐ Not speaking English *proposed* difficulties for them finding a job.

☐ Many students *portray* immature concepts.

☐ Through education a person's financial well-being usually is *enlightened*.

With prepositions, dissonance in word choice is even more difficult to get at because explanations rarely clarify. (We "hear" that to *dispense of* and be *rid with* are wrong but are hard put to explain why those prepositions are not interchangeable.) Many unfamiliar prepositional phrases are nonetheless called for in formal academic writing (and if we add to these the prepositions associated with non-finite verbs, as in *alerted to, interrupted by*, etc., the list is even longer), which tends to be more heavily qualified than informal language. Many of the prepositional qualifiers are set pieces, more like single words than phrases (*regardless of, in relation to, as a result of*, etc.) which students have heard or read but not always mastered. In addition, we find the influence of other languages upon the choice of prepositions—particularly where the influencing language depends on fewer prepositions and therefore motivates the student to reduce the large vocabulary of prepositions in formal English or to choose uncertainly from among them.

This passage, by a native-born New Yorker with a Spanish-language background, reflects such a problem:

> For me, I think that the people will be *satisfied of* what they had done for themselves and that someday *on the future* they will find a good *opportunity of* work and won't have to be depending on nobody to get it's things. With a college degree you won't have to *suffer of* needs *on your future* and you won't make your child suffer either.

The most common error with prepositions, which dominates the above passage as well but is not confined to students with Spanish-speaking backgrounds, is the substitution of *of* for other prepositions. Thus we find many errors like these:

Erroneous form	*Correct form*
a good opportunity of work	to
first step of success	toward
to dispense of	with
alerting the student of what is needed	to
students that graduate of school	from
their education depends of	on

But many other types of errors occur as well (including the substitution of other prepositions for *of*):

regardless to	~~of~~
in the eyes on this person	of
a frightening insight to our involvement	into
has played a part into changing the game	in
few regrets on the life of my parents	in
to identify to	with
I reached into the conclusion	—
to my opinion	in
in the financial problems everyones got	with
he can train himself for receive better pay	to
you must meet to their standards	—
a job on the field	in
for one to pursue into higher education	a
aptitude toward	for
deals with crime on his own way	in

Errors of the sort we are noting here pose many questions for the teacher. They are, in a sense, "advanced" errors. Students at the least experienced level of Basic Writing rarely make them, choosing instead to stay within the error-safe limits of a basic vocabulary. But since there is no way of acquiring a new register except by trying to approximate it, whatever the cost in error, the teacher must consider carefully what his response should be to the so-called "egregious" vocabulary errors students tend to make at this stage of their development as writers. Should the teacher advise the student, as he himself was probably advised, to reject words of French or classical origin wherever an Anglo-Saxon alternative comes to mind, to avoid heavy qualifications that call for unfamiliar prepositions, to write in a "simple" style, without trying to sound academic? And when the student ignores this advice, producing a brand of formalese that echoes the bombastic styles of more experienced writers, should he be criticized for affecting a style that is not his own or credited with trying his hand at a style he has yet to master? Are excess and exaggeration merely stages in the acquisition of the new style or do they set the writer in a direction that leads away from the possibility of communication with himself as well as with his reader?

To answer these questions requires sensitivity to the individual student's use of language and an appreciation of the various reasons students can have for writing words they would not ordinarily speak. Often, for example, students are revealing stylistic preferences when they select the formal, albeit less manageable, words over the ordinary ones (an option that is ever-present in English with its Latin–French–Anglo-Saxon synonymy). This preference may have been nurtured in a linguistic culture that distinguished sharply between high or formal occasions and ordinary events. However ineptly they might manage the academic style, such students have nonetheless come to associate a formal idiom with serious events such as sermons or public speeches—or by extension, academic lectures and essays. I recall the indignation of a group of BW students who came to complain to me about their teacher's inclusion in the class assignment of a poem that contained obscenities. "We don't come *here* for that," one student protested.

Not only may they feel constrained by the academic situation to shift registers, they may enjoy the sound and look of the new words and more elaborate phrasings of the unfamiliar register. To add to one's stock of words—more particularly to appropriate for one's own use the formidable jargon of the "others"—can be a gratifying kind of acculturation as well as a strategy for survival. A gesture of participation, it may well mark an advance in the attitude and skill of the student even though it fails to achieve its end. Most writers can remember in their own writing histories a period of self-conscious emulation of the formal style, heavy with long words and stiff with the set expressions and elaborations of that style. Were writers to wait to use such words and phrases until they could manage them perfectly, they would not learn to use them at all. Learning is a sequence of approximations, some of them quite far from the intended mark, and it is not unusual for a student to sound worse before he sounds better.

The sense that something "higher" than vernacular English is called for in an academic paper is also nurtured by the models teachers give their students, either through their own styles of writing and talking or through the writing they select as exemplary. The student, for example, who is expected in a College Entrance Examination to choose paragraph 1 as the more effective and interesting paragraph might infer from that experience that simplicity does not in fact pay off:

Paragraph 1

His days were rich in formal experience. Wearing overalls and an old ? eater (the accepted uniform of the private seminary), he sallied fᵥ th at morn accompanied by a nurse or a parent and walked (or was pulled) two blocks to a corner where the school bus made a flag stop. This flashy vehicle was as punctual as death: seeing us waiting at the cold curb, it would sweep to a halt, open its mouth, suck the boy in, and spring away with an angry growl. It was a good deal like a train picking up a bag of mail. At school the scholar was worked on for six or seven hours by half a dozen teachers and a nurse, and was revived on orange juice in midmorning. In a cinder court he played games supervised by an athletic instructor, and in a cafeteria he ate lunch worked out by a dietician.

Paragraph 2

His days followed a set routine. He wore overalls and an old sweater, as everyone else did in his school. In the morning, a parent or nurse walked the two blocks with him to the corner where he met the school bus. The bus was always on time. During the six or seven hours of the school day, he had six teachers. The school also employed a nurse and a dietician. Games were supervised. The children ate in the cafeteria. Orange juice was served during the morning session.⁶

Furthermore, the "simple" styles of even well-known writers rarely appear simple to students, for the simplicity of written language is not *simply* a return to conversational style. Rather, it is the final achievement of a writer, a dynamic activation of complex thought through the medium of the common language. But this language is "common" only to readers who have been long apprenticed to the literary culture. As simple as a passage from Orwell may sound to someone habituated to prose of that kind, it is far from simple to students for whom the subject, the mode, and the style are all strange. To urge a student to emulate such "simplicity" without exploring it thoroughly is to push

6. From Benjamin S. Bloom, J. Thomas Hastings, and George F. Madaus, *Handbook on Formative and Summative Evaluation of Student Learning* (New York: McGraw-Hill, 1971), p. 797.

him far beyond his verbal resources and encourage the very formalese a writer such as Orwell was careful to avoid. Uncertain of just what makes Orwell so praiseworthy, the student is likely to select those features of the writing that impress him as different or difficult.

We must recognize, too, that much of the writing English teachers promote, consciously or unconsciously, is not simple, even by the standards we apply to Orwell. The aesthetic that dominates English teachers' judgments has generally been shaped by years of exposure to belletristic literature, and their pleasure in the arrangement of words, in the exploitation of rhetorical options, or even in their custodial responsibilities toward the tradition of letters has made them the most likely agents of the high style. Here, for example, in the letter of a high-school English teacher to *his* teacher in graduate school, we find the same failure to discriminate between the archaic and the formal, the idiom and the cliché, that we find in student writing that is striving toward a more formal register:

> I wish to express my apology for not attending the final session but personal family business required my presence elsewhere. I think it would be wise to get on with the main intention of this letter—one incomplete term paper. I have been busily working on it but a few obstacles have proven to be a chronic hindrance to its completion. In the first place, the untimely closing of the library prevented my using their facilities when it would have been most convenient. Secondly, the state required my taking twelve credits this semester. Most important, this is examination week and I have been engaged in their preparation and grading. During this time I let all other work take a back seat to my prime responsibility. I hope the completed paper will be worthy of your patience.

Nor have we mentioned yet the other incursions of formalese upon the consciousness of students who, like the rest of us, must read, or try to read, the literature of the many bureaucracies that control our lives—the instructions of the government, the catalogues of colleges, the texts of other teachers, the letters of businessmen, and the pronouncements of people in high office. The student who defined "good" writing as "writing you can't understand," or the student who complained that she deserved a higher grade on her essay because she had read it to her friends and they hadn't understood it, or the class that ranked a piece of gobbledygook above a passage by Mark Twain—such students have merely accepted the models that society offers them. Styles—even bad styles—come from someplace, and it is important to remember this when responding to a piece of student writing that offends or amuses or bewilders in its effort to approximate the high or formal style of academia.

Students are easily misjudged by the styles they attempt to assume as writers. Here, for example, is a passage that bears a teacher's familiar exclamation and injunction: "Jargon! Make it simple!!"

> It can be said that my parents have led useful live but that usefulness seems to deteriorate when they fond themselves constantly being manipulated for the benefit of one and not for the benefit of the community. If they were able to realize that were being manipulate successful advancements could of been gained but being that they had no strong political awareness their energies were consumed by the politicans who saw personal advancements at the expenses of dedicated community workers. And now that my parents have taken a leave of abscence from community involvement, comes my term to participate on worthwhile community activities which well bring about positive results and to maintain a level of consciousness in the community so that they will know what policies affect them, and if they don't quite like the results of the policies I'll make sure, if its possible, to abolish the ones which hinder progress to ones which well present the correct shift in establishing correct legislation or enactments. In order to establish myself and my life to revolve around the community I must maintain a level of awareness to make sure that I can bring about positive actions and to keep an open mind to the problems of the community and to the possible manipulation machinery which is always on the watch when progressive leaders or members of the community try to build effective activities for the people to participate.

The writer of the above passage could be viewed as someone who is using (and abusing) "fancy" words to impress his reader. But again, he could be seen as someone who is struggling to develop a language that will enable him to talk analytically, with strangers, about the oppression of his parents and his own resolve to work against that oppression. Certain words and phrases, worn with use, may be fresh to him (one can imagine how the word "manipulate" must serve to illuminate and group the experiences he has in mind). Or he may be finding, in this stiff and distant idiom, a way of transposing his deepest concerns into a language that protects him from the curiosity and sentimentality of strangers, even as it allows him to think about what has happened to him in terms that have wide application. To be sure, he has not mastered the style. It is dense with jargon, weighted with generalizations that keep us from feeling what he feels or knowing what he, through anecdote and description, could help us know. But to weave personal experience into analytical discourse, to be the stuff of one's own conscious conceptualizing, is difficult at the beginning. The "easy" merging of experience with idea that we find in essays such as James Baldwin's "Notes of a Native Son" or George Orwell's "Such, Such Were the Joys" or the even greater distancing of self from experience that is so impressive in Hoggart's *The Uses of Literacy*—these are the achievements of mature and gifted writers. The writer who has begun to advance into the complexity of the new language is almost certain to sound and feel alien with the stock of words, routines, and rituals that make up that language. Yet there is no way to gain the use of these unfamiliar forms except by trying them out, even at the risk of sounding funny or phony. The teacher in such a situation has the delicate task of encouraging the enterprise and confidence of the student who is moving in this direction while at the same time improving his judgment about both the forms and meanings of the words he chooses.

Stages of approximation to the formal style

So far, we have considered only the mistakes BW students make with the words they use. But in order to understand more fully how vocabulary affects what they are able to say as writers, we must now consider more generally the types of words they use and the types they leave out. Here we find, as with punctuation and syntax, that the BW student usually works with a basic stock of words which serve to name or qualify or predicate only in the most general way. His dependence upon these words keeps him from being precise in his writings and, very likely, in his thoughts, for writing is as much a way of exploring thought as getting down what has already been thought. If the writer has words to choose from, he is led into making differentiations that might otherwise not occur to him, and these differentiations affect the quality of his thought. If we look at the vocabulary in the writing of three different groups of freshmen—the basic, the intermediate, and the advanced writers—we see how closely our judgments of maturity in writing are related to vocabulary.[7]

Basic writers
Three features of vocabulary stand out in papers of the basic group: a preponderance of vague nouns and ambiguous pronouns, a dependence on basic verbs, and an absence of modification. For reasons that are not always clear, or the same, writers at this basic level often fail to name the object or person or idea they are writing about. We have seen in the chapter on syntax how this evasion of the subject entangles the writer in passive constructions or inverted patterns—*it is, there is*, etc. (*In college it is more of a responsibility than an obligation. I mean to say that it is not only a small group but merely a large number of these students who don't really know how to read or write*).[8] But even where sentence patterns follow the natural order, subjects tend to be but vaguely named: a method of teaching is labeled *this idea*, controversial issues are called *certain things*, or independent study is referred to as *this way*. Words like *way, idea, aspect, factor, cause, fact, example* are misused and interchanged (*New York has many aspects and one is open admissions. . . . Whatever you learn it will increase your knowledge to better understand the factors of the world. . . Here are some of the examples of why I feel. . .*).

But the favorite word is *thing*, the all-purpose noun that parallels the all-purpose *that* of syntax or the all-purpose *comma* of punctuation. No noun comes so easily or covers such a range of "things":

☐ Now things are organized people are made to think so they understand the reason for things.

☐ There are new things they see in college that they may haven't thought of.

☐ When talking to a college friend you tend to see how quiet they react to certain thing which gives one a feeling of wanting to get this way.

7. To make this comparison I have drawn material from the writing folders of 200 students who were classified, on the basis of their writing, as basic, intermediate, or advanced writers. I am indebted to Kathy Roe for her initial analysis of the material.

8. See Valerie Krishna, "The Syntax of Error," *Journal of Basic Writing*, Spring, 1975, for a fuller description of this problem.

☐ In college there are too many things required to take.

☐ He checks out certain things before he gets into it.

☐ Reading has to do with English. History, thing of this nature I don't seem to be able to get across with.

The verbs of this basic vocabulary are the common verbs of the language—*make, get, have, be, put, bring, give, cause, keep,* etc.—and like the basic nouns they are used for all purposes. We see in the following sentences how a dependence on these verbs affects both meaning and style. Frequently, the basic verb dulls the edge of meaning:

☐ College *has* and open chance for students to really experience and *bring forth* their feelings about themselves and others.
(provides, discover)

☐ For some men too many Humphrey Bogard pictures *show* masculinity out of a cigarette.
(Too many Humphrey Bogart pictures cause men to *associate* masculinity with cigarette-smoking.)

☐ Also cultural background *gives* this change in behavior.
(encourages or fosters)

☐ The city would be *over* a lot of its crime.
(rid of)

☐ The pressures and worries was too much on the brain therefore being weak.
(The pressures and worries overtaxed and weakened the brain.)

☐ We are just starting to *put* strong laws.
(enforce)

☐ Another way for a person to *have* greed is gambling.
(reveal)

Where the right verb (or the verb form of a noun the writer already knows) cannot be summoned up the writer will often use several words to get at his meaning, producing an awkward as well as an inexact statement:[9]

9. Broderick, in a study of formal and informal written English, finds support for the hypothesis that formal written English may have a larger inventory of verbs than informal, that these verbs tend to have greater syntactic potential than verbs used only in informal written English have, and that proficient writers have larger inventories of verbs available to them than do non-proficient writers. (John Patrick Broderick, "Usage Varieties and Writing Competence: A Study of Formal and Informal Written English Elicited from Selected Groups of American Colleges," Diss., Georgetown University, 1972.)

☐ After junkies have asorved a great quantity of liquor it *causes a depression on their will power.*
(their will power diminishes)

☐ It *hurts their moral* and makes them feel ugly.
(demoralizes them)

☐ This lack of manner *can also be drawn from* the fact that . . .
(can be attributed to)

☐ *As children grow older meaning adults* . . .
(as children mature)

Basic writers modify their nouns and verbs with the common adjectives:

a lot	fast, faster	interesting
bad	good	many, much
better, best	great	more, less
big, biggest	happy	same
certain	hard	various
different	higher, lower	worse
easy	important	young, old

Except for the common intensifiers (*too, very, really, quite, hardly*), which are over-used, adverbs rarely appear. Words having to do with size, measure, magnitude, or quantity, whether verbs or adjectives, are frequently misused or confused. Words that cannot combine with *increase* or *decrease* are made to do so; quantities that don't conventionally have number are numbered:

☐ Psychology has *increased* my mind.

☐ The slum areas *decrease* their living conditions.

☐ Pressure can be *few.*

☐ A *little* percentage of people

☐ *Amount* of grown-up friends

☐ The space grew *less.*

Like all writers, the writer at this basic level is encouraged by his familiarity with the language, especially in its spoken form, to coast along with the words and phrases that slip into the mind like old habits. He does not choose words so much as fall into them: grades or programs or "things" are of a *certain* kind; trains or feelings or people are *good; it* is *really big* or *important* or *interesting,* etc. Most of the means of differentiation—the choice of precise words, the listing of words where no single word can carry the meaning, the use of examples and explanations to illuminate words like *good* or *thing*—seem to be unavailable to the writer at this stage, perhaps because the words he needs to explore his meaning are not in his active vocabulary or because he is unaware of the reader's need for specificity or because he has learned few of the writer's strategies for getting beyond or below the general term. The result is a style that resists the complexity and individuality of the writer's thought or, worse, encourages him to use words without connecting them to his thoughts or to the reality he has experienced.

The intermediate writer

The borderline between what we are calling *basic* and *intermediate* writing cannot be sharply drawn. Students whose writing strikes the academic reader as being beyond basic may yet retain traces of the basic style. Here, too, we can find misused words:

☐ He then arranges classes into a schedule *encompassed* around a job.

☐ So somebody has to start the *initiative* move.

Pronouns and nouns can still be vague or inappropriate:

☐ I agree that there are certain classes that are required for your field of work, but I feel *that* should be as far as it goes.

☐ In order to find out *things* you must do *it* yourself. There's no way people will come up to you and tell you what is required as they do in High School. This takes a lot of responsibility and maturity to be able to cope with *this.*

And the formal vocabulary occasionally gives out:

☐ They encourage me to *hang in* there.

☐ Students like to be *wise guys* and give the teacher a hard time.

Nonetheless, the vocabulary at this stage has many resources that are missing at the basic level. The student has by now, for example, become adept at altering the forms of words, a skill that saves him many syntactical snarls and circumlocutions. Where he may have been able to use the verb *exist* before he now uses *existing* and *existence* as well; *benefit* can be shifted to *beneficial, approximate* to *approximation,* and so on. Furthermore, he has acquired a stock of nouns and verbs, adjectives and adverbs that enable him to identify and label the experience, process, or event he is discussing. Thus where a basic writer might say, "We didn't get the test and he put the term paper off," the intermediate writer says, "One test was cancelled and the term paper deadline was extended. This courtesy from the professor. . ." Not only has the student distinguished between the two actions—cancelling and extending—but he has identified both actions as a courtesy (and, in the process, avoided a vague pronoun reference).

In short, the intermediate writer has words to work with. He has verbs that rarely, if ever, appear at the basic stage. Here are but a few, randomly drawn from a collection of intermediate essays:

accustom	eradicate	pamper	stem
advocate	fade	penalize	subdivide
cater	falter	preserve	suggested
demolish	fluctuate	prod	warn
destined	inclined	provoke	witness
emerge	modify	regulate	
entailed	neglect	rely	

In place of the all-purpose *thing* or the vague *it* or *this* the intermediate writer has more nouns for naming:

☐ Those who feel that going to college is a lark and persist in maintaining *this attitude* can be found among the drop-outs.

☐ These *anti-pollution* devices or units should be made mandatory for all *buildings, automobiles, buses, ships, planes* or any other *contributors* of air pollution.

Where the basic writer might say *these things they give me to read,* the intermediate writer will say *these letters, brochures, and pamphlets,* a list that comes closer to suggesting the deluge of literature the student received before going to college. The intermediate writer is not as likely to settle for *various types* of criminals, with future references to *these criminals;* he mentions *pickpockets, rapists, addicts, organizations such as Cosa Nostra.* Lists of any kind, in fact, are rare at the basic level whereas the writer at the intermediate level is likely to over-use them, as if the process of selection that goes on within the mind of the mature writer has not yet been internalized.

Finally *good, bad,* and *important* give way to more informative adjectives (e.g., *hostile, honest, permanent, thorough, specialized, impatient, watchful, monotonous*). The *-ly* adverbs that occur often in formal writing appear for the first time (e.g., *realistically, adequately, fluently,* *efficiently, repeatedly, recently).* Multiple adjectives also occur, but seldom with any gain in precision:

☐ He is interesting, well-read, and informed.

☐ A college degree is not the solution for making a person responsible and self-sufficient.

☐ They need to solve social, political and economical problems.

The idea that a writer begins with is seldom fully formed. Submerged in his mind, it must be drawn to the surface by words. But once the words are there, the writer begins testing them against the thought that evoked them, discovering his meaning as he chooses and rejects. Fluency is largely a matter of having ready access to many words and therefore being able to bring them quickly to the surface. Precision, however, comes from the habit of testing the words that come to mind against the thought one has in mind. And it is this habit of choosing that seems crucial to precision. The intermediate writer's vocabulary may give him a wider range of words to choose from than the basic writer has. But it does not guarantee better choices. For this, the writer must also have acquired criteria for precision that guide him in his choice of words. The absence of adverbs at the basic level is probably less a problem of not knowing certain words than of not being in the habit of articulating the conditions under which a statement holds or the manner in which an action is taken. Often the words a writer needs in order to be exact are already in his vocabulary, but the writer does not seek them out. Perhaps he is not aware of the extent to which a reader depends on words to understand what is in the mind of the writer or perhaps he is not in the habit of noticing closely the phenomena he writes about. Just as the painter's eye catches details of color and shape that the ordinary eye ignores, so the writer learns to name and note and relate with an exactness that would not occur to the non-writer. What we observe in the best of the writing from this intermediate group is not simply a larger vocabulary but a greater tendency to produce sharp delineations of scene or event. Here, for example, is a sentence written by an intermediate writer. Below it are the words a basic writer might have used instead:

When a young woman was found murdered in the vestibule of her
When a ...... woman was ..... murdered near .... a
building last summer in Brooklyn Heights, neighbors had heard her
building .... people ...... heard her

cries for help but not one came from behind their bolted doors to
scream.......but no one came............................. to
rescue her.
help her.

The intermediate writer has advanced on several fronts. Not only has
he packed more information into his sentence than the basic writer
would be likely to give to his reader, but by the juxtaposition of humane
and violent images (*her* building, *vestibule, neighbors, young* versus
murdered, cries, bolted doors) he has suggested the chilling immorality
of the event. Something in the writer's preparation has given him not
simply words but a judgment about words that has enabled him, in
turn, to express his own perceptions of this event.

But when the intermediate writer attempts to write on more abstract
topics or when, even in reportage, he attempts to relate clauses or
statements, he is not always as successful. (Even in the sentence above,
for example, the time relationship between the two clauses is muddled:
it was not *when* the woman was *found* murdered but *as* she was *being*
murdered that the neighbors heard her cries and bolted their doors.)
Experience in the real world tends to support description and narration.
The writer of the above passage, for example, has not seen the murdered
woman he writes about but he has seen murders enacted in movies or
read about murders in stories or newspapers. He can locate Brooklyn
Heights in his mind and may even have been there. Words like *young
woman* and *neighbors*, like all words, are of course abstractions but
they don't feel like abstractions. They don't cut the writer off from his
experience in quite the same way as words of analytical discourse do.
The vocabulary of logical relationships, so important in analytical writing, is in this sense more like the language of mathematics than of
everyday life and the intermediate writer is characteristically unsure of
himself in using it. He may not be certain of the kind of relationship a
word signals. (A student *begins* an essay, for example, with *moreover*.)
Or he is simply not in the habit of bringing relationships to the surface
of his thoughts by means of words such as *therefore, although, in addition* or by transitional sentences or whole paragraphs. Once conscious
of the need to do this, he may manage the transitions clumsily—by an
announcement, perhaps that a certain subject is about to be discussed
(*I will now proceed to discuss* . . .) or by some personal assurance that
there is good reason for what has been said or is about to be said (*My
major reason is* . . . , *My statement is based on personal experience* . . .,

Another reason why I feel . . . , I can use myself as an example of this . . .). Ready with sentences, he is still not ready to spin webs of academic discourse.

The advanced writer

The advanced writer's greatest gain in vocabulary is in the use of relational words, phrases, and sentences that are only beginning to appear at the intermediate level. Here we find a sudden flow (at times an inundation) of words and phrases that point up connections. Not only do we find most of the idioms of connection, both logical and rhetorical, that produce the web of discourse in analytical writing but we find the syntactical structures that underlie many of these idioms. Thus we find not only words like *consequently, subsequently, therefore, unfortunately, yet, accordingly, otherwise* or phrases like *what's more, not to mention, above all, as far as, the exception is,* but also paired constructions that complicate sentences in ways that less experienced writers usually cannot manage—*while x also y, it is not x but rather y, as much x as y, the more x the more y, if x then y,* and so on.

☐ More privileged students, *while* far more advanced in many scholastic subjects, *also* show a lack of skill in reading and writing.

☐ While it is true that there are a great number of jobs which require little or no reading and writing abilities, the brunt of the jobs fall into categories which *not only* require a well-poised person *but also* one who can handle all types of instructions, vocal and written.

☐ Also, if teachers were to insist on these subjects [reading and writing], *not only* would society be less ignorant *but* it would encourage those who have talent and imaginations to develop their potential abilities and write books.

☐ *Of all things* taught (*and indeed* of all things one must learn in order to prosper in this society) writing is the *most* difficult.

☐ *The more* people there are *the harder* it becomes and *the greater* the need to get a good high school and college education.

As several of the sentences above also illustrate, the advanced writer often describes or identifies an object or relates an idea in more ways than one. This was beginning to happen at the intermediate level, but now we find greater boldness in packing appositives, alternative words and phrases, and modifiers into sentences.

□ No matter what one writes—be it a short story, a letter to a friend or associate or a purely business letter—one presents his character in what he writes.

□ There will always be the ones who are slow, those whose minds wander, those who need constant attention or who are simply apathetic.

□ It will become a ghetto school in a ghetto environment—misguided community control, self-centered teachers.

□ This is a familiar theme on which many popular articles (nine out of ten of which are entitled "Why Johnny can't Read") have been written.

Vocabulary is of course not the only influence here. The ability to juggle contradictions, exceptions, and multiple levels of meaning requires syntactical fluency as well. Syntax becomes itself a kind of vocabulary, offering patterns for subordination and balance without which the enlarged vocabulary is useless.

Advanced writers, because of their readiness with words, rarely produce vague references to *things* or *it*. In sixty samples of advanced freshman placement essays, the word *thing* appears only five times and *something* only twice. And even here, the writer generally goes on to make the reference precise. Here, for example, the word *something* is not the crutch it is likely to be at the basic level.

□ You wonder if the best preparation for joining society is something you never learn in school: strengthening an ability to maintain your own values and goals under the pressures of a society penetrated by the mediocre.

Seldom are there pronoun reference errors, except those caused by carelessness (disagreement of number or gender between pronoun and referent, for example). With access to nouns that name attitudes, ideas, tendencies, feelings, events, the writer has less need for *it* or *this*, except where these pronouns help reduce redundancy.

Prepared syntactically to balance and subordinate in a variety of ways, secure with the vocabulary of connectives, and ready with the longer Latinate words of formal English, the advanced freshman writer appears to be so much ahead of his peers that his own shortcomings as a writer are easily overlooked. Yet here, too, we find imprecision. He has learned the melody of formal English but the words are not always exact. Distinctions may be unclear ("No education can be *total*, it must be *continuous*"; "It is not an *inherent* fault but a more *generalized* one"). Combinations may be dissonant ("A kind of *apathy flourishes*"; "Housing and values are *subnormal*") or redundant ("a *detriment* and a *roadblock*"; "no general *awakening* or *enlightening*"; "too *jumbled* and *mixed*"). Most important, for all the gains in vocabulary that the writer at this stage can claim (particularly where a word signals the acquisition not simply of an alternate expression but of a new concept—as with *taboo, legacy, ecology, neo-illiteracy*, etc.), the pre-packaging feature of language, the possibility of taking over phrases and whole sentences without much thought about them, threatens the writer now as before. The writer, as we have said, inherits the language out of which he must fabricate his own messages. He is therefore in a constant tangle with the language, obliged to recognize its public, communal nature and yet driven to invent out of this language his own statements. But invention is difficult at these early stages when the clichés and conventions of the formal style are fresh to the writer and before he is confident or knowledgeable enough to translate more freely into language that is closer to his thoughts. Thus we find limitations in the "advanced" student's writing of the sort I. A. Richards describes:

> A child of eight is constantly made to feel that he is not understanding something. At eighteen he may misunderstand nearly as often, but the testing instance, which makes him realize that this is so, infrequently arises. Unless either his company or his studies are exceptional, he will rarely be forced to face any such disagreeable facts. For he will have acquired enough skill in the reproduction of more or less appropriate language to disguise most of his failures both from the world and from himself. He can answer questions in a way which may convince everybody, himself included, that he understands them. He may be able to translate difficult pasages with every sign of discernment, write passable essays and converse with great apparent intelligence upon many subjects. Yet in spite of these acquirements he may be making at innumerable points what Mr. Russell once called, in connection with the words *number* and *two*, a "purely prudential use of language." That is, he may be using words not because he knows with any precision what he means by them, but because he knows how they are ordinarily used, and does with them what he has heard other people do with them before. He strings them together in suitable sequences, manoeuvres them aptly enough, produces with them pretty well the effects he intends, yet meanwhile he may have not much more inkling of what he is really (or should be) doing with them than

a telephone-girl need have of the inner wiring of the switchboard she operates so deftly.[10]

Writing at this stage is often heavy with predictable phrases:

tangible results	extensive vocabulary
solid background	serious intentions
present unrest	mutual cooperation
ultimate solution	prior preparation

Sentences are studded with adverbial conjunctions:

In many elementary schools a hatred rather than a need for learning is taught, and in such an atmosphere it is hard for learning skills to develop. *Fortunately*, in Junior High School they tend to eliminate some, but not all, of the irrational dislike of learning produced in elementary school pupils. *However* a dislike of performing academic feats is here induced into the pupil. *In other words*, although one does learn in Junior High School, he finds the application of his knowledge tedious and for the most part unfruitful. *Furthermore* . . .

Figurative language (which rarely appears in basic and intermediate writing) tends to be heavy-handed:

☐ A dictionary is not a book one goes to as a last resort but rather a wonderland of images, a valve for the outlet of the imagination.

☐ In this academic world we have witnessed the fruition of democratized education and subsequently, the destruction of several centuries of highly developed temples of cultures. Where once students bowed down reverently before a monumental legacy of learning, there is now a cheap shop of trinkets and baubles that are theirs.

Unsatisfactory as these metaphors may seem to the experienced reader, they reflect a confidence with the written language that is characteristic of the advanced freshman writer, a confidence that also shows itself in the social judgments such students make, almost always (as in the passage above) placing themselves among the talented or educated or lucky and looking (usually down) upon the "others" as failures:

☐ A school can seize upon a child of my background and introduce her to a great many new areas of literature as she grows older; but if I had not come into school from a home environment where reading

10. I. A. Richards, *Practical Criticism* (New York: Harcourt Brace, 1929), pp. 304–5. Reprinted by permission of Harcourt Brace Jovanovich, Inc., and Routledge & Kegan Paul Ltd.

was as much a process of nourishment as eating I suspect that I might have turned into one of the semi-literates that seem to make up the bulk of this country's high school graduates.

☐ A high school graduate with superior aptitude should by all means go on to college. Having superior skills, this student will probably excell in college as well as upon graduation from college and be able to find work. The superior student might not seek employment upon graduation, but instead pursue advanced graduate work. Another type of student is the high school graduate who lacks the necessary skills for college work. In some instances, with remedial work, such students might eventually suceed in college. For the most part, however, college is wasted on those unprepared for it. This type of student would do better to seek employment upon graduating from high school.

Still, the advanced freshman writer has clearly not completed his own apprenticeship, and the basic writer, whose difficulties are the focus of this book, need not be abandoned, as many of his more advantaged peers seem ready to do. The basic writer usually understands this better than his teacher. He understands, further, that vocabulary is at the root of many of his difficulties with writing. This is doubtless why he spends his money on books that promise to build his vocabulary. But the acquisition of new words or new meanings for old words at the age of eighteen and at the pace that is dictated by the remedial situation demands more than this. Little has been done as yet to help the student grapple with the college vocabulary. What has been done tends to help him more as a reader than as a writer. Yet vocabulary looms as perhaps the most formidable and discouraging obstacle he faces in his struggle for advanced literacy, making him feel almost as a foreign-born student might feel before the vast lexicon of another language. What follows are merely some of the obvious strategies suggested by his plight.

Suggestions for teaching vocabulary

We know little about how adults acquire new words, most studies having concentrated on concept formation among children and on the relationship of concepts to word meanings. While certain that performance on vocabulary tests is highly predictive of college performance, we can be equally certain that learning to pass a vocabulary test is not the same as learning to use the academic vocabulary in writing. Furthermore we sense, if only from our own experiences with words, that there are limits to the rate at which we can acquire new words, that there are degrees of difficulty with words, depending on everything from the physical characteristics of words to the complexity of their referential meaning; and that the latter kind of acquisition is what a student's entire education is about, not what the basic writing course can aim for during its brief encounter with the student.

Part of the task of teaching vocabulary in the basic writing course is therefore to decide what realistically can be done in a short time to help a student cope with the academic vocabulary. At least three kinds of learning are involved:

1. learning about words;
2. learning words;
3. learning a sensitivity to words.

To learn about words is to acquire the kind of information about words as physical, grammatical, and semantic entities that makes analysis possible. To learn words is to absorb specific words into one's active vocabulary. To learn a sensitivity to words is to become aware of the process whereby exact choices are made in writing. I will discuss vocabulary study under each of these headings.

Learning about words
So much has been written about words—their nature, the changes they undergo through time, and the effects they have upon people—that the teacher must struggle not to unload on the student bulks of information that have little to do with his immediate difficulties with words. To be sure, certain general insights about words may have a direct bearing on a student's vocabulary development, but such insights are more likely to come about inductively, through specific encounters with words, rather than through introductory lectures on words. Students tend, for example, to mistake words for the things words refer to or to think of them as having meanings that are not, or ought not to be, affected by shifts in time or situation. The mastery of the academic vocabulary is probably as much, or even more, a task of accepting specialized meanings for words the student already knows in different contexts as it is of learning completely new words. Education itself might be described as the process whereby students learn to associate new concepts with familiar words or familiar concepts with new words. To the student who has learned the popular meaning of *ego*, the introduction in

psychology class of a new meaning may cause him to resist the concept, as if accepting it were consenting to a linguistic betrayal that threatens to wipe out not just a word but the reality that the word refers to. But no amount of abstract discussion about multiple meanings can succeed so well as one such encounter in making the point.

But if we consider the formal (rather than the contextual) ways in which words can be made to shift meaning we are closer to the kind of practical information about words BW students need. This requires a return to the subject of affixation, specifically to the system whereby prefixes and suffixes are added to words in order to shift grammatical class or to change meaning. Far less regular or pervasive than the inflectional suffixes that indicate tense and number, the derivational prefixes and suffixes are nonetheless frequent sources of error in BW papers as well as important features of the formal vocabulary. The long words that pose such difficulty for BW students can often be broken down into stems plus a variety of affixes, as with *bi dia lect ic al*, and even though the meaning of many prefixes may be too various for productive paradigms and the list of suffixes producing specific grammatical classes too lengthy for memorizing, an ability simply to see that words can be broken down into smaller units made up of stems and affixes increases a student's control over words.

But there is more to be gained than this from a close look at certain prefixes and suffixes. Some affixes, for example, still carry dependable information that can help the student deduce the meaning of unfamiliar words. Prefixes indicating number, for example, are stable in meaning: *uni-, bi-, tri-, quadri-, tetra-, pent-, multi-, mono-, poly-, duo-, omni-*. Certain affixes give fairly invariant indications of smallness: *mini-, micro-, -let,* and *-ette* (the latter can also indicate "imitation" or "feminine," however). A number of prefixes suggest, dependably, relationships of sequence and space: *anti-, pre-, intro-, pro-, post-, re-, sub-, supra-, inter-, intra-, in-* (to be distinguished from the negative *in* as in *intangible), ex-, circum-, com-*. Still other prefixes suggest various kinds of negation: *non-, in-, un-, anti-, counter-, contra-, dis-, mis-, mal-,* and *pseudo-.*

With even this limited number of prefixes a student gains access to a large number of meanings. And if such forms can be combined as James I. Brown has combined them in his "Master Word" table with important root elements, the student not only increases his vocabulary but develops a sense for the way roots and prefixes combine to form meanings that bear a close relationship to dictionary definitions. Brown's "Master Word" list consists of fourteen master words whose twenty prefixes and fourteen root elements pertain to over 14,000 words in *Webster's Collegiate Dictionary* and a projected 100,000 words in an unabridged dictionary. His table (page 214) lists not only the prefixes and roots, with their meanings, but the variant spellings of both forms.[11]

Students working with such a list can be expected not only to remember the key prefixes and root elements as they occur in the table but to recognize the various forms as they appear in other words and to gain some confidence in approaching such words analytically.

We have observed the difficulties BW students have with derivational suffixes. As efficient readers, speakers, and listeners they are likely to give closest attention to the beginnings of words. English, furthermore, is a language that depends to a high degree upon context rather than form to indicate the grammatical classes of words. There are, as a result, many "grammatical homophones" in the language, words that keep the same form for different grammatical classes (*clean* can be a verb or an adjective; *early*, an adjective or an adverb; *love*, a noun or a verb; etc.). And finally, where suffixes serve to indicate class, they do so with such a variety of forms that no paradigm is possible. As we saw at the beginning of the chapter, the BW student has difficulty predicting which derivational suffix is appropriate for a specific word and therefore appears to attach or omit suffixes in random ways, at one point deriving an adjective or noun by means of the wrong suffixes (a *destructional* way, there should be *preparance*), at another producing the wrong grammatical class (without *supervise*, who *resemblance* the Godfather). In the one instance the student chooses the wrong suffix from within the right derivational class; in the other, he is wrong about the derivational class itself. For the former problem a list of the common derivational suffixes is of no use. For the latter, a list of suffixes arranged according to patterns of derivation (suffixes that derive nouns from verbs, verbs from nouns, nouns from adjectives, etc.) could be useful in eliminating certain errors (noun suffixes in verb positions, as with *who resemblance*), but unless the student can make swift grammatical calculations he is likely to find the method too laborious.

As with other major trouble spots in formal English, there are no snappy solutions to word-class derivations because the phenomenon

11. From James I. Brown, *Efficient Reading, Revised Form A* (Lexington, Mass.: D.C. Heath, 1976), p. 128. Reprinted by permission of the author.

Prefix	Its other spellings	Its meaning	Master words	Root	Its other spellings	Its meaning
1. de-	......	Down or Away	DETAIN	Tenere	Tain, Ten, Tin	To Have or Hold
2. inter-	......	Between	INTERMITTENT	Mittere	Mitt, Miss, Mis, Mit	To Send
3. pre-	......	Before	PRECEPT	Capere	Cept, Cap, Capt, Ceiv, Ceit, Cip	To Take or Seize
4. ob-	Oc- Of- Op-	To, Toward, Against	OFFER	Ferre	Fer, Lat, Lay	To Bear or Carry
5. in-	Il- Im- Ir-	Into	INSIST	Stare	Sist, Sta	To Stand, Endure or Persist
6. mono-	......	One or Alone	MONOGRAPH	Graphein	Graph	To Write
7. epi-	......	Over, Upon or Beside	EPILOGUE	Legein	Log, Ology	Speech or Science
8. ad-	A- Ac- Ag- Al- An- Ap- Ar- As- Al-	To or Towards	ASPECT	Specere	Spect, Spec, Spi, Spy	To Look
9. un-	......	Not	UNCOMPLICATED	Plicare	Plic, Play, Plex, Ploy, Ply	To Fold, Bend, Twist, Interweave
com-	Co- Col- Con- Cor-	With or Together				
10. non-	......	Not	NONEXTENDED	Tendere	Tend, Tens, Tent	To Stretch
ex-	E- Ef-	Out or Formerly				
11. re-	......	Back or Again	REPRODUCTION	Ducere	Duct, Duc, Duit, Duk	To Lead, Make, Shape or Fashion
pro-	......	Forward or In Favor of				
12. in-	Il- Im- Ir-	Not	INDISPOSED	Ponere	Pos, Pound, Pon, Post	To Put or Place
dis-	Di- Dif-	Apart From				
13. over-	......	Above	OVERSUFFICIENT	Facere	Fic, Fac, Fact, Fash, Feat	To Make or Do
sub-	Suc- Suf- Sug- Sup- Sur- Sus-	Under				
14. mis-	......	Wrong or Wrongly	MISTRANSCRIBE	Scribere	Scribe, Scrip, Scriv	To Write
trans-	Tra- Tran-	Across or Beyond				

itself is too complex and unruly. But there is something to be said for
fixing in the student's mind the nature of the problem. It is helpful to
be aware of the massive number of suffixes English uses to derive word
classes and to add information to stems. It is even comforting to learn
that verbs and adverbs are derived from a very few of these suffixes
(verbs mainly from *-en, -ate*, and the infamous *-ize* and adverbs mainly
from *-ly* and the equally infamous *-wise*). Nouns and adjectives, on the
other hand, are derived from a large number of forms, some of which
can be usefully called to the student's attention.[12]

Common noun suffixes that indicate only part of speech

-acity	-ness	-tude
-hood	-ty	-ship

Suffixes that form many abstract nouns

-ance	-ation (-tion, -ion)	-dom	-mony
-ence	-ism	-ery	-ment

Suffixes that indicate agent

-eer	-grapher	-ster	-stress
-ess	-ier	-ist	-trix

Invariant noun suffixes

-ana	-chrome	-gram	-latry	-phobia
-archy	-cide	-graph	-meter	-ric
-ard (-art)	-ee	-graphy	-metry	-scope
-aster	-fer	-ics	-ology	-scopy
-bility	-fication	-itis	-phone	

Invariant adjective suffixes

-est	-form	-wise	-like
-ferous	-genous	-less	-ous
-fic	-scopic	-able (-ible, ble)	-ose
-fold	-wards	-most	-acious
-ful			

Once equipped with a working list of derivational suffixes, the student
should be encouraged 1. to observe closely the make-up of words that
he encounters in his reading or produces in his writing (can the student,
for example, locate the source of his difficulty with *stimulization* if he
compares it with *realization*); 2. to make predictions about unfamiliar
words (how much, for example, can he predict about *mellifluous*,

12. The lists that follow have been drawn from Lee C. Deighton's valuable study
Vocabulary Development in the Classroom (New York: Teachers College Press,
1959).

lexicographer, monochrome, bellicose, and the old standby *antidisestablishmentarianism*); 3. to generate lists of words that take the same suffixes or prefixes (*anthropology, ornithology, paleontology, philology,* etc; *lexicography, lithography, photography,* etc.); and, perhaps most useful, 4. to practice word-class shifts in the context of phrases or sentences:

A.

1. audible (adj.) ———(noun)　　3. anarchy (noun) ———(adj.)
   The sound is not audible.　　　His thoughts suggest anarchy.
   The ———— is poor.　　　　　His thoughts are ————.

2. suffocate (verb) ———(noun) 4. resembles (verb) ———(noun)
   He will suffocate.　　　　　　He resembles his father.
   We will die of ————.　　　　There is a ———— between
   　　　　　　　　　　　　　　him and his father.

B. Fill in all possible blanks (note that not all words have forms for all classes) and write sentences for each word.

Noun	Verb	Adjective	Adverb
initiation	initiate	initial	initially
courage			
	believe		
		envious	
			psychologically
		strong	
		etc.	

Learning words

Whatever their resources as speakers in non-academic situations, BW students are at a great disadvantage in college because not only must they learn, as other freshmen must, a formidable number of new words —many of them long words of Latin and Greek origin—but they do not know many of the words their teachers assume they know. This deficiency shows up most clearly in their writing, where words outside the basic vocabulary are usually either missing or erroneously used. The vocabulary of specialized terms associated with such subjects as psychology, biology, or literature is much easier to isolate than what might be called the vocabulary of general literacy, which includes both various classes of words and various ways of using words. Within such a vocabulary we could include:

1. Words that allude to events, places, and people that are assumed to be commonly, if but vaguely, known (Gandhi, the French Revolution, the Nile, etc.).
2. Words that serve as formal equivalents to concepts already familiar to the student in different words (as *atheist* is the equivalent to "someone who doesn't believe in God").
3. Words that serve to identify complex historical movements (Renaissance, Marxism, evolution, etc.).
4. Words that, although part of the nomenclature of certain fields, are also used in the wider culture with variant meanings (in literature, for example, such terms as *fiction, drama,* or *novel*).
5. Words that are intended to initiate highly specific academic activities (*define, compare, generalize, document, illustrate, prove, summarize, interpret,* etc.).
6. Words that are used in deliberately ambiguous ways in order to enrich or refine meaning (*irony, figures of speech,* etc.).
7. Words that articulate relationships such as addition, negation, condition, or causation (*moreover, therefore, however,* etc.).
8. Words that represent Latin- or Greek-based synonyms for familiar words (i.e. *initiate* or *commence* for *begin*) and that tend to give an academic flavor to the writing and speech of teachers.

Text writers and teachers, who have spent years acquiring the language of their professions, tend, like most people who have mastered a skill, not to see the water they swim in. Information, concepts, specialized terms rush from their pens and mouths as naturally as everyday talk while students, especially BW students, struggle to stay above the waves. The teacher of a remedial writing class cannot hope to prepare his student for such a deluge. Words, for the most part, must be learned *in* contexts, not *before* contexts, and in the entire course of a student's training, not in his one or two semesters of "remediation."

Much should be written about the approach to vocabulary in regular college courses, particularly at the introductory level. Teachers who take the trouble to find out will discover serious gaps between the vocabularies they *expect* their students to have and the vocabularies they in fact have. We can assume, for example, that an introductory psychology lecture that includes in its first twenty minutes such words as the following can only reinforce the student's habit of not expecting to understand what teachers are talking about:

legacy, mechanism, theological, philosophical, neural, rational, modalities, synthesize, empirical, apperceptive (briefly defined), therapeutic, milieu, stimulus-response (briefly defined).

At the other extreme, the movement to re-write textbooks so as to eliminate difficult words and shorten sentences threatens to remove from the student both the subject in all its complexity and the challenge that almost defines studenthood—the experience of being just so far over one's head that it is both realistic and essential to work at surviving.

Like the books Bacon tried to classify, some words are to be tasted, others to be swallowed, and some few to be chewed and digested. Doubtless there are many words that students who are considered well prepared for college know but superficially. College is (or ought to be) the place, in fact, where over time such words develop deeper resonances as the student experiences them in fuller contexts. Freshmen who, for example, can briefly identify a proper name like Marx are not likely to have read what he wrote or understood his significance in intellectual history. They have a light acquaintance with the word but one that nonetheless keeps them from blankness when the word occurs in a text or lecture. Not "at home" with the word, they have at least a sense of its neighborhood, which helps them to cope with the total message.

The process whereby such students acquired these staples of the academic vocabulary has usually been slow and indirect, much slower than the BW student can now afford. But because the words are in a sense superficially known at this stage it is not unrealistic to suggest that with an imaginative and adult use of film, tapes, pictures, books, and even puzzles a student could acquire quite painlessly a large number of useful academic words. Biographical films, for example, in a field such as science would quickly equip a student not only with important scientific terms but with human situations from which to view the unfolding of scientific knowledge.

Many of the words students do not know refer to concepts or relationships they do know and can express in other ways. Here it is

possible to build upon the student's vocabulary, pointing out equiv-
alencies between the words he knows and the words he is learning but
also refining meaning by comparing roots and affixes, looking words up
in the dictionary, and observing the words in various contexts—all of
which tasks serve to fix words in the memory much more efficiently
than rote memorization.

There remain the words that lie deep in the context of particular subjects and must be learned there rather than in skills classes: the
nomenclature of a subject, which in a field like biology, for example,
includes not only words specific to biology (probably the most formidable of naming systems) but a number of general scientific words such
as *adaptive, kinetic, synthesize, viscosity* and general non-scientific
words common to any analytic discussion such as *component, con-
comitant, elongate, fluctuate, inhibitory, phenomenon.*[13] Finally there
are conceptual terms which are nurtured throughout a course—the
concept of *irony*, for example, in literature, or *ecology* in biology, or
perception in psychology.

Students can thus be expected to have different kinds of difficulties
with the words they encounter in courses. In some, the semantic burden
is staggering, especially where students have difficulty making close
observations of words. Faced at times with as many as ten to fifteen
new words on a page, as might happen in biology, the student has
difficulty not only finding ways of remembering the words of Greek
and Latin origin but also managing to keep from confusing words that
are roughly similar in appearance (*neuron-nephron, automatic-auto-
nomic, uterus-ureter, systematic-systemic,* etc.). With other words the
problem is not formal but semantic: certain words, while familiar
enough in the context of ordinary situations, take on different, technical
meanings. Thus the term *independent variable,* important in a subject
such as psychology, is bewildering to many students because the word
"independent" suggests that the variable *cannot* be manipulated,

13. In my comments on academic vocabularies I have depended very much upon
two reports prepared for this study: Valerie Krishna's report "The Language of
Introductory Biology" and Gerald Kauvar's report "The Language of Introductory
Psychology," both unpublished. The authors were City College writing teachers
who took introductory courses, one in biology and the other in psychology. As
students in the courses they experienced the language tasks of each subject and
observed the experience of other students. Their reports attempt to describe the
language "problems" in each subject and to recommend ways of helping students
cope with what seemed to them a formidable academic task, even for college
teachers.

whereas it is the independent variable that *is* manipulated in an experiment. Or again, in a discussion on visual perception the word *texture* is certain to be associated with such tactile sensations as roughness or smoothness rather than with the visual distinctions between figures and backgrounds. Words of this type must be learned not through verbal definitions but through experiences that enable the student to visualize the meaning. (The anatomy class is in this sense the perfect model for vocabulary development, for here names meet with their designata. Unfortunately the "body" of other subjects is not accessible.)

The teacher who becomes aware of the dimensions of the vocabulary problem for BW students might well ask how in his modest semester or two, with all the other skills he must attend to, he can possibly help his students learn new words. The answer is, of course, that he cannot do much to reduce the corpus of words his students have yet to learn, but he can introduce techniques for learning them that will make the task easier. And here, although there are doubtless rich opportunities for the development of multi-media approaches to word learning, the homespun method of keeping a personal vocabulary notebook in which the student enters the word, the pronunciation, its meaning, the sentence or phrase in which it was found, and the source, remains helpful. Alfred Westfall reported over twenty years ago on a successful vocabulary course at Colorado A & M built around this method. Students were expected to add thirty words a week to their notebooks, the words to come from their work in other courses. Class time was spent sharing vocabulary entries, discussing the words, and developing good definitions. Students taking the course demonstrated significant vocabulary gains as well as a greater resourcefulness with words.[14]

Even with such preparation, however, the BW student is not usually ready to cope with the traditional vocabulary load of introductory courses in subjects like psychology, biology, sociology, or history. Where skills teachers are linked as consultants to content courses or where courses in reading and writing are integrated with content courses, students may find the task somewhat less formidable. The skills teacher has developed antennae for trouble spots and can often predict where the concept load is likely to become too heavy or where an explanation must be expanded. He is also more inclined to integrate writing into the course, a practice which content teachers are increas-

14. Alfred Westfall, "Can College Students Expand Their Recognition Vocabularies?" *School and Society*, January 13, 1951, pp. 25–28.

ingly reluctant to follow despite the fact that writing serves to tell both student and teacher how much has been truly learned. The skills teacher can also prepare, under the guidance of the content teacher, supportive materials for the course—glossaries of terms, dictionaries of key concepts, study manuals to accompany the texts and lectures. And perhaps most important, he can help the content teacher become sensitive to the language he uses, which, while transparent to him, is often utterly opaque to his students.

Such assistance to content teachers would not be necessary, some might argue, if the content teachers were teaching, but the traditional stance of the college teacher as dispenser of information and concepts rather than teacher of individual students, the traditional format of large introductory courses, and the relative preparedness of college students in the past have combined to produce a teaching situation that discourages exchange and allows both students and teachers to pretend that they understand one another. The writing teacher, because he regularly must read what students write and meet with them to discuss their work, knows something about their levels of preparation and the pace at which they can be expected to move ahead.

It may be, however, that nothing short of a major reform in the design of introductory courses will address the problem. Still for the most part committed to terminology and taxonomies and to hierarchies of learning that are prescribed by administrative rather than epistemological realities, these courses serve mainly to separate majors from non-majors rather than to introduce all students to distinctive ways of observing and interpreting the life around them.[15]

Learning a sensitivity to words

Writing is a process which by giving us more time to form sentences greatly multiplies the number of choices we face. This is the beauty and the pain of writing. It permits a writer to search for a day for the word that fits his meaning or it may freeze him for weeks in indecision as the options for this word or that rhetorical strategy pile up. But in his search, the writer is doing more than retrieving words from his memory; he is advancing his thought. As he discriminates among words,

15. M. L. J. Abercrombie's *The Anatomy of Judgment* (New York: Basic Books, 1960) is an excellent introduction to this kind of reform. See also Douglas Barnes's valuable report on language in the classroom in *Language, the Learner, and the Classroom* (New York: Penguin Books, 1969).

he discovers the ramifications and the qualities of his ideas, and this, more than any improvement in style, is the value of attending to words.

But the BW student is not in the habit of exploiting his opportunities in writing. For him the "right" word is usually the word *someone else* has in mind (the teacher, most often), not the word that helps him tease out his own meaning, and to the extent that he attends to words at all it is to wonder whether they are correct or appropriate but not whether they are precise. The process whereby writers generate choices is of course not observable, but students can experience the process synthetically through exercises such as the following:

1. *Substitution practice.* In one form of this practice, words from a thesaurus entry can be substituted for an underlined word in a passage and the student (or class) asked to describe the shifts in meaning (denotative and connotative) that occur with each substitution. In another form, words from the student's own writing can be circled and students asked to generate as many options for the word as they can think of. The writer, in turn, can defend his choice by showing how the options depart from his meaning.

2. *Observation of first drafts.* One of the most important facts about the composing process that seems to get hidden from students is that the process that creates precision is itself messy, littering the page with so many deletion marks and emendations as to make some manuscripts almost indecipherable. Yet the scrutiny of such manuscripts, whether they be facsimile copies of Keats's *Eve of St. Agnes* or the first draft of a teacher's memo to the executive committee, is instructive: it reproduces for the student a map of the writer's debates, which, in turn, encourages the student to hesitate over his own words. At first the teacher in conference must usually articulate the debate for the student, raising questions about certain words the student has used and searching with the student for better ones, but in time the student hears his own questions and initiates his own debates.

3. *Reading.* Teachers disagree about the importance of reading in a writing class. Some worry that reading will become a substitute for writing, especially in programs where teachers of English literature are required, under the exigencies created by open admissions policies, to teach the rudiments of writing but end up teaching literature just the same. Others believe that books and essays should be used as models which students deliberately imitate, a method of instruction that reaches

far back into the past. Still others would use reading to spark discussions which in turn generate theme topics.

These approaches are largely product—rather than process—oriented. That is, they pose tasks for the student that require him to look at a piece of writing as something that *contains* its meaning, as a pound of sugar might be said to contain its weight or a word in the dictionary is perceived to *be* its meaning. The text stands outside, separate from the reader, impersonal and invulnerable, like some ancient tablet that the archaeologist struggles to decode. It is a "classic" or a "model" or a "priming pump," and when the student writes *his* papers, it does not occur to him that he is a writer producing reading; he remains a writer producing writing. This alienation of the student writer from the text robs him of important insights and sensitivities, for it is only when he can observe himself as a reader and imagine that a writer is behind the print of the page that he understands his own situation as a writer. (The student who refers to the author of *The Great Gatsby* as "they" is already in difficulty with the text.)

First, then, in what might be called a writing approach to reading is the *fact* of the reader's response. And then, not a correction of that response, but an effort to understand it, to discover what in the text or the reader's experience created it. Then the reader shifts perspective and tries to imagine the writer's intent, to decide why he used this word instead of that, moved in this direction instead of that, or chose to expand upon one point and not another. Using the text as his terrain, he tries, in short, to map the thinking of the writer and finally to see in relation to that map where he, as one reader, traveled.

Reading in this way, the student begins to sense that the meaning of what he reads or writes resides not in the page nor in the reader but in the encounter between the two. This insight makes him a more careful writer and a more critical reader. As a writer, he must think about the kinds of responses his words are likely to arouse; as a reader, his growing critical stance encourages him to raise questions about what he reads, to infer the author's intent, and even to argue with him. And of course these same critical skills can then be turned upon himself when he writes, for the process of writing utterly blurs the line that many college programs draw between reading and writing when they have the two skills of literacy taught not simply in different courses but even in different departments. It is encouraging to note, however, the move to introduce writing instruction along with reading at the earliest stages of elementary education and the effort at the upper levels to require writing across the curriculum.

Conclusion

I have been presenting the academic vocabulary as a formidable yet solid fact to which the BW student must adjust—a "given." There is much linguistic realism behind this, since languages that have become as institutionalized as the academic languages have are more difficult to change than people. Nonetheless, if we distinguish between the goal of acquiring a working use of academic English and the process whereby that goal is achieved, the burden of adjustment to other kinds of linguistic realities falls on teachers and the people who design college curricula.

Generally the student is motivated to increase his vocabulary. It is the one part of writing instruction that needs no sales talk. Still, vocabulary growth is almost always slow, so slow that a vocabulary test is likely to be the least sensitive measure of progress during a semester. For all that a teacher can do to equip a student with information about words and with strategies for learning them, there appear to be stubborn (and doubtless individually different) limits to the pace at which words can enter our active vocabularies. For the most part, we piece together the meanings of words by encountering them over time in a variety of contexts. Yet college is, almost by definition, a place where people come together for a short time to be immersed in words—and where their mastery of the meanings of these words is what is always being tested. Even students who are prepared for the immersion have difficulty with vocabulary. What, then, is to be done about the unprepared student?

I have made several suggestions. First, it is probably possible to reduce somewhat the number of words students must learn in introductory courses. This raises the question, well worth raising, of whether the concept of the introductory course as a survey of a field and a glossary of special terms is pedagogically sound for any student. A further reduction might come about if a distinction is made between words that are essential to conceptualization in particular disciplines and those that serve the secondary role of perpetuating the stylistic preferences (and excesses) of academicians. (Here the problem of textbook and lecture styles must be explored.) As a further check on vocabulary size, students with serious vocabulary deficiencies might be discouraged from taking courses with heavy vocabulary loads until they have had time to work on basic vocabulary problems.

Second, the responsibility for vocabulary development must be shared by all teachers and not isolated in the "remedial" wing of a college, as if vocabulary were a prerequisite course rather than the medium of instruction in all courses. Here the possibility of combining skills and content instruction offers the skills teacher a real vocabulary world to work in and the content teacher expert help in assessing vocabulary difficulty and developing vocabulary materials. Third, the skills teacher, relieved of the responsibility of teaching specialized vocabularies, can turn to some of the rudimentary vocabulary problems we have seen in BW passages. Some of these problems—unfamiliarity with idiomatic expressions and semantic blunders—reflect the students' superficial and random exposure to formal written English and will probably disappear with time and close editing. What seems more important is to build criteria for precision—through skillful questioning, through cultivating a sense of audience, through the close examination of precise passages —so that the student begins to push past the limits of his customary vocabulary, searching for better words and phrases. As this is happening, the student can also be learning more about words—about prefixes and suffixes and word class and about the process of generating word choices—so that he is more willing to take risks.

Finally, the teacher as mediator between the languages students bring to class and the language of the academy must himself serve the students both as translator and model, trying not to lean so far toward the students' language as to misrepresent the tasks of the academy and appear foolishly adaptive, nor yet to appear so bound by the academic conventions as to be insensitive to the difficulties they pose for others. More than any exercise in word discrimination, the teacher's personal use of the language, his attentiveness to the words he, as well as his students, uses, his pleasure in precise language and his courtesy in offering, within the context of his talk, ways of understanding unfamiliar words, are the best forms of vocabulary instruction. They nourish the student's will, without which the academic language is too large and tedious and complex a dragon to slay.

7
Beyond the sentence

Up to this point, we have been examining the sentences students write, but we have not attended closely to the ways in which these sentences combine to produce passages. Yet the mature writer is recognized not so much by the quality of his individual sentences as by his ability to relate sentences in such a way as to create a flow of sentences, a pattern of thought that is produced, one suspects, according to the principles of yet another kind of grammar—a grammar, let us say, of passages.

"There is not a sentence," wrote Whitehead, "which adequately states its own meaning." The statement suggests that the quality of an idea is not to be found in a nucleus or thesis statement but in the sentences that follow or lead up to that statement. An idea, in this sense, is not a "point" so much as a branching tree of elaboration and demonstration.

This distinction is useful in approaching the difficulties BW students have beyond the sentence, for it is inaccurate to say, although many teachers say it, that BW students have no ideas, if by "idea" they mean what is conventionally meant by an "idea"—that is, a "point" or general statement. Not only do BW students produce essays that are full of points but the points they make are often the same ones that more advanced writers make when writing on the same subject. The differences lie in the style and extent of elaboration. Once having identified some of these differences, we should find it easier to decide what the content of instruction ought to be when the student moves from the sentence into the open field of discourse.

One of the most notable differences between experienced and inexperienced writers is the rate at which they reach closure upon a point. The experienced writer characteristically reveals a much greater tolerance for what Dewey called "an attitude of suspended conclusion" than the inexperienced writer, whose thought often seems to halt at the boundary of each sentence rather than move on, by gradations of subsequent comment, to an elaboration of the sentence. The BW essay tends, as a result, to be made up of "sentences of thought" rather than "passages of thought," and although the essays are not always short, they tend to be so because of the difficulty the writer has in staying with his point beyond its initial formulation.

Here, for example, a student attempts to answer the job-market question (whether it makes sense, in the light of a shrinking job market, to go on for a college degree):

> Yes, being that today's jobs are being made impossible to get without a college degree with the to high school graduates.
>
> College is a significant of keeping the mind open for advance and more learning after high school.
>
> The U.S. future education in college is good also, because it help's the mass production in this country it provides teaching job. Let's one person help another.

Another student, writing on the question of whether college encourages students to be immature, produces a longer essay, but again its thought units are bounded by one or two sentences. And his staying power diminishes as the essay progresses:

> Maturity with a good college education makes better human beings.
>
> I find it very hard to believe that college encourages students to be immature.
>
> I am a perfect example because I have had only a high school education which I feel was not enough to take me through this fast moving world. I just felt I had to go to college to learn more so as to deal with the environment.
>
> We can look at the leaders of the world today, I am sure that common sence alone could not put them where they are they all had to have some college experience.
>
> In years or Centrys ago people was dying because their minds were lazy they belived in a lot of supersticion because they could not think

of any other reason for what was happening to them. Now things are organized, people are made to think so that they can understand the reasons for things.

I have realized that in life whatever is worked for are more apprieated than whats not worked for. I have never had life easy and I am not sorry. If many people should tell you what they have gone through to be where they are today you would be shocked.

Students whos family did not prepare money for their college education grantidely should be helped to persue college.

Another thing is that if a student does not wish to attend college he or she does not have to go.

If we all fight for aid the government will help.

Sometimes or the other the college student will find his education valuable as he encounter with the outside world.

One senses in such passages that the writer is cut off from the thoughts that might be awakened in less restricting situations. The mind is not allowed to play upon the topic, to follow out the implications that lie within statements, or to recover the history of the idea as it developed in the writer's mind. Instead, the writer moves abruptly from one point to the next, abandoning as he goes all possibility of elaboration. We see this even more clearly when a BW student's passage is compared with a passage written by a more experienced freshman writer. In Essay 1 below, for example, the writer, a BW student, is making two main points: that if a person seeks personal enrichment college might make sense but that if he seeks a good job that requires no degree, college makes no sense. In Essay 2, the writer touches upon the first point but follows out the implications of the second for most of the essay:

Essay 1

It makes a lot of sense for a young person getting out of high school today to go to college for a degree if to him this is what he wants.

If a person feels that by getting a college degree would make him a better person although the jobs to fit his education might not be in demand of course it makes sense.

On the other hand it does not make sense to spend all that money to go through college to become a stenographer. If after high school you find a good job, which you feel that you can spend the rest of your life doing and enjoying. I see no sense in going to college then.

Essay 2

In view of the above statistics, it appears that a young person getting out of high school should not go on for a college degree. The jobs that will have the most openings are those that require little training in academic subjects.

In today's world, more and more people are urged to receive as much academic experience as possible. This view tends to ignore the fact that when these people have completed their education, there will be few job openings that fit their particular skills.

Many people are more adapt at taking apart a radio than in diagramming sentences. These people should be encouraged to receive mechanical training rather than receiving a B.A. in English. There should be no stigma to manual labor. A person who does not do well in school should not be encouraged or forced into a college when he will not be able to complete with scholastically brighter students.

Our society has forgotten the need for so called "untrained" personnel. The young person getting out of high school today will often go on to college, even if it does not interest him, as a result of social pressure. A secretary who is proficient in shorthand will be many times more useful to her employer than a college graduate who is a two-finger typist who couldn't find a job. There is a great demand for workers in such fields as plumbing who know what they are doing.

While receiving training for these jobs, courses in literature, language or mathematics might be taken to broaden a person's outlook, but the goal of being well-trained in one's field should not be forgotten.

I believe that if a young person has a desire to go on to college, he should be encouraged to do so; however, the person who shows greater interest in the non-academic fields should also be encouraged freely to follow what interests him. Society should encourage all to excel in the areas to which they are best suited.

In yet another essay by another more experienced freshman writer, the contradictions that lie within the topic are given even fuller play, with the result that the writer herself is dissatisfied with her conclusion.

Everyone these days is apparently going to college; there must be some logical reason for this. Now, it seems to me that, although statistics seem to point to the fact that there are few openings in jobs for college degree holders, they neglect to mention the financial side of it. Anyone holding a degree, particularly professional degrees such as M.D.'s, will get jobs with a much higher salary than, say, a repairman or secretary. This, I believe is the main attraction to high school graduates—good money. I suppose many don't consider the possibility of not finding one of these fabulous, money-making jobs.

In my opinion, high school students should think twice about going to college. They should really consider what they want to get, or need to get, out of a college education. If you really have ambition and feel a "calling" in a certain field, I say more power to you—if you've got the money. If you plan for a degree simply for the money, you should probably try to pick a career in which there is likely to be openings in the future. If you're one of those people who just wants to learn, you better make sure you have either some sort of mechanical skill, or rich parents.

In general, I think it's a really good idea for all high school students to have the college experience. However, with society in the ridiculous, mind-killing condition it is now, people graduating from high school have to look out for their own survival. Taken in this light, it does not make sense for all high school graduates to go on to college, if these statistics are to be believed. They would wind up with too much competition for jobs and probably only get totally messed up in the end. So, if it is possible for young people to hold on to their heads and their pride in themselves without being able to have the opportunity of a college education, it would seem to make more sense for less people to plan for a college degree, but to try to learn a mechanical skill. This conclusion is really hard to come to and accept because of the implications involved; a society more full of robots and less full of people. However, I believe that people alive and performing as robots is better than people dead on the street from hunger.

A reader's sense of order and development in a piece of discursive writing depends upon the writer's ability to stay with each thought in the line of his discussion long enough to mark it as important. Otherwise it is difficult to know what thought is connecting with what as the writer makes his way through his essay. To the BW student, however, the demand for elaboration is likely to be viewed as a demand for mere bulk and, being unfamiliar with the ways writers generate their material, the student falls back on the strategies that enable talkers to support and extend their conversations with one another. Often these are strategies, however, that discourage deliberate, thorough inquiry of the sort demanded in analytical writing. Two strategies in particular dominate student writing well beyond the BW stage: the substitution of common wisdom in the form of platitudes or routine affirmations for careful individual inquiry and the drift from stated general purposes toward personal reverie.

The following essay has, for example, something of the quality of the casual exchanges speakers have with each other when they lack the time or energy to develop their thoughts. Like the fillers "you know" or "you understand," essays like this nurture a sense of accord by drawing upon generalizations that are so broad-based and familiar as to be unassailable—or so, at any rate, the writer probably hopes:

> Yes. I feel it makes sense because Its always good to better your Education. High School isn't enough. I think you ought to try to go further on to be successful in Life to make yourself a better person. Plenty of people should go to College and get a degree BA or PHD. or A.A. just to be something. You'll never Know what you would turn out to be if you just try. Sometimes opportunities only Knocks once and then no more and then you wind up no where. In Some cases people have never gone to College and still have accomplished Something in Life but you still have a better chance when you go to College.

In the following essay, the writer, also responding to the question about jobs and college, seems unable to get into the topic by approaching it directly and chooses instead the oblique route of reverie, which, as it turns out, draws her further and further from the formal topic:

> I decided to come to College because it was something to do. I'm not a lazy person, at least I don't think so. I love to work and do all kinds of things try new activities. I am the type of person that has the attitude of easy come easy go. No matter what happens, I really have to think whether if is something to cry about or not. I know this actually doesn't have any thing to do with the paper given to us. But I hope it will lead to it.
>
> I don't like to read, I guess thats because I haven't done alot of it. And also I really don't know how.
>
> I feel that the society today is a little to much for me to handle. To tell you the truth I just don't care any more about who the president, or governor, or senate is, because you can't change it.
>
> The job I really want is to be a police woman. I don't want to be a news reporter or a famous book writer. I just want to be myself. I don't expect to become a college professor. But with my luck or my attitude I'll probably want to be that If I really get into it. Whatever that is?
>
> I don't speak another language. Although I worked In a Greek

Coffee Shop. And before I know it I was speaking the language, understanding, writing and reading. I thought it was fantastic. I would really like to learn any language possible. I don't even know if I'm going to stay in college. I guess you would say I live day by day. Which is true.

I hope the world be a better place to live and the society be understandable about the way other people want to live and learn. I'm sure things will change. If not for better for worst. Like they say, we the children are the leaders for tomorrow.

Although common wisdom and reverie can figure in the generation of ideas about a subject, the inexperienced writer tends to use them as substitutes for ideas. They encourage the flow of words and sentences without engaging the writer in the real struggle of articulation. We get a sense of this struggle when we turn to essays where the student does attempt to address a question or problem, even though his ability to hold on to his idea is not yet well developed. At the most rudimentary level of development, the writer appears to have made a rough sorting of his points, which he often separates by indentations or extra space. But neither the points themselves nor their relationships are well articulated. Rather the passage has more the quality of a writer's inner, pre-verbalized thought, not yet shaped for communication. The reader must look hard to see even the traces of a pattern of development. Thus in the following essay on the college question, the writer begins by observing a correlation between low-paying jobs and limited education. Next he considers the job prospects of college students and notes that the unskilled jobs will have been given out and that even in the area of skilled jobs there will be unpredictable fluctuations, owing to demand. But the writer does not yet see the pattern of his thought clearly enough to mark it for his reader, who without more articulation is likely to dismiss the passage, as the teacher of this student did, as "totally disorganized":

According to the figures which were distributed. The people with little, Higher education have gotten more jobs than people with degrees. The people who get jobs as secretaries and Stenographers probably would received the smallest salary. Since there jobs are so simple. They will be looking for benefit. Because of the time they have spent in school. The most popular jobs would be filled the quickest by unskilled laber which would be trained on the job.

As a person who has benefited through mistakes he has made in his pass life; Same jobs, for example engineers were in demand but now they are very rare. Because there was such a big production made about the field and the benefits. Today the teaching field will probbely become the thing of the future mostly because the population explosion.

Without a sharp awareness of his proposition or purpose a writer has, of course, great difficulty remembering where he is going. The ability to hold larger and larger units of discourse together (from paragraph to essay to term paper to research paper) is in fact an important measure of a student's intellectual growth, and writing can be viewed in part as a technology for holding vast and complex units of thought together. But the task of remembering and constantly returning to one's purpose in a piece of writing is difficult, particularly for the inexperienced writer. Getting sidetracked or shifting points in midstream are thus common flaws in BW passages. Frequently, students are drawn away from their stated purpose by the magnetic power of personal preoccupations, as with this writer whose enthusiasm for psychology finally dominates the essay. (An experienced writer would not necessarily exclude this content but would find a way of relating it to the question. Much of what this writer has to say about psychology, for example, could be used to illustrate the point that college can be personally and socially rewarding without necessarily guaranteeing a better job):

> Yes, if this is what the person wants to do in life. My self I'm thinking of psychology, this is one think in life i like most. Psychology is a good field to work in because of the type of people coming up today.
> Psychology has helped me in my home and around my friends. Psychology is very interesting to me and I see life a little better. I'm looking to become a Psychologists, it is going to help me in my work as a manager.
> A College Degree is good to have when getting a job and if you know the work well it's not needed. For myself both college degree and experence is good.
> I have three jobs for me now as a manager, with the aede of Psychology it well make it better.
> I think Psychologists should be demand in all business offices and all people who work with people should have a psychology back ground. This will help them to help people and to understand them a little better.

Often a student begins to write his essay before he has arrived at what might be called a starting idea so that his essay, rather than being the development of an idea, is the record of an idea developing. In a sense, of course, writing is a process whereby an initial idea gets extended and refined, but here I am referring to a stage in the composing process that has probably been internalized by experienced writers—the stage when the writer picks up certain tentative paths that seem to branch out from his propositions, or pushes his proposition far enough to discover that it is at odds with what he really wants to say, or immerses himself in his data, hazarding guesses here and there as to what they mean, but resisting any formulation that secures order at the cost of comprehensiveness.

The BW student, pressed usually by time and unacquainted with the ways writers build their ideas, is likely to begin writing before his ideas have undergone this period of incubation. Here, for example, a BW student is trying on the one hand to make some sense out of the facts that have been given him on employment prospects while at the same time composing an essay that requires him to have already digested these facts:

> I think so because all the jobs on this sheet request some kind of college education, like to become a physicists or psychologists you need a college background. it is impossible to get these jobs with a high school diploma. with a diploma, you might be able to get a job, as repairmen Hospital attendants or a salesmen or secretary in a little office. jobs in most demand is in the teaching field, especially in the college and universitys. Elementary school have 56,300 all they need is an experienced baby sitter with those children because soon you won't be able to get a job without an college education. and I fell that they need more teaching staff because they only have 17,00. All of the jobs that is kind of important don't have a good rating, like mechanics and repairmen, when your car or television break without them you would have to buy a new one anytime something happens to it.
>
> The important have to get more people, and the only way to learn is to go to college.

The writer has produced a jumble of observations that seem to have no relation to each other nor to his concluding sentence. Yet there lies within what he *has* written, an incubating idea that would be worth nourishing—namely, the observation that discrepancies of status and pay between white- and blue-collar workers do not necessarily correlate with the social importance of the work being done.

In another essay illustrating the problem of premature formulation we find a complete but unconscious turnabout in the writer's purpose, the first part of the essay criticizing the strictness of parents and the second criticizing the disrespectfulness of the young. The conflict between the two points could be reconciled in a more complex and interesting idea that is latent in the essay—namely, that the rigidity of parents is linked not only to their own authoritarian upbringing but to their sense of waning authority over the young:

> During the life of which I will be growing up, I don't like the idea of my parent trying to run my life. Because the way our parents was brought up is different these days. And I think they should try to understands how we feel. Times have changes and they cannot keep us back. Regardless of whatever they said we till is going do our thing. Because I'm a person that like to party. And parents don't like to see me going out every weekends. So some weekends I stay home just to please them. My parents try to keep me in the house. But they just don't know that by keeping in the house, won't solve the problem. I like to party, but I also like to do my work in school. Then when weekend come I be somewhere in the streets. I guess the way my mother's was brought up was not to go anywhere. After school come straight home and all that other kind of stuff.
>
> Kids today that are growing up are getting very wild. Since they reach a certain age. That why parents of today are having many problems with them. So they figure if they lock there kids up they might become better children. But if they only new, that they would end worst than how they was. One thing I noticed was that oure parents had to respect there parents. Do you think the kids of today would do that. No they just disrespect there parents.
>
> I may love to party but I think respect come first. If a child don't respect there parents its not always the child fault. Its sometime have to do with the parents. Maybe while they was growing up the parents spoiled them. That sometime be the biggest problems. Because when the child reach that certain age when they see everything they want. And the parents can't give it to them. It bring a great big deal of a problem. That's when the child stop disrespecting her parents. It happen many times. When the child is young. She received anything she want. But after when she get older. She start asking for too much thing, which the parents can'nt afford. They start throwing back in there parents face about how they used to buy this for them. And

since they reach a certain age the parents don't want to buy nothing
for. To spoil a child is a bad thing. Unless you know how to handle
them when they reach that certain age. This is my expression about
life.

Observing these various flaws in the BW student's management of
even short pieces of discourse—the absence of "play" upon ideas, the
restriction to oral strategies for elaboration, the difficulty with framing
and holding on to a central or organizing idea—the teacher often
concludes that thinking rather than writing ought to be the focus of
his instruction, that in fact once the student has "learned to think" the
task of writing down his thoughts will come easily. Such an interpretation tends to isolate the student's difficulty with writing from the
linguistic situation he finds himself in and focuses instead upon the
functioning of his brain, proposing various types of thinking tasks
designed to develop the mind. Thus if we view the production of a
written essay as involving at least three different levels of performance
—the generation of a thought, which may not involve the mediation of
language (the matter is greatly debated), the transposing of the thought
into language, and finally the transposing of that language into writing
—the teacher of "thinking" assumes 1. that the student's writing
problems reflect something approaching a dysfunction or retardation
of the conceptualizing faculty itself and 2. that this condition will (or
may) respond to direct instruction that concentrates upon the thinking
process rather than upon writing. The teacher in such a pedagogy is
an initiator rather than a mediator and the student is learning to think,
not becoming conscious of the ways in which he can control his
already-developed faculty for thinking.

Such a view can be criticized on at least two grounds. First, it too
often confuses the analysis of thought with the generation of thought.
That is, it assumes that because thoughts, once they have been generated, can be shown to reflect various patterns of logic which can be
analyzed and reproduced, it is possible to generate thought through the
analysis of logic. But both experience and research tend to contradict
this assumption. We are much too ignorant about where and what the
wellsprings of thought are to be ready to propose a pedagogy that will
draw from them directly. Rather, our ignorance forces us to move about
with our pedagogical strategies like someone witching for well water,
waiting for the vibrations of a slight willow branch to signal the location of springs. We can observe in many students over the course of

their training in college an increase in their specifying and generalizing powers, but we cannot link this growth to particular forms or subjects of instruction. "Thinking," writes Susanne Langer, "employs almost every intuitive process, semantic and formal (logic), and passes from insight to insight not only by recognized processes but as often as not by short cuts and personal incommunicable means. The measure of its validity is the possibility of arriving at the same results by the orthodox methods of demonstrating formal connections. But a measure of validity is not a ground of validity. Logic is one thing and thinking is another. Thought may be logical, but logic itself is not a way of thinking."[1]

We do not, in short, understand how people learn to think or be logical. We can theorize about hierarchies of thinking tasks and even suggest developmental patterns of growth that correlate with such hierarchies (although we are on shaky ground when we attempt to draw analogies from research on children to the thought processes of young adults), but we are still ignorant spectators of the phenomenon of "getting an idea" or relating one idea to another.

The second weakness of the "thinking" pedagogy is that it minimizes both the intellectual sophistication of the students and the extent to which "thought" is narrowly equated with those styles of thinking and ordering that dominate academic discourse. The point has by now been made often, and probably most cogently in William Labov's much-anthologized chapter "The Logic of Nonstandard English,"[2] that the ability to conceptualize must be defined broadly enough to take into account the different forms that conceptualization takes in different cultures and classes. While it is obvious that the BW essays we have been considering are far from acceptable examples of academic essays, even the poorest of them can be seen to contain propositions that could lend themselves to development in the academic style. Nor are the papers as "disorderly" as a first glance might suggest. Often the underlying order of a paper is logical by conventional standards although the writer has not made the connections between statements explicit. At other times, the basis of order is derived from non-academic models. The student, for example, who wrote the following

1. *Mind: An Essay on Human Feeling* (Baltimore: Johns Hopkins Press, 1967), Vol. 1, pp. 148–49.

2. In *Language in the Inner City* (Philadelphia: University of Pennsylvania Press, 1972), pp. 201–40.

passage on the word "reality" (a topic that could easily engulf a practiced writer) was influenced by the shape and tone of the evangelical sermon:[3]

> Reality is what I say it is, I say is to live for "God". It's real or I such say that he is for real and he is more real if you know that your just here on earth for just some time, maybe fourty year, fifty, eighty years, but who realy knows. I guest nobody here on earth knows. You know in "good book," I mean the "Bible," it said that there is two kinds of life, this kind of life, that where living on earth and the life where he lives. This is reality to know that I'm just here for a short while because I donn't know when he is coming for me (death and passing away of the body) I'm glad I wont pass away just my body. But I have to take under consideration that there are other people that were born before me and there turn has to come before me. Because its just a line, your just waiting to be called.
>
> A funny thing happen to me when I went to the A.P. shopping for food. I was with my wife and we got all the food that we can get for us to eat for two weeks. Something distriked my eye when I was about to pay for the ideoms. There was a book on the counter by the cash-register and this book (books) where for people to buy. It was publish by Readers Digest and it said "How to live a *longer* life in nine easy steps". This was realy funny to me because people of today are trying to prolong life, I mean a lot of people, doctors inventing something like a heart transplant (thats just one ex.) How far can you get. Like in the story of Edgar Allan Poe, Allegory and The Masque of the Red Death and Bartleby the Scrivener. Death comes and there no way in the world that you can stop it because the lord comes like a shadow at night, or the angle of the Red Death.
>
> This is reality if people can see it but thay have eye's but they cann't see and they have ears but they cann't hear.

And this writer's statement on the plight of the uneducated captures the rhythm and powerful authenticity of spoken language:

> Being 28 years old—and having worked at most of the no-where jobs available, for with-out any schooling, or training. After many-many of these kinds of job's and the jails and institutions that they lead too—i sort of realize one must be some what concerned with, where and just who he is,—having this choice—and the chance to work for certain goal's—and to brake out of this cycle, i can't find any more rewarding purpose for self then to spend the next few

3. I am indebted to Kenneth Bruffee of Brooklyn College for this example.

years in school. My advice to anyone—coming out of High School today—would be to stay in school—for at least four year of college. If not to a masters—in a city like N y.

The separation widens between the classes—before one knows it— they are caught in a grnd—of never ending responsibility just to take care of the basic's of living—with-no or little chance to better— themselves or the society around them—my head trip—now adays— is one of concern for the society i do live in my thought's—i fully realize my inability to express this concern—verbally. Whereas an experance of back to school can only make a better more content human—out of me and somewhat if i am lucky to be able to find some purpose in being a live i am sorry, i dont have very much to say.

These are clearly not analytical passages as that term is used in academia, and any translation of the ideas that dominate either piece into the language of academia would be certain to sacrifice the very qualities that give life to the passages. The opening sentence of the above passage, for example, with its cresting of modifiers, would probably "harden" into a proposition something like this (and it would be followed by a fuller description of the cycle of poverty and by an account of the way in which education affects the job prospects of ghetto youth): "For the person who has grown up in an urban ghetto, college offers a chance to break the cycle of disadvantage and failure that will otherwise control his life."

Many teachers would view any such transposition as an intolerable kind of academic colonizing, discouraging the student from developing his "native" talent with language and imposing upon him a model of competence that is by comparison barren. Yet the differences we note grow out of real situations that will not dissolve simply because of our preferences for expressive over discursive, for personal over public, or spoken over written styles. The student who wrote the passage on college did not choose his style but was confined to it by his unfamiliarity with the conventions that govern academic or discursive writing, conventions that would require him, for example, to address directly the question posed to him (which had to do with job prospects for college graduates, as reflected in some predictions about job possibilities in the seventies) and to defend those parts of his answer that would be open to argument (the assumption, for example, that education is a cause rather than a symptom of social and economic inequality or that one can "prove" a case with an example). To ignore either the force of his statement *or* the fact that it is not a piece of analytical writing would be to misjudge both his abilities and the nature of the task ahead of him.

Central to this task is an understanding of the expectations and needs of the academic or professional audience, for we see many evidences in BW papers of the egocentricity of the apprentice writer, an orientation that is reflected in the assumption that the reader understands what is going on in the writer's mind and needs therefore no introductions or transitions or explanations. The academic audience is, however, the least submissive of audiences, committed as it is, in theory at least, to the assessment of new and as yet unproven interpretations of events. The writer is thus expected to make "new" or arguable statements and then to develop a case for them, pushing his inquiry far enough to meet his audience's criteria for fullness and sound reasoning. The beginning writer is of course not prepared to meet these expectations, but his awareness of them helps him make sense out of the conventions that govern academic discourse.

Of these conventions, at least two seem basic to the student's understanding of his task: the convention of ranging widely but in fairly predictable patterns between concrete and abstract statements, between cases and generalizations; and the convention of explicitly marking the logical and rhetorical relationships between sentences, paragraphs, and larger units of composition. Let us consider briefly each of these conventions and the skills that underlie them.

BW students are often said to be "concrete" rather than "abstract" thinkers, or to lack "conceptualizing" powers. What their teachers seem to mean by such diagnoses is that the students lack the vocabulary and habits of generalization that are associated with academic writing. These habits require that writers not only make abstract statements in a language that has been especially developed to extend the ladder of abstraction beyond conventional needs but that they be able to move back and forth between levels of generalization in the interest of supporting their abstract statements. It is a mistake, in other words, to think that the problem for the student lies simply in learning to make more abstract statements rather than in developing greater play *between* abstract and concrete statements. The problem in most BW papers lies in the absence of *movement* between abstract and concrete statements. Papers tend to contain *either* cases or generalizations but not both. If anything, students seem to have more difficulty moving from abstract statements *down* to more concrete levels than they do moving up the ladder of abstraction.

It is not difficult to see how the purposes of academic writing give rise to a wide interplay between abstract and concrete statements nor why this interplay poses difficulties for inexperienced writers. Committed to extending the boundaries of what is known, the scholar, as we have noted, is constantly proposing generalizations that cover the greatest possible number of instances. This requires both that he make statements that have broad applicability and that he defend them by the support of cases, arguments, and explanations. The student, on the other hand, has not been responsible as a speaker for the advancement of formal learning. His "propositions" seem to come unbidden, without the strain that is associated with the formulation of thesis statements. He has been free to express opinions without a display of evidence or recount experiences without explaining what they "mean." His movements from one level of generality to another are more often brought on by shifts in the winds of conversation rather than by some decision of his to be more specific or to sum things up. For him, the injunction to "be more specific" is difficult to carry out because the conditions that lead to specificity are usually missing. He may not have acquired the habit of questioning his propositions, as a listener might, in order to locate the points that require amplification or evidence. Or he may be marooned with a proposition he cannot defend for lack of information or for want of practice in retrieving the history of an idea as it developed in his mind.

Similarly, the query "What is your point" (what is the statement under which all you have said is subsumed) may be difficult to answer because the student has not learned to cope with the conditions under which students generally must write, conditions which do not allow for the slow generation of an orienting conviction, that underlying sense of the direction the writer wants his thinking to take. Without this conviction, he cannot judge the relevance of what comes to his mind as one sentence branches out into others or one idea engenders another, gradually crowding from his memory the direction he initially set for himself.

Or again, the writer may lack the vocabulary that would enable him to move more easily up the ladder of abstraction. This becomes especially apparent when a student is asked to write on a topic that does not lend itself to narrative answers but requires instead that the writer abstract from the topic the underlying thought or proposition. One essay question, for example, presents a scene between a father and his child. The child is watching and enjoying some birds and the father intervenes to teach him the names of the birds. The episode is intended to illustrate a contrast between two ways of experiencing the world—the child's direct way, through his senses, which, according to the author of the passage, gives the child a capacity to enjoy beauty, and the adult's way, through objective analysis, which involves the acceptance of society's way of classifying the world. The student is asked whether he agrees or disagrees with the author.

In their responses, some students will fail to find in this passage anything but a literal contrast between the ways of children and adults:

> As I read the paragraph, in fraunt of me, I have consider the main point of it is to say is that when you are a infant growing up it is not hard for you to see or hear. but when you get older it become very hard to do this. So you need the help of man made tols like glasses or a hearing aid.

Or again:

> I disagree on the fack the paragraph sed that when get old you must get it secondhand. Whell that is not true becatuse they are a god meney of older people hou can see a hear beter than the year one and this is true all over.

More often, however, the student will perceive the general point that underlies the concrete situation but will have to forge out of a non-analytical vocabulary a way of writing about it. The following writer, for example, is making a point that learning theorists would support, namely that the infant's world is less highly differentiated than the adult's, but must strain her vocabulary to meet this special purpose. (The results can often, in fact, be refreshing. Thus in this passage "a talent for the mass" carries a fresh meaning, but one that reflects not so much the writer's choice as her restricted vocabulary.)

> My understanding is that parent delusion their children at a early age. As the child gets older he starts to separate one from another. With help from the parent. Their talent is lost at an early age for beauty.
>
> To a certain extend I agree with the father. He is only teaching the child about life. The reason I feel that children are desluion easy because they are innocent.

They start life and to them everything goes with everything. That to say they don't relate anything to anything. its all one big mass. That why many lose this talent, which we have with mother nature.

When a child starts separating one from another then they notice the other side to things. Everything has two sides. This I would image this period starts between the ages of 5 year to 10 years.

Then as they look they compair and criticizes. This is when they start losing their talent for the mass which everything is beautiful. The father is only breaking him in for the real world. As they taught us. But who is to say who's right? For children are influence by their parent. So its a cycle we play on each other. Until somebody gets hip on to it and changes it.

If we compare these answers with the answer of a more experienced freshman writer, we can see more clearly the function of abstract words in academic discourse, which is not simply to substitute more prestigious abstractions for the words of daily life (although the following passage bears traces of such a motive as well) but to provide a conceptual frame within which to examine a particular case. Thus the writer of the following essay, because of her acquaintance with certain concepts in the psychology of learning, is able to "connect" the isolated episode described in the essay question to an "official" view about child development:

I believe the author of this short exposition is explaining how he sees the creativity and imagination of children stifled by their elders attempts to "educate" them. Since young children's perceptions are more often physical than intellectual, the author states, adults feel they must provide children with what the adults consider objective knowledge of a subject, in addition to the emotional knowledge which the child readily acquires through his own sensory mechanisms.

The author's premise is undoubtedly true, for, from the time they are born adults are anxious for their children to "learn", whether the subject in question is toilet training or advanced mathematics. I believe this sharing of knowledge can be a beautiful, healthy experience for both child and adult; I make this statement with equivocation, however, by stating that the opportune time for this communication is the time when the child desires to learn. In this manner, the child receives the full benefit of the information, and retains it well, because his desire is the motivating force.

Giving a child knowledge is exactly that, not forcing something upon him for which he sees no need or desire. After a child has recorded and absorbed all the sensory experiences of a particular subject, he will be prepared, and eager, to learn the other aspects of his new discovery. It is at this time that learning becomes a true human communication, and a joyous discovery.

The author of the passage has in a sense already learned a way of thinking and writing about child development that serves her purpose here, providing her not only with conceptual terms such as *physical-intellectual* or *emotional-objective*, but with an over-all strategy of developing her point. The writer, to be sure, has "wrapped things up" with sophomoric aplomb, but the ability to recognize the situation described in the essay question as a "case" and to go on to use the case to explain a concept about learning marks an advance toward the academic model.

The difficulties BW students have with making deliberate shifts away from or toward the points of highest abstraction are of course at the root of their difficulties with organization as well, for while accomplished writers rarely proceed along set designs of the sort teachers and texts often impose upon their students, they depend upon their ability to make retrospective maps of where their thinking has taken them so that no matter how far-ranging a term of thought may be, it is always possible to return to the point where it began and pick up once again the main line of development. Even where the writer is experienced, this task of controlling the direction of an essay while at the same time giving play to the ideas that are generated along the way is probably the most taxing part of writing. It should not surprise us that even a writer of Tolstoy's stature should include among the major skills demanded of a writer the skill not only of selecting *one* out of a number of ideas and images but of *remembering* it. Much as the person who crochets creates, by a deft looping and interlocking of a single thread, a design of great intricacy, so the writer beginning with the thread of his idea slowly "works" it into a paragraph or an article or a book. But for him, the pattern as well as the product is being developed as he goes. Each sentence, each term of thought, leaves a deposit out of which the next sentence or thought is generated. And it is this open-ended, existential situation that makes every piece of writing both unique and potentially bewildering. The writer, if he cannot know precisely where he is going, must nonetheless know where he has been so that he can mark the pattern of his thought for his reader.

Order is a way of arranging units so that they appear to be parts of a developing pattern. The sense of orientation that results from such an arrangement creates a pleasure called understanding. Thus in academic discourse, where the patterns of development are likely to be difficult to follow, a system of alerts and reminders has been developed so that the reader will not feel lost. This system includes 1. words that identify the bases of sequencing between sentences and paragraphs (spatial, temporal, topical, etc.) or knit the key elements of one sentence to the next (pronouns); 2. sentences and subheadings that serve as bridges between parts, and 3. paragraphs that reveal to the reader the writer's intention with respect to the development or elaboration of individual sentences (whether stated or implied in the paragraph). Although useful, even at times essential to a reader's understanding of a piece of analytical writing, these rhetorical conventions are too often taken to be the *sources* rather than the *signals* of order, and the student is encouraged to use them before he has a clear sense of what they mean. (The student who, intent upon putting her new "connecting" vocabulary to work, *began* her essay with "Moreover . . ." was clearly a victim of such instruction.)

For the BW student, instruction in organization must begin, not with the techniques writers use to help their readers follow them, but with the more fundamental processes whereby writers get their thoughts in the first place and then get them underway. Teachers often use the word "idea" in their instructions to students. "A sentence," they are likely to say, "is a complete idea." Or again, "A paragraph is a group of sentences that serve to develop a main idea." Or, "A topic sentence is the statement of a main idea." Yet students are not always certain of how a writer recognizes a main idea when he has one or how he sets about finding one if he doesn't. Usually they are persuaded that they don't have the sorts of ideas people write about, and when they are asked to produce an idea for an essay, they tend to sit and wait for one, or worse, to block all access to their ideas by worrying about how to get started when there seems to be nothing to start with.

For these reasons, it is well to consider directly some of the conditions that are favorable to the generation of ideas, for these are the conditions that ought to pertain in a writing class. It is important to note, for example, that ideas generally seem to be spawned in data— whether the data be fragments of remembered sensations or opinions or the carefully wrought texts of famous writers. And although much time has been spent arguing about the kinds of data that are appropriate for composition classes—whether, for example, literary texts or social studies or language or some other content should provide the base of information from which students draw their ideas—the more important issue is probably whether the student is led gradually and with awareness from relatively simple to more complex tasks of conceptualization, for it is largely by observing themselves "get" ideas that students begin to understand the difference between facts and inferences, subordinate and superordinate statements.

There is room here for several types of instruction. At the most basic level, the student can be introduced to the *concept* of levels of abstraction, first by having to select a governing word for simple word sets and then by selecting a governing sentence for sentence sets.[4] The purpose of such exercises is not, however, to teach students how to make inferences or move up the ladder of abstraction but rather to demonstrate to them that they already know how to do this and that accomplished writers simply make deliberate use of this faculty for sorting and connecting when they compose.

Once aware that the term *topic sentence* implies a *relationship* among sentences, in which the topic sentence is the superordinate statement, the student should be ready to try developing his own governing statements by making inferences from small pools of data, preferably non-print data at first so that the shift from observation to generalization is as sharply drawn as possible. Students may, for example, arrive at inferences from pictures that have been grouped so as to encourage generalization. The following thesis statements grew out of such an assignment:[5]

> *Slide group showing couples*
> Old couples sometimes look more like brother and sister than man and wife.
>
> *Slide group showing a variety of pregnant women*
> Not all expectant mothers react the same way to their pregnancy; some are joyful, some are sad, but others are afraid.
>
> *Slide group showing men at war*
> War changes men. Some for better, some for worst.

4. For a lucid introduction to the concept of abstraction which uses this approach, see Alan Casty's *Building Writing Skills: A Programmed Approach to Sentences and Paragraphs* (New York: Harcourt Brace Jovanovich, 1971), Chapter 8.

5. I am indebted to Mary Epes of York College, City University of New York, for these examples and for having introduced me to the idea of using photographs during the initial stages of paragraph writing.

Slide group on children
Children playing alone can become very involve in a animal or object.

Once having generated such statements, students often find that their own experiences provide even better data than those in the photographs. Thus the last generalization above developed into the following essay, which demonstrates a first step in the subordination of three cases to a governing or organizing statement:

Children at Play

A child playing alone can become very involve in a animal or a object.

Walking through Kings Park I notice a little boy sitting with his leg folded on a bench, he had a bag with something in it resting between his leg. A bird sitting on the edge of the bench. It look as though from the expression on the little boy face he was quit surprise at the bird. He start feeding the bird something from the bag. Although the boy alone he having a good time with the bird.

A boy was sitting on my friends porch. He have a puppy on a leash. The look in the boy eyes and smile on his face show much love and care for the puppy. He seem as though he was able to discuss problem he face in school that day with the puppy.

There was this little girl who attended the camp I worked in last year who was lost in the woods. When I found her she was staring at something in the bush, whatever it was she found it quite amusing. When I call her she just continue staring at the object. Until I finally walk up to her and tap her on the shoulder. She look up at me and start to smile. she found a butterfly who keep her company and also help her forget the fact she was lost.

Children when involve in play seem to be very tense and are very careful in what they do. They concentrate on that and nothing else.

At the next level of difficulty, students can begin working with printed data from tightly controlled sources such as the lists, tables, or graphs to be found in books like *The World Almanac*. Bewildered at first by the density of the information in such sources, students usually find after studying them carefully that they can discover patterns or develop questions that in turn lead to fertile topic statements. The following paragraphs, written in response to assignments of this kind, demonstrate an improvement over the unfocused and unsupported paragraphs BW students are likely to produce at the outset.

Paragraph based on a list of forty-six major kidnapping crimes committed over the past 100 years:

March 1, 1932: Charles A. Lindbergh, Jr. kidnapped from his home in Hopewell, N.J. Found dead after $50,000 ransom paid.

December 7, 1970: Giovane E. Bucher kidnapped by revolutionaries in Rio di Janiero. Freed after release of 70 political prisoners.

These two cases separated by 38 years show the trend in kidnappings from yesteryear to today. From the years 1874 to 1968 kidnappings were confined to the purpose of gaining money. Some of the sums demanded were large, such as the $600,000 demanded for the release of Robert C. Greenlease. Others as the 1500 demanded for the release of Marlon Parker were not so large. Then on September 4, 1969 the U.S. Ambassador to Brazil E. Burke Elbrich was released after demand for publishing manifesto and 15 political prisoner were released. This was not a move to gain profit. It was a political move by the revolutionaries to get their ideas published and some of their men back. From 1969 to 1971, there were 13 cases of political kidnappings, either for the release of political prisoners or imprisoned terrorists. This is a large number for the 2 years time, especially since in the 32 years before the first political kidnapping there were none at all. So the trend of the motive has definatly gone from profit to politics.

Paragraph based on a list of salaries for individuals across a range of jobs:

Salaries in the United States have no formal ground. Politicians whose jobs are the most frustrating and complex make less money than those whose jobs are the lease complex. For instance, Johnny Carson makes one million dollars a year to sit behind his desk and ask movie stars and other people of prestige a bunch of unintelligent questions. The President of the United States, on the other hand, went through numbrous years of college, many political positions which included a lot of knowledge and hours of work to make less than a quarter of Johnny Carson's salary. Walt Frazier is another example. Walter Frazier makes two hundred and ninety thousand dollars a year to do his job while an intern only makes eleven thousand dollars a year after he has gone through eight years of college.

After working with single sources of data, students can move to more complex arrays of information. They may work with data that seem to occur in more "natural" settings—the cases described in books designed to prepare students for the law school admissions tests, the problems posed in simulation-gaming texts, which attempt to simulate the settings of real problems, complete with primary sources and conflicting points of view, or the data that students themselves gather through interviewing and reading. The important point is that the base from which the student generates his ideas may widen gradually, but the purpose in each exercise is to arrive through the observation of data at a position that can be formulated in one sentence.

The sentences derived in these ways are interpretations of data rather than statements of facts, and as such they are both individual and open to argument. The writer cannot assume, that is, that anyone else has responded to the data in the way that he has or even for that matter seen the data at all. (In classes where students read one another's papers, this becomes obvious.) Thus his own conclusion (which becomes his topic statement) about the data must be either proved or, where this is not possible, given the kind of support that will persuade his audience. Thus we see that the seeds of paragraphs lie in the statements students develop from their data. In simple exercises, the proof of a topic sentence is built into the exercise, but as generalizations broaden or give rise to new questions, the task of establishing one point leads to the making of another, which in turn sets up new demands for proof or support to which the writer must be sensitive. It is one order of difficulty for a student to observe from a table of statistics on the population of New York City boroughs that, despite an over-all rise in the city's population, Manhattan has been losing people over the past twenty-five years, but quite another for him to explain why this has happened. Such a question calls not only for new information but for a more ambitious kind of synthesis than was demanded by the tables.

As the complexity of writing tasks increases and the student pushes deeper into his ideas, the ability to make conceptual maps of where he is going or where he has been becomes an essential skill. It is a difficult skill to isolate for the purposes of instruction. Indeed, it is doubtless related to the process of intellectual maturation in ways that are beyond the control of the writing class or the student himself. Just as sentences appear to "grow up" along with the children who use them, so probably do ideas. But writing is a skill that involves a highly self-conscious use of our linguistic and intellectual resources. It demands from the writer a sustained accountability for his thoughts: he must stay with his points or depart from them in ways that make sense to his readers; he must recognize his commitments to explain or illustrate or prove; he must observe proportions; he must, in short, keep track of where he has been and look toward where he is going or risk losing both his line of thought and his reader.

To meet such responsibilities, the writer needs to in some way visualize his thoughts, to sort consciously and shift and divide his ideas in accordance with a pattern that may have been determined at the beginning or that may be emerging only as he advances into his subject. And just as the perception of sentence structure or word structure requires the learner to view sentences and words in unfamiliar, more abstract ways, so the perception of paragraph and essay structure demands a way of thinking that the student needs to practice. At least two types of instruction are valuable here: training in the perception of structure, which involves practice in "seeing" structure in a wide range of written materials; training in the recognition of thought patterns that figure often in conventional writing tasks for college. We will consider each of these briefly.

Training in the perception of structure should begin with the observation that we are surrounded by examples of language structures. Not only do business letters, newscasts or columns, soap operas, and sermons have their distinctive structures but many of the statements we make ourselves follow the patterns of classic folk structures whose forms are so familiar as to be invisible. Thus such oral rituals as wishes, superstitions, curses, fables, or riddles are distinctive structures that students can quickly become conscious of.[6] (A superstition, for example, is a cause-effect structure with non-logical connections between the two; a riddle is an analogy with a key part missing.) From here the student can begin to consider (and imitate) the more intricate structures of poetry, taking note of the ways in which thoughts themselves are distributed so as to create the forms.[7]

After some experience with seeing and imitating "closed" forms, the student can begin to search for patterns and themes from more "open" discourse, first in belletristic literature, where forms are easier to isolate, and finally in analytical discourse.

Whatever the novel or story a student is asked to read for this type of analysis, challenging structural questions and problems are there to explore, and they need not "kill" the novel for the student. Indeed

6. I am indebted to Marie Ponsot of Queens College, City University of New York, for having pointed out to me the value of folk forms in teaching writing.

7. Kenneth Koch's *Wishes, Lies, and Dreams* (New York: Random House, 1970), although an account of his work with children writers, is a rich source of ideas on structure for teachers of older writers as well.

they can heighten his sense of the writer's achievement. The following sample lesson presents the steps a student might go through in working on a structural feature that appears in Richard Wright's novel *Black Boy*. The lesson, which focuses upon one of the several lists that appear in the midst of Wright's narrative, is part of a sequence of lessons in which the student has already worked on description, dialogue, and narrative and moves now into analysis.

Steps in analyzing a piece of writing
1. *Look at your subject and keep a list of your observations.* The only way to analyze something, whether it is an event, a problem, or a piece of writing, is to look at it steadily, thoroughly, carefully until you see something. Like description, analysis depends almost entirely upon your ability to notice things. If you have difficulty with this step, it is probably because you are not certain what to look for and therefore have the impression there is nothing to see.

The following questions may help guide your observations:

a. What are the parts?
b. What gets repeated from one part to the next?
c. What is unexpected or contradictory or missing?
d. If what you are analyzing is part of something larger, how does it connect with the larger unit?

2. *On the basis of your observations, make some general statement about the subject you have observed.* If you think the reader needs more than one sentence to understand what you mean in this general statement, go ahead and say as much as you think he needs. There is no easy formula for reaching this general statement. It is your idea, based on your observations, and it will be only as good as your observations. If it is a good idea, it will draw together a number of your observations under one heading, and it may show how what you observed is part of an even larger design.

3. *After you have made the general statement, go on to show how it "fits" your observations.* In other words, prove your case.

Sample Assignment
Supposing you are asked to analyze the following list, which appears in Chapter 2 of *Black Boy*:

Up or down the wet or dusty streets, indoors or out, the days and nights began to spell out magic possibilities.

If I pulled a hair from a horse's tail and sealed it in a jar of my own urine, the hair would turn overnight into a snake.

If I passed a Catholic sister or mother dressed in black and smiled and allowed her to see my teeth, I would surely die.

If I walked under a leaning ladder, I would certainly have bad luck.

If I kissed my elbow, I would turn into a girl.

If my right ear itched, then something good was being said about me by somebody.

If I touched a hunchback's hump, then I would never be sick.

If I placed a safety pin on a steel railroad track and let a train run over it, the safety pin would turn into a pair of bright brand new scissors.

If I heard a voice and no human being was near, then either God or the Devil was trying to talk to me.

Whenever I made urine, I should spit for good luck.

If my nose itched, somebody was going to visit me.

If I mocked a crippled man, then God would make me crippled.

If I used the name of God in vain, then God would strike me dead.

If it rained while the sun was shining, then the Devil was beating his wife.

If the stars twinkled more than usual on any given night, it meant that the angels in heaven were happy and were flitting across the floors of heaven; and since stars were merely holes ventilating heaven, the twinkling came from the angels flitting past the holes that admitted air into the holy home of God.

If I broke a mirror, I would have seven years of bad luck.

If I was good to my mother, I would grow old and rich.

If I had a cold and tied a worn, dirty sock about my throat before I went to bed, the cold would be gone the next morning.

If I wore a bit of asafetida in a little bag tied about my neck, I would never catch a disease.

If I looked at the sun through a piece of smoked glass on Easter Sunday morning, I would see the sun shouting in praise of a Risen Lord.

If a man confessed anything on his deathbed, it was the truth; for no man could stare death in the face and lie.

If you spat on each grain of corn that was planted, the corn would grow tall and bear well.

If I spilt salt, I should toss a pinch over my left shoulder to ward off misfortune.

If I covered a mirror when a storm was raging, the lightning would not strike me.

If I stepped over a broom that was lying on the floor, I would have bad luck.

If I walked in my sleep, then God was trying to lead me somewhere to do a good deed for Him.

Anything seemed possible, likely, feasible, because I wanted everything to be possible. . . . Because I had no power to make things happen outside of me in the objective world, I made things happen within. Because my environment was bare and bleak, I endowed it with unlimited potentialities, redeemed it for the sake of my own hungry and cloudy yearning.[8]

This seems at first sight to be a strange list. Wright has been telling about how he tried to sell his dog, and suddenly he stops with his narrative and begins this list. At the end of the list, he says that he was creating a substitute world for the real one that was so unpleasant. In other words, if we look carefully at this list we might even get an idea of the kind of world young Wright escaped to. Are there any resemblances to his real world?

After thinking about the list in this way, trying to figure out why Wright included it, what connection it has with the rest of the book, you should begin a close observation of every item in the list. Before you turn to the next page, see how much you *see* in the list.

Step 1:   *Observations*

Parts: The list has twenty-five items. The opening and closing passages are different from the list and they have similar words— "possibilities," "possible," "potentialities."

Repetitions: All except one of the sentences in the list begins with *If* and ends with some kind of result. Of the twenty-five statements, more than half (fourteen) bring good results and the rest bad (good health or good luck; bad health, death, or bad luck). The things you do to get good luck or health don't seem much different from the things you do to get bad luck. Good and bad luck are found in unpredictable things: human secretions like spit and urine; strange actions like kissing your elbow, itching, touching a hunchback, pulling a hair from a horse, walking under a ladder or over a broom, throwing salt, covering a mirror, typing a sock around the neck.

Omissions: None of the typical formulas for success are on the

8. From Richard Wright, *Black Boy* (New York: Harper & Row, 1966), pp. 81–83. Copyright 1937, 1942, 1944, 1945 by Richard Wright. Reprinted by permission of Harper & Row, Publishers, Inc., Mrs. Ellen Wright, and Jonathan Cape Ltd.

list: work hard and you will succeed; save and you will be wealthy; etc. Not much attention is given to money, success, power, but only to survival (health, death). Nothing you *do*—like work, study, take care of your health—seems to change things. Luck is the only thing that seems to work once in a while.

Connection with larger work:

Before the list: Wright attempts to sell his dog in a white neighborhood and is treated rudely.

After the list: Wright begins talking again about his dread of the white world and tells about the murder of a black woman's husband.

Step 2: Idea

Main Idea for Analysis: In Wright's world, there is no logical connection between what you do and what happens to you. It is not a reasonable world and cannot be controlled by being reasonable. The only kind of control that might work in this crazy world where nothing but trouble seems certain is luck or magic (control through non-rational means). Everything is *not* up to you; it is up to something outside of you which you can't control.

Step 3: Analysis

General statement

The list of superstitions in Chapter 2 of *Black Boy* gives the reader an idea of the kind of world that makes sense to Richard—a world controlled by magic.

Explanation of statement

In magic there is no clear logical connection between what you do and what happens to you, between an act and its consequences. In the so-called rational world, there *is* a connection. If a person works hard, he will probably be rewarded; if he shows imagination and ambition, he can go far. His future is up to him, not to some mysterious outside power.

Use of observations to illustrate statement

But in magic you never know. If you spit on something, it may mean luck. If you urinate on it you may be dead. If you kiss an elbow, pull a hair from a horse, tie a sock around your neck or do any number of ridiculous things, you may be dead or alive, sick or well, depending on the superstition. Life cannot be figured out or controlled. It is full of danger and terror, a crazy mixture of nuns and devils, spit and stars.

This list of superstitions reflects the way the world

Showing
connection
with
the rest
of the
book

looks to Richard. It reflects a crazy world of lynchings and hunger and "Jesus Saves." The "logical" formulas for success in America hold no promise for him. If he has ambition, he will be punished. If he reads books, he will be dangerous. If he develops fully his talents and powers as a human being, he will most likely be dead. In a world surrounded by the irrationalities of racism, it is no wonder that young Richard feels safer and happier with magic. In a world of "reason" he always loses. But in a world of magic, he is bound to win some of the time. Magic, for him, opens up the world of "possibilities."

Assignment: Analyze the list on page 14 or the list on page 113 of *Black Boy.*

Follow the steps given above: Make observations on parts, repetitions, omissions, and connections. Write down the main idea you get from your observations. Develop that main idea into an essay that makes a general statement, an explanation of the statement, an illustration of the statement, and a concluding statement.

The final step in this general training for the perception of structure should move the student into so-called non-literary materials, where the structure is in some respects more sharply marked and yet more difficult to detect because of the abstract nature of the language and ideas. Here the most effective models for analysis are often total books, rather than fragments of books or essays. Not only does a book allow a longer time for the student to observe the process whereby an idea is explored, but structure seems often to be easier to perceive in large works than in small extracts. Care must be taken, however, to choose books that have well-defined over-all structures and to use a special method of reading that itself requires training.[9] The method can be visualized as taking place in three concentric circles, with the inner circle involving the sentence-by-sentence examination of passages for the purpose of identifying the links between sentences. After five to ten pages of such reading, the reader moves to the middle circle, where he reads at a more natural pace, attempting to identify the nature of the links between paragraphs. Finally, in the outermost

9. The "concentric circle" method I describe here is an adaption of a method of reading originally advocated by Edward Prokosch for students learning the vocabulary of a foreign language. The method is described in William G. Moulton's excellent handbook *A Linguistic Guide to Language Learning* (New York: Modern Language Association, 1966), pp. 19–20.

circle he reads at a scanning pace through the rest of the book to identify the relationship between chapters.

The method can be illustrated with a book such as Ruth Benedict's *Patterns of Culture*, which is ideally organized for this kind of assignment. Conceptually, the first chapter is the densest and requires the student to move sentence by sentence, even word by word, through the initial formulation of the author's main idea, namely that understanding the various cultures of the world is more important than ranking them according to the values of one's own culture. Beginning with the first sentence, "Anthropology is the study of human beings as creatures of society," the student must attempt to see what words or concepts in one sentence give rise to the sentence that follows. In this instance, the author selects the concept *society* for further definition and then, in subsequent sentences, moves toward the idea of cultural *differences*. The last sentence in the first paragraph contains three words that stress difference (*distinguish, others, different*) and the first sentence of the next passage begins an expansion on the notion of *differences*. What should become apparent as the student moves in this exacting way through the first stages of the book is a "seeding" process whereby sentences give rise to sentences and paragraphs to paragraphs. Innumerable questions need to be raised at the inner circle of analysis —what do words like *society* or *culture* or *custom* mean here? Why does the writer take this step instead of that? What other sentence might have been engendered from a given sentence? Why did the author stop here with her examples or her paragraph, etc.? Where can we expect her to go in the next paragraph or chapter? Proceed slowly, thoroughly, without worry about finishing the chapter. The experience of thoroughness is what matters here. If some of the chapter is left over, students can complete it on their own.

This immersion in the first chapter of the book prepares the student to move more easily through the next two chapters, which form the conceptual introduction to the work. The second chapter, for example, picks up the idea that cultural diversity comes about because individual cultures *select* to emphasize some things and not others, but the direct statement of this idea occupies only five of the thirty-three paragraphs in the chapter, the rest simply providing illustrations of the point. The pattern is an easy one for the attentive student to observe as he moves in his middle circle of concentration through the chapter.

Chapters 4, 5, and 6 conveniently fall into three case studies of Indian societies, which can be read at the scanning tempo of the outer circle, with primary attention to the categories that are used to discuss each culture (birth, puberty, mating, death, etc.). The final chapters clearly break with the middle chapters and can be quickly identified as returning, this time with larger strokes, to the themes introduced in the opening chapters.

Such an approach has required the student to perceive structure at three levels and to use reading techniques appropriate to each level. In addition to acquiring new information about other cultures, the student can discover through the book a way of organizing a description of any culture. He is ready, therefore, to approach a writing assignment that asks him to describe one feature of his culture. He may decide, for example, to describe the courting stage of the mating ritual in his world. His task would then be to collect observations on that one feature (when does courting begin, are there taboos, special forms of dress or language, etc.). Once having gathered information under these sub-heads, he has automatically generated his paragraph divisions as well. He has acquired a way of ordering certain kinds of information that is conventional to a specific academic subject, a conceptualizing tool that will enable him to generate, sort, and even remember his data.

The second kind of training in structure aims at familiarizing the student with prototypic thought patterns that transcend even the intellectual classifications of specific disciplines. If, that is, there appear to be recurring thought patterns that are evoked by specific situations or tasks and that in turn lead to fairly predictable forms of writing, then the student should be able to learn about these patterns in advance so as to avoid the laborious, perhaps impossible, task of amassing on his own, in one or two semesters, the working capital of written language.

Let us think of the writer in a college situation as someone who is being asked regularly to make various types of written statements that give rise to fairly predictable patterns of elaboration. We can call both the statement and the pattern it generates a *basic thought pattern* and attempt to identify those patterns that seem to figure most often in academic assignments. At least seven will be considered here as basic to instruction at this level and they will be presented below as prototypic statements writers are called upon to make and then develop across a range of forms and subjects.

1. *This is what happened.* The writer, whether he has been asked to describe a laboratory experiment, write a story, or recount a historical event, faces the task of telling what happened. It requires him to

organize his material in a time sequence, an organizing task that comes to him more "naturally" than any other because of the dominant part narrative plays in everyday life and lore. His difficulties with the pattern are caused usually by the omission of some step in the unfolding of the narrative or by the failure to mark adequately for his reader his movement through the time sequence, a skill that often requires a deft use of verb forms and an ability to use words that signal chronological order. Various exercises encourage the use of this vocabulary. Students can be given jumbled blocks of sentences and asked to reassemble the sentences in a correct time sequence, introducing the appropriate words for signaling structure. In another exercise a teacher has cleverly devised a controlled writing assignment that requires the student to incorporate time words into a semi-constructed narrative:[10]

> *Instructions:* Using all the phrases in Group A in the order in which they appear, write an essay about getting from home to school. Make as much use as you can of the connecting words in Group B.

Group A	Group B
getting from my house to school	first
the alarm clock rings	last
cut it off and go back to sleep	and
turn on radio	when
go into bathroom	as soon as
wash up	if
put on clothes	once
eat grub	since
get my books and leave	the first thing
stop at store	next
get newspaper	after
head for train	
get to station	
wait for #2 train	
ride it to 96th Street	
change to the uptown Broadway line to 137th Street	
get off the train	
walk up hill to school	
get half way	
ready to come back home	

10. I am indebted to Kenneth Libo of City College, City University of New York, for this exercise.

Example: Getting from my house to school is the hardest thing for me to do all day. As soon as *the alarm clock rings*, I know it means the beginning of the ordeal. If I'm in a lazy mood, I *cut it off and go back to sleep*.

2. *This is the look (sound, smell, or feel) of something.* The attempt to re-create for someone else the experience of one's own senses is commonly encouraged in beginning writing classes, although subsequent college assignments most often require the student to interpret or recreate what has come to him through print or formal lectures, to picture what is not (and may never have been) before him. Where descriptions are required, they are generally non-expressive or so-called "objective" descriptions, as in the description of a dissected frog in biology or the description of a place or person in a social studies class. Courses in architecture often introduce exercises in "seeing" and music courses in "hearing," but in all such assignments the goal is generally to present what has been experienced through the senses in an impersonal and analytical manner that leads the reader to accept the descriptions as having referential truth, that is, as being verifiable by other observers.[11]

Innumerable exercises exist for demonstrating to students how precise language must be in order to re-create in someone else's mind even the simplest of shapes or settings. Such exercises generally require one student to describe an abstract shape or unfamiliar object that only he has seen and the rest of the class to attempt to reproduce the object or array from his description of it. Descriptions of this kind often require the writer to use such familiar spatial sequences as *left to right, top to bottom, outside to inside*, etc., and to select words and phrases that signal spatial relationships. The vocabulary is large and often unfamiliar to the writer. It includes some of the troublesome pronouns (*in which, into which*) and innumerable words that indicate geographical direction, immediate position in relation to other objects (*parallel to, perpendicular to, adjacent to, background, foreground*, etc.), and physical shape (*oval, triangular*, etc.).

When we add to the task of description the aim of describing not

11. No attempt is made here to distinguish among the different techniques of observation associated with different academic subjects, but clearly the introduction to a subject is largely an introduction to its conventions of observation and description. See H. L. M. Abercrombie, *Anatomy of Judgment* (New York: Basic Books, 1960), for an excellent analysis of this kind of learning and the methods that encourage it.

only the neutral shapes and positions of things but the sensations they evoke in us, the task is for some even more difficult. Here the inexperienced writer tends not to realize the extent to which his reader depends upon descriptive details if he is to see or feel what the writer saw or felt. A rather simple demonstration of the role of detail in description will often make the point more effectively than innumerable injunctions to use details. A good descriptive sentence or passage can be pruned of its modifications, as this sentence has been:

> There is a building standing now where the house in which we grew up once stood, and there is a tree where our doorway used to be.

When asked to describe the images that come to their minds with such words in the passage as *building, house, tree,* students are certain to offer a wide range of images, from palm trees to spindly city trees, from cottages to skyscrapers. They will thus experience directly the abstract quality of nouns, which enables individuals to read into them their private images. Then the original sentence can be restored so as to reveal the author's images:

> There is a housing project now where the house in which we grew up once stood, and one of those stunted trees is snarling where the doorway used to be.
>
> —James Baldwin, "Fifth Avenue Uptown"

This should be followed by a lesson in focus, which can be introduced visually by two simple figures:

Figure A Figure B

The concept of focus can then be applied to a simple writing assignment in which students are asked first to develop a list of observations and then to group them under one "covering" word. Let us say the list contains various features of a classroom:

1. room is 20 x 20
2. walls—no pictures, pale institution green
3. 35 side-arm chairs (faint pastel color) with hard plastic surfaces that can't be carved on

4. an empty teacher's desk
5. windows—shut, weather-stained
6. few wads of paper near the wastebasket
7. film of dust over everything
8. cigarettes flattened on the floor
9. air—stale and dusty
10. fluorescent tubes on ceiling that cover everything with blue
11. a half-erased grammar lesson on the board

A student may decide that the word "non-room" covers many of the details, suggesting that the room has no interest or life, little trace of the students who have listened and learned and even slept there. With this central idea, a plan such as the following can emerge and the student is ready to begin his description.

The furniture is non-furniture. No one seems to have lived with it:

4. the desk drawers are empty, the surface blank
3. the 35 side-arm chairs with their hard plastic surfaces have no names, initials, or telephone numbers carved on them

The color of the room is a non-color:

2. the walls are a pale institutional green
3. the chairs are faintly pastel
10. fluorescent tubes glare down making everything cold blue

Nothing human remains, except here and there some classroom litter:

8. a few cigarettes lie flattened against the floor
6. a few wads of paper lie near the wastebasket
11. a half-erased grammar lesson remains on the board

3. *This is like (or unlike) this.* Probably no statement is called for more often in academic assignments than the statement of comparison. Not only is comparison a way of understanding the world around us, it is a convenient examining device for teachers who, by asking students to compare one work or era or person or idea with another, can net two answers with one question. In their daily lives students are constantly making comparisons—between one friend and another, one course and another, one stage of life and another. The written comparison is simply a more thoroughly developed, more consciously organized attempt at something students have done from infancy on. Yet many things are likely to go wrong with written comparisons unless students are given a frame within which to visualize the relationships among the

parts of the comparison. The following method of introducing the comparison will serve the student well during his first comparisons. Later, he can get rid of at least some of the scaffolding.

Step 1:   Decide what the *grounds* for the comparison are.
Example:

Members of comparison	Grounds for comparison
Western cowboy and James Bond spy	Movie heroes

Step 2:   Construct a comparison frame which includes the following information: points of similarity (+); points of difference (−); illustrations of points of similarity and difference.

A *Points of comparison*	B *Cowboy*	C *Spy*
1. Adventurous (+)	Never does a day's work. Gun battles, saloons, holdups, but no routine.	Luxury hotels, airports, exotic cities, dramatic meetings, mystery, but no routine.
2. Skill with weapons (+)	Quick on the draw, fast, fancy rider, agile, clever, equal to enemy.	Walking arsenal of electronic weapons: radios, tapes, special explosive devices, cars, etc.
3. Women (−)	Faithful, innocent type whom he eventually marries.	Overnight companion whom he doesn't see again or whom he plans to betray.
4. Methods (−)	Confrontation, showdown at the ranch.	Deception, disguise, intrigue.
5. Motive (−)	Get the bad guys. Be a good guy. Protect the underdog.	Do a job, carry out an assignment. Do a day's work. No patriotism.

Step 3:   After you have filled out the frame, begin writing your comparison. In an introductory paragraph, try to *summarize* the main points of your comparison (Column A). Then take up the first point of comparison (Frame 1) and use it as the opening sentence of

your second paragraph. Go on to illustrate and explain the point as it applies to both members of the comparison. When you have covered the point, go on to the next point, etc.

Step 4: After you have filled in the evidence, bring your comparison to a conclusion. Here you have several possibilities. You might want to state your own preference for the cowboy or the spy and explain why. You might want to go on and suggest what the differences between the two heroes reveal about the differences between their societies. Or you might want to make some general observation about heroes.

4. *This (may have, probably, certainly) caused this.* The search for causes is so constant and deep an urge among people of all cultures and ages that a teacher can hardly be said to "teach" the pattern of thought to students. Like the ability to compare, the ability to construe causal connections between events that have been either linked chronologically into a chain of "things that happened" or simply imagined through the medium of inherited myths and theologies is part of an unfolding intellective power that begins with infancy and continues, at least in the lives of some, until death, producing in every age brilliant, overpowering explanations for the phenomena that concern humankind most deeply. Almost every "subject" the college student studies exists because sustained, systematic attempts have been made by many people to get at the causes of certain phenomena and these attempts have produced not only an accumulation of information about the phenomena but also methodologies that have generated their own languages and histories, even, some would say, their own cultures.

For the student, then, the difficulties he is likely to encounter with the cause-effect pattern are rooted not in his lack of experience with the form but in the *quality* of his experience, in the largely intuitive and frequently simplistic unreasoned answers he is in the habit of giving (and getting) to the questions of causation. Generally little in his formal education has prepared him to detect complexity, let alone cope with it in causal explanations. At best he has been exposed to the explanations of others—mainly of his teachers and the authors of his textbooks—and has learned to repeat these explanations in testing situations as evidence of his having learned the causes of things, of wars, depressions, crime, literary achievements, or the floating of a frog on water. Thus, although the explanations of others may have been hard-won, involving years of watching and thinking and moments of spontaneous insight, the student acquires them often by a simple act of memorization, never experiencing for himself the difficulty—or the impossibility—of locating the causes of things. Rarely, for example, will he encounter effects that illustrate an orthodox causal nexus. When he does, it will probably be within the frame of a laboratory or quasi-laboratory situation where various controls enable him to isolate the phenomenon from all entangling conditions and events. And even here, he is likely to have great difficulty posing the questions that will lead to fruitful causal reasoning. To learn to ask such questions is, or ought to be, the chief burden of his instruction in a subject.

When we select for causal analysis effects that will not yield to laboratory study because they are too multi-dimensioned to be observed and controlled in that way, the possibility of coming up with direct or simple causes is slim, particularly where such refractory elements as human beings, either in groups or as individuals, are part of the phenomenon. Thus even the "simple" question of what causes students to be late to class or what causes them to drop out leads quickly into a maze of interrelated conditions that are difficult to fit into a cause-effect statement. The challenge here is not to come up with *a* cause but to explore as fully as possible the environment or context within which a particular effect seems to occur. To carry out such a task the student needs a way of writing about effects that does not clamp him into single-minded or closed explanations. This is in part a matter of having to think in more complex ways about causes but also of developing a style of discourse that encourages the writer to entertain multiple explanations.

Writing inclines us to consider matters sequentially, line after line, whereas the realities we try to account for often involve simultaneity; writing tends to "set" things whereas causal thinking requires the writer to suspend certainty in order to consider probabilities and alternatives. As sorting and structuring aids, outlines may be less useful here than flow charts or networks. The latter devices make it easier to envision and write about processes and systems, whereas outlines are more useful for material that is hierarchically arranged, according to levels of generalization.

Several types of words help to make explicit the kinds of relationships that dominate complex causal explanations, and often they are unfamiliar to the student writer. There are the words and phrases of simultaneity (*meanwhile, at the same time, while this is taking place*);

of alternatives (*on the one hand, under this condition, under that, viewed another way, from this perspective*); of probabilities (*possibly, probably, in all likelihood*); of conditions (*in the event that, if this occurs, if we can assume, under the circumstances*); of appearances (*at first glance, it appears, it is commonly regarded, some would claim, it must seem to some, a closer look reveals*); and of results (*thus, consequently, as a result, we can conclude*).

Beyond having the vocabulary and ordering devices of causal analysis, the student needs the experience of moving into the thick of a phenomenon and discovering the difficulties that accompany any responsible attempt to account for it. The phenomenon may be a local event about which little or nothing has been written, possibly something that has happened within the class itself; or it may be something that has awakened widespread interest beyond the campus and generated already a number of inquiries and explanations (a decline in college-entrance-test scores, perhaps, or a rise in unemployment among teenagers). The aim in exploring the phenomenon is not, however, to come up with a neat causal explanation for the event but to gain a respect for its complexity, to develop a taste for facts and information and a tolerance for answers that apply in some contexts but not in others or that point up the need for new questions.

5. *This is what ought to be done.* This statement is conventionally cast in a problem-solution pattern, although the same purpose underlies the design of utopias. In the conventional problem-solution pattern, which will concern us here, the procedure for arriving at solutions dictates the appropriate structure for most written proposals. First, the writer must identify the problem, describing its effects and locating the most likely causes of these effects. Next he must generate as many possible solutions as he can, deferring judgment upon any of them until he has exhausted his imagination, and the imaginations of others, on the task. Then he must assess the solutions, attempting to predict the unwanted mutations that are liable to be embedded in the "solutions." Thus the maritime union that succeeded in "solving" the problem of long absences from home by negotiating three-month vacations for its members later discovered that it had also apparently contributed to an increase in divorce, alcoholism, and suicide among its ranks. Or again, cities that have attempted to rid themselves of slums by initiating vast urban renewal programs have found too often that they have not only destroyed viable neighborhoods and dispersed the

poor into more expensive, more alien quarters but created new slum areas as well. In assessing solutions, the student can learn to classify effects under a number of organizing concepts that figure in problem-solving and are suggested by such phrases as *advantages-disadvantages, short-term–long-term, optimal-minimal, cost-benefit.*

Finally, there must be an attempt to show how the solution can be implemented, what the stages of implementation will be, what it is likely to cost in hours, energy, money, etc., to put it into effect, and how the results will be measured. In short, the statement "this is what ought to be done" generates the conventional proposal form, one of the most common forms of referential writing outside academia but also a form that provides the student with a procedure for thinking through a problem. Work on this form lends itself to small-group teaching, and, thanks to the bunglings of the great at all levels of society, there are always examples aplenty of failed "solutions" on which students can sharpen their wits. Exercises of the following sort, drawn from actual experience, enable students to practice problem-solving through the misjudgments of their elders.[12]

City X and the Tree Crisis

In 1960, City X, a capital of a developing country, had a population of 400,000. By 1975, the city's population had increased to 1,600,000. To accommodate this 400 per cent growth, large portions of formerly wooded areas were cleared to build homes, to obtain wood for construction, and to provide wood for cooking.

As a result, large areas surrounding the city have been denuded of trees. Tropical rains, common in this part of the world, have washed away the topsoil, leaving an infertile, sandy base and serious erosion problems. Several years ago the government decided to reforest these denuded areas. They called in reforestation experts who proposed extensive refertilization of the area and large plantings of trees suitable for the climate. The experts came up with three different proposals. Two of the proposals were acted upon; the third is now under consideration.

1. The first proposal was to grow saplings some distance from the city and then transplant them in the denuded areas. This was done, but the soil of the city areas differed so much from that of the initial planting area that the striplings did not survive the transplanting.

12. A number of useful guides to what has come to be called "creative problem-solving" are now available for the teacher who has not tried this approach. See, for example, Edward DeBono's *New Think* (New York: Basic Books, 1967) and Sidney J. Parnes's *Creative Behavior Guidebook* (New York: Scribner's, 1967).

2. The second proposal was to plant striplings in the denuded area itself, to fertilize the ground and erect a chain fence around the planted area so as to protect the trees during the growing stages. Ultimately, the planners believed, the people would realize the environmental and esthetic benefits of having trees and not cut them down. The plan, however, was abandoned not long after it was begun because people from the surrounding area kept taking the expensive chain fence in order to fence in their domestic animals.

3. The third proposal, now awaiting approval, is to announce to the people that the government is undertaking an extensive program in planting fruit trees in the denuded areas. People will be informed of how the trees will ultimately bear fruit, which they will be able to consume themselves. Knowing this, the planners feel, the people will forego their immediate needs and not cut down the trees for fuel.

The third proposal now awaits government approval. Meanwhile the need for fuel grows. Wood is being imported into the city from further and further out and the price of fuel is soaring. From being 14 per cent of the average family budget in 1970, fuel is now approximately 33⅓ per cent.

Analyze the solutions that have been attempted or proposed so far, explaining where the planners went wrong or are likely to go wrong. Then offer a proposal of your own.[13]

6. *This is what someone said.* The ability to re-present in summary form what someone said or wrote is central to many academic tasks —to test-taking, where summary is often the main method of testing comprehension; to the preparation of book reviews, critiques, or arguments, where the writer must begin by giving a neutral summary of the text he is about to analyze or argue with; to note-taking, where the student records for future study what he is reading in a text or hearing in a lecture; and to essay-writing, where the writer often finds it useful to make summary statements as he proceeds through a complex piece of discourse or when he reaches the end of an essay and wishes to bring what he has said together.

13. In such exercises students frequently limit *their* solutions in the same way as earlier planners did. For example, they are likely to continue searching for a way to plant trees rather than begin exploring new, inexpensive sources of fuel. And they are likely to miss the political ramifications of issues—the possibility, for example, that a department of agriculture might be interested in extending its own activities and therefore see trees as the only solution to the problem.

Despite the importance of this skill in college and even later, where the professional must often reduce long memoranda and reports to their essentials or pull out of digressive committee discussions a compact statement of what got said, most composition texts—and teachers—give little attention to summarizing except to warn students that they ought not to confuse a "mere" summary with a critical or analytical statement. Yet we find little evidence that students are able to summarize effectively. If we examine the skill, we can even see good reasons for their difficulties with the form.

We must recognize first that the term "summary" is used to cover at least four different types of writing: the synopsis, the abstract, the précis, and the paraphrase. The synopsis gives the summary of a story, relating the main events in the order of their occurrence. An abstract reduces non-literary works such as articles, reports, or chapters largely for the reader's convenience (to save him the time of reading the full document or to help him decide whether he wishes to read the complete work). The précis not only summarizes the contents of a work but suggests the style and proportions of the original, often by key words or phrases from the original or by quoting the author directly. The paraphrase re-phrases or translates a passage so as to clarify its meaning.

All these forms of summary except the paraphrase (which might more accurately be called a translation) require that the writer condense a total work in such a way as to preserve its intellectual structure. This task becomes especially difficult when the intellectual structure of a work does not mirror the rhetorical structure. Thus an essay writer often delays stating his dominant idea until the end of his essay and the reader realizes only retrospectively how the parts contribute to the whole. The summary of such an essay involves a re-ordering of the contents of the essay, not simply a listing of what each paragraph is about. Yet most of a student's experience with summarizing has encouraged the latter approach, particularly where the student's main encounter with summarizing has been with stories or plays. But even where a summary follows the order of presentation of the work, the student is involved in an implicit critical act, choosing some features of a work and ignoring others.

It is seldom an easy task, this attempt to identify main points in their natural habitats, surrounded by the flora and fauna of elaboration. Students must approach it gradually, beginning with one-sentence

summaries of paragraphs and moving on to longer passages and longer
summaries. They should be discouraged from summarizing as they
read but instead urged to read a work carefully and completely first.
Then they should try to state *in one sentence* what the main point of
the work is. After this, they can return to the work and attempt to
identify the parts. Each part should in turn be summarized and the
student should try to determine how each of the parts relates to the
main point of the essay. Does one part, for example, serve to illustrate
the main point; does it consider arguments against the main point or
does it give historical background in order to explain the origins of
the main point, etc. When the bases of connection between the parts
and the main point have been identified, the student is ready to write
his summary, which begins with the statement of the main point and
then summarizes each part, noting at the outset the nature of its
relationship to the main point.

In his early summaries, the student should make no attempt at
quoting from the original or attributing ideas to the author (*the
author says, continues, goes on to, emphasizes,* etc.). But as his ability
to write abstracts increases, the refinements of summarizing can be
introduced, including the ability to quote selectively from the original.

Probably no form offers the student as much practical help as the
summary. It encourages him to read closely but with an eye for the
total pattern of thought in a work. It gives him exercise in grouping
details under general categories and in detecting prolixity and flawed
organization. Finally it prepares him to distinguish between a summary
and an interpretation or analysis.

7. *This is my opinion (or interpretation) of what someone said.*
As we have noted, BW students are often unprepared for the fact that
academic readers have been trained to reject the opinions of others
unless they are supported by appropriate evidence. But evidence is
not, even for academicians, an everyday way of winning arguments, so
it should not surprise a teacher when a student openly questions the
necessity for something beyond a statement of approval or disapproval
(I liked—or didn't like—this, or I agree, or I thought this was interesting or dull). "This is so," the student seems to be saying, "because
I'm telling you." And this may well be support enough in the company
of his peers. (Certainly it is not an unfamiliar method of persuasion for
parents and teachers.) But the academic reader has been trained to
expect more in the way of support when he is reading within an

academic framework and the BW student must be alert to this expectation.

As our prototypic statement suggests, a critical response may involve agreement or disagreement or simply an observation. It may direct the writer to seek ways to bolster his disagreement with someone else or it may prompt him to account for the effectiveness or failure of a particular work. The former response produces the sort of argument he might be asked to conduct in a social science or political science class; the latter, the sort of analysis he might be expected to write in a literature class. For each of these approaches there is, of course, a tradition of strategies and styles, and the teacher is certain to have difficulty deciding what is "basic" and what must be taken up in subsequent courses.

Probably the most important point to be made about statements of opinion or judgment is that they must be backed up by some kind of evidence or support which assures the reader that what is being said to be true of the real world is indeed true. The writer establishes that someone else's-statement is not true by demonstrating that the information in a work is either erroneous or incomplete, or he establishes that it is true by lending the support of additional information to the statement. Two sorts of problems arise in this kind of assignment. First, the student lacks information and cannot therefore make his case even though he suspects that a good one might be made. Second, the student is uncertain of how much evidence he needs to make his point with an academic audience. The answer to the first problem is obvious—the teacher must either control assignments so that the information students need to support their judgments is contained within the assignment (as it is, for example, in literary works, where most arguments can be supported by citing from the text) or he must introduce the students to key sources of information that will serve them in particular subjects or topics.

On the problem of knowing when one has given enough evidence to persuade an academic reader, the difficulties are more subtle. Almost everything worth writing about is also worth arguing over, but it is not always clear just what constitutes an adequate argument in specific cases. One writer may take a volume or more to make his case among his peers while another leaps within the limits of a personal essay from an account of his experience to a generalization that embraces mankind—and both may gain acceptance from their peers.

Thus Piaget will attempt to describe the world as children perceive it by drawing extensively upon laboratory observations to support his point. But Orwell will use in one essay his own recollected experience as a student at an English boarding school to generalize about children's perceptions of the adult world. Each writer has set for himself a different task, different in scope and in kind of analysis. In doing so he has had in mind his own resources as a thinker and writer, the nature of his data, the demand of the marketplace, and the realities of his work schedule.

Students are limited in even more stringent ways. They usually work within narrow time frames, sometimes no more than a class period, never any longer than a semester. In *their* marketplace, where credits and grade points are the currency, the demands are most often for examination essays, short papers, (two to five pages), reviews and critiques (five to ten pages), or research papers (ten to twenty pages), and rarely do they have an area of expertise to exploit in their assignments. At the same time, they encounter, in their readings, the writings of scholars whose standards for fullness and specificity are way beyond the beginning student's capabilities. So great, in fact, is the gap between what students write and what they read that the two products are rarely connected in their minds or practice.

Yet if we accept the idea of academic genres, of certain basic forms students are expected to produce and teachers have defined in their minds if not in their instructions, there is no good reason why models of these genres cannot be presented to students so that they can locate on the sliding scale of "proof" just what constitutes adequate evidence for their purposes. Much of the student's ability to cope with college assignments will depend not so much upon knowing how to prove things as knowing how proof is defined in the various situations he must think and write in. For such purposes, an anthology of exemplary student writing, gathered from the work of students in many classes (both advanced and remedial), would serve as an excellent text for this part of the BW course. Essay contests held for students in all sections of a writing course also produce models that can later be inexpensively anthologized. Teachers themselves should also carry out the assignments they give and take occasion to revise student papers in demonstration lessons so as to bring them closer to the academic model.

The statement of opinion or judgment conventionally begins with a neutral summary of the work being criticized. This is followed by an announcement of agreement or disagreement and then a presentation of the reasons for this position. In moving between what someone else said and what the writer is saying, the writer often makes use of words that mark the transition (*in my opinion; as I see it; however; my own view is;* etc.). He needs words that separate one reason or point from another (*first, second . . .; next; finally;* etc.) and words of praise and blame that maintain a tone of fairness and courtesy conventional to formal criticism (*the writer has failed to note,* or *does not go on to support,* or *appears to have missed,* or *seems to be unaware of,* or *mistakenly assumes,* etc.).

Most of the thought patterns we have been reviewing here are familiar to many teachers already as the topics of rhetoric, yet the presentation of the patterns in the form of statements rather than names not only helps the student understand and remember them but demonstrates how form, rather than being an arbitrary frame one imposes upon unruly content, lies embedded in the thesis or matrix statement that conventionally heads up a paragraph or essay. An analysis of such statements yields a conceptual plan that checks the students' tendency to move associatively from one sentence to the next in the ways illustrated in our samples.

If, as I suggested earlier in this chapter, the task of composing beyond the sentence involves an ability both to hold to one's stated intent and yet allow oneself a full or appropriate measure of elaboration or even digression, we might view the ability to assess a sentence for its implicit conceptual possibilities (cause-effect, narrative, problem-solution, etc.) as addressing most directly the first problem, the problem of knowing where one is committed to going, within the limits of the matrix, or organizing, sentence. An ability to recognize implicit thought patterns in sentences should at least help the writer generate the major points he intends to cover.

To assist the student with the other task—that of elaborating upon his points—the Christensen scheme for identifying levels of generalization offers him an excellent means of gauging his ability to go *into* a point.[14] Thus if the student is able, not only to increase the number of second-level statements that follow his first-level generalizations but to move into third and fourth levels of elaboration and then return

14. Francis Christensen, *Notes Toward a New Rhetoric* (New York: Harper and Row, 1967), pp. 52–81.

to a first level to pick up his path, he is clearly in control of the process that overwhelmed him in earlier essays.

Finally the writer must learn the courtesies of the essay form, those conventions that have developed because of the distance between the writer and his audience. Here we can include the conventions of introducing his idea, of providing transitional sentences at the junctures of his thought or alternate statements where a point may need emphasis or clarification, and of concluding his statement in a way that gives satisfaction to his reader. Numerous freshman texts devote chapters to these features of the academic essay, often demonstrating the form by ingenious diagrams as well. At the outset, however, a simple set of imagined responses from a listener may serve to generate a basic essay form:

Listener	Writer's Response
1. What's your point?	Thesis statement.
2. I don't quite get your meaning.	Restatement in different words.
3. Prove it to me.	Illustration, evidence, argument.
4. So what?	Conclusion.

Conclusion

We have ventured in this chapter beyond the sentence for several reasons. First, by looking even briefly at passages rather than individual sentences we have been able to determine whether the difficulties BW students have with school writing are confined to grammar, spelling, and punctuation or whether their relatively limited exposure to written language has other ramifications as well. And here we have found unmistakable evidences of oral rather than formal written styles of development and of misinformed or partially informed ideas of what the academic model is supposed to be. At the same time we can see here some of the same kinds of writing problems other freshmen have —the failure to stay with a line of thought, to elaborate or to push into the thick of an idea, where contradictions and real questions arise.

Tempted as writing teachers are to take on the entire responsibility for their students' intellectual growth, they would probably be wise to assume that a few years of steady reading, writing, talking, and listening in an academic setting are certain to increase the intellectual tenacity and spanning power of their students. For the struggle to bring about instant intellectuality by direct intervention will take time away from more profitable albeit less ambitious types of instruction.

Which leads to another reason for this chapter—namely, to suggest what *is* basic to the BW student "beyond the sentence." Here I have tried to suggest three needs—the need to experience consciously the process whereby a writer arrives at a main idea or point; the need to practice seeing and creating structure in written language; and the need to recognize specific patterns of thought that lie embedded in sentences and that point to ways of developing large numbers of sentences into paragraphs and essays.

Finally I have intended to suggest in this chapter that there is no reason why the BW student must wait until all his sentence problems have been dealt with before he can begin to work on the organization and development of academic papers. While it is true that papers with large numbers of basic errors in grammar and punctuation are likely to be poorly organized and inadequately developed as well, the two deficiencies are not causally connected. Furthermore, the student is almost certain to find his progress beyond the sentence more gratifying, for it seems to link him more directly to his recognized powers and, therefore, to the deepest purpose of education as Dewey has defined it: "the transformation of natural powers into expert, tested powers, the transformation of more or less casual curiosity and sporadic suggestions into attitudes of alert, cautious, and thorough inquiry."

To the reader who has come this far, it should be clear that the purpose of this analysis of basic writing has not been to minimize the importance of the "small" and conventional tasks the academic writer must master nor to establish some kind of hierarchy of tasks that ends up with either correctness or developed discourse being postponed as teaching matters until "next" semester. What I hope has emerged from each section of this analysis is both the "connectedness" of basic writers' difficulties in one area with those in another, all of them reflecting upon the quality and extent of the students' formal education, and the saving preparedness of these same students as thinking and speaking young adults to begin the hard work of learning to write for college. In the next chapter I will examine what a commitment to this task means for students, teachers, and the schools they both work in.

8
Expectations

The expectations of learners and teachers powerfully influence what happens in school. If we do not already know this in our bones, we can find it documented in studies of learning. It is a truth both reassuring and disturbing, reassuring because it reminds us that not all students who have been judged academically inferior are necessarily or natively so, disturbing because however unsound such judgments may be at the outset, they do tend gradually to fulfill themselves, causing students to lag behind their peers a little more each year until the gap that separates the groups begins to seem vast and permanent.

The sentences and paragraphs we have been looking at were written by students on the wrong side of the academic gap. We have sorted and analyzed various features of their writing in order not only to describe what goes wrong or what is missing but to understand the logic that underlies their behavior as writers. And finally, we have derived some principles and even some practices from these observations for the guidance of teachers. Little has been said, however, about the ways in which BW students can be expected to improve nor about the responsibilities of teachers and institutions in bringing about this improvement. Before we do this, we should perhaps be reminded of the very limited ways in which we can discuss growth in writing.

Few people, even among the most accomplished of writers, can comfortably say that they have finished learning to write, nor even that they always write as well as they can. Writing is something writers are always learning to do. When we speak, therefore, of a student's "learning" to write we have in mind that student's reaching a level of proficiency that seems appropriate for his age and situation but not the level he will be confined to for the rest of his life. Let us say it is the level a student must reach before a school exempts him from direct instruction in writing. But this level has by no means been absolutely or clearly defined either. Definitions of proficiency in writing vary widely from school to school and from teacher to teacher, with the widest agreement at the lower rungs of the skills ladder, where correctness and basic readability are the concern, and the widest divergencies at the upper rungs, where the stylistic preferences of teachers come into play. But even within the province of error, there are disagreements about the importance of different errors and about the number of errors an educated reader will tolerate without dismissing the writer as incompetent.

Then there are disagreements about the rates at which students can be expected to gain control over various features of their writing. Formal instruction proceeds by plans which are in turn bound by budgets and institutional timetables. But the learner also has his private timetable and improves, often, in seeming indifference to outside schedules, lagging behind or lapping over the finishing lines of courses. Some lessons bear immediate fruit, some fall by the way, and others lie dormant until one day the student bursts out in an "I see!" or produces a piece of writing that moves him, seemingly overnight, to a new plane of competence.

We have but the crudest of instruments whereby to measure such changes and must wait upon further research to document in a systematic way the progress of BW students. But given the alarming state of their writing when they arrive at college, it is important to note, if only by citing examples, the fact that BW students *do* respond to instruction, often in dramatic ways, and that while matters at the outset are perhaps worse than anyone imagined, the prospects for improvement are better than most teachers expect.

Thus we can expect within a semester of instruction a clear indication of control over errors in punctuation and grammar, provided this is a feature of instruction either in the class or in conferences. Errors will remain, but for most students the errors should begin to appear residual rather than dominant. Students often have sound criteria for correct forms but tend not to see what they have written. For such writers, the improvement in a particular feature may be swift, as in the following example, where several lessons in proofreading and punctuation enabled the writer to rid herself of most of her punctuation errors.[1]

Passage written early in semester

Yesterday I saw something horrible. As I was walking down the street. I saw a man and his dog. Though this was a average man and his dog. This was a man beating his dog to death. Which made me sick. I scream for him to stop, Though I didnt get any answer from the man . .

I decide to call the police to have thi man arrested . . The police took so long to get here. So that I went after the man with a broom. Swinging the broom with no luck, The Police finally came and they took the man away and sent the dog to a animal shelter.

Passage written one month later

I am the smartest girl in this class. This isn't a conceited statement, but a true one.

I started this class February 4, 1974. I didn't know anything about English, till I got myself interested in this class. This was a very great step for me. For the reason that I'm learning extremely fast.

The first assignment we had was a writing assignment. I made so many mistakes that it was truly ridiculous. The teacher returned my paper for me to correct it. The teacher helped me correct it and find the reasons why I made the mistakes.

The second writing assignment we had was a little more difficult. I had my heart in this assignment not to make any mistakes, but I was wrong. I made fewer mistakes but they were there. This time I had to find them myself and understand why I made them. I found most of them but I really couldn't understand how I made such idiotic mistakes. This is where proof reading comes in. If I had proof read my papers there wouldn't have been that many mistakes.

The third writing assignment was a great challenge for me but I was determined to get it right. I wrote with all my new technique and I did really great. My teacher thinks it's a great improvement. Now you know I'm the smartest girl in the class.

Some students make such impressive strides within a semester

1. I am indebted to Betty Rizzo of City College for this example. In all such before-and-after examples, the "after" samples bear many marks of revision (crossed-out words, corrected punctuation, etc.), suggesting that the students have acquired the important habit of going back over their sentences with an eye to correctness.

that one can only conclude that competence lay, at the outset, barely below the surface of their performance, even though they seemed to start at the same level of skill as other students in the class. The writer of the following passages, for example, discovered early in the semester that writing gave him access to thoughts and feelings he had not reached any other way. During the semester he produced a deluge of extra papers and worked doggedly at the formal assignments. We see from the two passages below, both on the subject of childhood, the measure of his improvement in one semester. Both essays were written in a class period.

Essay written at beginning of semester

Harlem taught me that light skin Black people was better look, the best to suceed, the best off fanicially etc this whole that I trying to say, that I was brainwashed and people aliked.

I couldn't understand why people (Black and white) couldn't get alone. So as time went along I began learned more about myself and the establishment.

Essay written at end of semester

In the midst of this decay there are children between the ages of five and ten playing with plenty of vitality. As they toss the football around, their bodies full of energy, their clothes look like rainbows. The colors mix together and one is given the impression of being in a psychadelic dream, beautiful, active, and alive with unity. They yell to eachother increasing their morale. They have the sound of an organized alto section. At the sidelines are the girls who are shy, with the shyness that belongs to the very young. They are embarrased when their dresses are raised by the wind. As their feet rise above pavement, they cheer for their boy friends. In the midst of the decay, children will continue to play.

Improvement that pervades the student's writing in this way is exceptional. Still, even where the gains are largely confined to such highly measurable features of a student's writing as subject-verb agreement, verb forms, or punctuation, one often notes a shift in tone, a more confident, deliberate air that may be in part, at least, a consequence of having learned how to control certain troublesome features of written English. One senses such a change in the following passages. For the first passage, the writer was asked to comment in an in-class essay upon the decline in reading and writing skills among students. The second question asked the student to comment upon the claim made by some that college encourages immaturity. Not only is the number of errors reduced from fifteen to five but the response begins to take on the shape of an essay:[2]

Essay written at beginning of semester
on reading and writing skills

Adults and children are not reading and writing to their levels. The problems people not reading and writing lies on the instructor and his ability. I been to schools that doesn't have the equipments for teaching.

A person can cope with the problem if they determine to learn. With today's progress, I have learn to read and writing on my level. My level of reading and writing are on the high school level. I can and has learned to read and write college level also. My writing does needs some improvements. The main point of the passage, is that reading and writing is valuable to life. Without the knowledge of reading and writing life is almost useless. On the other hand, it is determination that prohibits us to cope with that problem or any problems.

Essay written at end of semester
on college and immaturity

While I'am in college I work part time. Not including the enormous responsibilities at home that I try hard to forget about while in school. I have the cooking, cleaning and shopping to do at home. Also I have homework and studying to do. When a person has responsibilities and knows how to cope with them he is apt to be mature.

While I'am in college, I gain more knowledge. The more intellectual a person is, the better he can face society. The knowledge you obtain may change your personality. The knowledge I obtain makes me aware of my career. By knowing what my job is about I can face it with less concern. Some people get a job and don't know anything about the job. And some may know a little but that's not sufficient. In order to approach a job with good qualifications you have to know what you are doing. College supply you with the necessary equipment to enable us to cope with jobs.

To me, a person is mature if he makes the decision to enter college. Accepting the fact you are going to school you have to struggle to stay in school. Responsibilities, making an important decision and the knowledge you obtain makes a person mature. And he gaines those going to college.

2. I am indebted to Gerald Gould of City College for this example.

Not all students improve in ways that translate so easily into numbers. Leveled for the purposes of placement and group instruction, they assert their individualities in a variety of ways—in their styles of learning, their paces and patterns of development, even in the features of their writing that resist or give way to instruction. The student who wrote the first passage below made slow, almost imperceptible progress during the period of formal instruction in writing. When she left the BW program after three semesters, the most marked change in her as a writer was not yet apparent on the page but was reflected rather in a shift in her attitude toward writing, and more broadly, toward achievement in academia. Somehow she learned to imagine herself as a college student and to feel the allure of books and study and the rituals of studenthood. A sample of her writing acquired three years after her placement essay was written demonstrates the measure of her progress:

Sample from Placement Essay
>(student was given choice of forty names to write about)
>   George Washington has contributed much; in making of American History. A general in the army during the American Revolution. He commened many victories; that lead the thirteen colonies to an independent United States. Later became the First President of the United States. His picture is shown on the one dollar Bill and twenty-five cent picence (quart) . . Parks, Streets, Cities, people and plases are named after this great leader. Mr Washington was an outdoorsman in the very sence of the word. He loved horse back riding and hunting. It has been said, "he cut down a cherry tree." Making his home in Virginia with his wife Martha.

Sample from paper written three years later
>   Many Americans believe that Puerto Rico is fortunate to be exempted from paying taxes. What most Americans do not know is that the tax exemption is not for Puerto Ricans, but for the American investors. The Industrial Incentives Act of 1947, continued even after commonwealth came into being. It authorized and incouraged private firms (American) to invest in Puerto Rico. This Act was enacted to supply jobs and hopefully raise the Island's economy. At first the idea was good; however, as time passed the Puerto Ricans received the short end of the stick.

The goals of a basic writing course are generally practical, namely, the development of a readable expository style that will serve for courses and, later, for professional or civic writing assignments. But there are always, among the students in basic writing, incipient poets and novelists who discover their power with written language early in the semester and who take their heads in directions quite far from the purposes of the course. Often they are impatient with the conventional tasks set for them in basic writing and cannot mobilize themselves to carry them out. Such students challenge the teacher to find ways of defining and promoting the goals of the course without destroying the student's new-found pleasure in writing. Often such students, although clearly promising as writers, have as much difficulty as their BW peers in developing a readable analytical style of writing, but where they are encouraged to continue their expressive and non-analytical writing at the same time they are developing competence with bread-and-butter prose, they are less likely to view school writing as a threat to their talents. The following descriptive passage was written by a student during the second week of the semester, after he had sat through several in-class essay assignments without producing more than three sentences. With the first assignment in description, however, he produced this remarkable account of a woman on a bus. From then on he surged through that semester and the next, writing reams of unassigned papers. His "school" writing, however, improved slowly, barely maintaining a pace with the other students in his class:[3]

A Little Old Lady

Their was this old lady on the bus and was she messed up. she sat in back in the middle seat and she drive all the attention to everyone on the bus it was not crowded and you can see her quit well as she tryed to set right in the seat. She was old, about 67 years of bad looks. I could not believe if she was ever beautiful at one time. He hair was like an jungle with a road dug deep in it. the color of her hair was a mixture of brown and Black which blened in on both sides of the road (part) of the head. The brown looked like it was burn and was tryed to be straighten. The black looked like an uncondition afro uncomb and had a lot of tint. the road (I mean the part) went down the right side of the head and looked to me as a road. Her hair did not come as far on her face so you can see her face very clearly. Her eye were big and from where I was sitting looked like they would come out any min. He nose looked like a skii jump, short and fast. Her mouth was small and when she smile (she did once) you just seen darkness all the way in. Her face was dark and she had a beard like

3. See the *Basic Writing Anthology*, City College of New York, 1972, for examples of the impressive achievements of BW students in fictional and expressive writing.

a man who has not shaved in two days. She wear a jumper that was two big for her. And it was short sleaved. her arm stuck out of the short sleave like a burn branch of a die tree that was cracked at all parts. She also had molds on both arm that were so big they looked like fruit that was trying to grown but dry up and died. She changed her prosition and now sat with a bag between her legs with made her set with her legs open in the back of the bus. Her legs were also like a black branch but dead for about 30 or more years. He knee caps looked like an old stub off an old oak tree that was burn almost to the ground. He shoes looked like a piece of leather first throwen in fier then in water and then give to the mice to eat. She just got up with the bags and walk lik she was the world off the bus and said thank you to the driver.

These few examples of writing, drawn mainly from the files of a few teachers, do no more than attest to the fact that some severely unprepared adult students managed to improve their writing significantly within a semester or two of low-intensity instruction (four hours a week plus conference time). To make a slightly larger generalization about BW students, we might consider what happened to the writing of fifty such students during a semester of instruction. Typical basic writers in all respects, with the usual errors in word forms, spelling, and punctuation and the usual inadequacies in development, the students were evaluated as writers on the basis of four performances, a placement essay and three departmental essays administered at different points during the semester. Rated on coherence, control over sentence structure, focus, development, organization, and care, almost all the students showed signs of improvement, and three-fifths gave evidence of over-all and marked improvement.[4]

	Number of students
0 = no improvement	4
1 = slight improvement	7
2 = some improvement (mainly in one area)	11
3 = significant over-all improvement	21
4 = marked improvement	7

4. I am indebted to Kathy Roe of City College for her work in developing the criteria of evaluation and for her analysis of the essays.

Several features of their writing over the semester are worth noting. In all cases where handwriting was an initial problem, handwriting improved to the point that there were no illegible final exams. Where students had started out with severe spelling problems, their improvements tended to be indicated less by correct spellings than by closer approximations to the correct spellings. Most of the final essays gave various signs of having been wrought—that is, of the writers' having intervened in deliberate ways to change their wording or correct errors or of their having attempted to follow the rudiments of a plan for developing their points. At least 50 per cent of the students managed to stay with their topics. In illustrating their points, students tended to limit themselves to one example drawn usually from personal incident or observation and rarely did they choose to develop more than one aspect of a topic statement. Generally, they placed themselves in positions of totally agreeing or disagreeing with a point, a characteristic of other freshman writers as well. Finally, although some students had extended control of their ideas beyond the sentence, most of them were still confined to the sentence as the main field of struggle and concern, a result that may well have reflected the priorities of the writing program rather than any developmental reality.

In any event, the group seemed ready, with the exception of perhaps five students, to move into a semester of work on the short essay, their difficulties at the level of basic correctness having become a matter of further practice and regular review. To be sure, there would remain many residual traces of these rudimentary difficulties with written English, and should their fragile competence go unattended and unpracticed for a semester or two, the students would most likely be back almost where they had started. But within a semester they had learned, finally, something about the sources of their difficulties with writing and they had given substantial evidence of their ability to overcome these difficulties at a pace that would warrant their continuing in college.

They would need two more semesters of instruction to complete their apprenticeship and, after that, frequent occasions for writing in their regular courses and regular editorial comments from the teachers of those courses. In short they would need what colleges used routinely to offer more privileged students on the assumption that the ability to write readable, carefully reasoned and developed prose does not come swiftly nor easily nor solely through the efforts of basic writing teachers.

Our concern here has been mainly with the first stage of the student's apprenticeship, a stage we have called basic writing. In many ways the most formidable stage of instruction for both student and teacher, it is nonetheless the stage where miracles often get called for, and anyone who presumes to write about the difficulties writers have at this stage is probably expected to come up, at the end, with a method (or The Method) to which teachers and programs can be discipled, a plan that settles once and for all what should come after what and what works best at each step along the way.

Yet our examination of the writing problems of unprepared college freshmen has revealed such a complexity of problems and possible solutions (and such large territories of pedagogical ignorance) that a search for The Answer begins to seem an inefficient way to start thinking about a course (or courses) in basic writing. Let me mention but a few of the variables that encircle any decision to teach basic writing in one way or another: there are the variations in competencies among students who are classified as remedial-level writers, the kaleidoscopic range of influences that lie beneath their mistakes and misunderstandings and the proclivities they have as individuals for learning in some situations rather than others; there are the wide differences among teachers, whose weak spots and strengths lead them to cultivate some strategies more eagerly than others and to see some problems as more important than others; there are the imperatives of institutions, which differ from college to college, affecting the degree to which a college is financially committed to training the unprepared freshman and the standard of performance that is demanded of the "regular" students with whom the BW student must ultimately merge; and there is, finally, the reluctant, subtle phenomenon of the written language itself, which frequently evades our strictures, slips between our strategies, or grows in spite of them, defying us to explain precisely why a student fails or succeeds in basic writing. We are, in short, too much in the dark to be evangelical. At best our awareness of these variables should make us sensitive to the worth of *various* methods and more clear-eyed about what we can and cannot expect of ourselves and our students within the two or three semesters we have to work with them.

To understand what tends to go wrong when our students write and to acquire the habit of reasoning about what goes wrong are pre-liminary steps to deciding how to teach basic writing. They are the steps that have concerned us here. The teacher who would move from here to the design of a course or courses must be prepared to make not one but many decisions. He must first define the province of basic writing in a way that highlights the specific work to be done over the period of instruction allowed him. In planning a composition course of three semesters, for example, a teacher may find a skills chart such as the following helpful in apportioning the work that belongs to each semester:

	Semester		
	1	2	3
1. Syntax			
a. Sentence completeness			
b. Basic word order (including direct and indirect questions, expletives)			
c. Basic modification (relative and adverbial clauses, phrases, words)			
d. Advanced sentences (parallel structures, periodic structures, variety, etc.)			
2. Punctuation			
a. Terminal			
b. Basic inner punctuation (series, participles, adverbial and adjective clauses, etc.)			
c. Basic quotation (direct, indirect)			
d. Academic quotation			
3. Grammar			
a. Regular standard inflections			
b. Basic agreement			
c. Basic tense formations			
d. Irregular verbs			
e. Tense consistency			
f. Special usage (case with pronouns, agreement in unusual contexts, etc.)			
4. Spelling			
a. Syllabication			
b. Key standard/non-standard variations			
c. Key sound-letter correspondences (including the troublesome vowels)			
d. Basic spelling patterns (doubled consonants, silent *e*, etc.)			
e. Demons (misspellings common to college freshmen)			

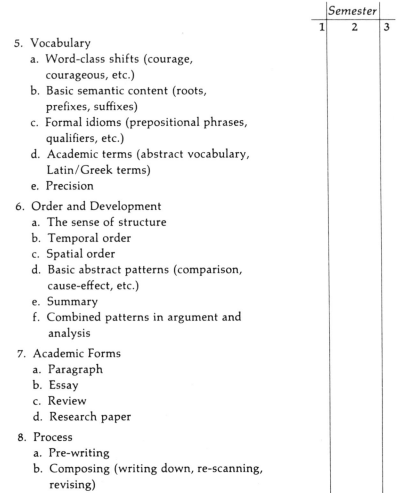

	Semester		
	1	2	3

5. Vocabulary
   a. Word-class shifts (courage, courageous, etc.)
   b. Basic semantic content (roots, prefixes, suffixes)
   c. Formal idioms (prepositional phrases, qualifiers, etc.)
   d. Academic terms (abstract vocabulary, Latin/Greek terms)
   e. Precision

6. Order and Development
   a. The sense of structure
   b. Temporal order
   c. Spatial order
   d. Basic abstract patterns (comparison, cause-effect, etc.)
   e. Summary
   f. Combined patterns in argument and analysis

7. Academic Forms
   a. Paragraph
   b. Essay
   c. Review
   d. Research paper

8. Process
   a. Pre-writing
   b. Composing (writing down, re-scanning, revising)
   c. Proofreading

Each of the items on the skills chart must in turn be examined from four pedagogical perspectives:

1. What is the *goal* of instruction? Is it *awareness, improvement,* or *mastery*? Under the category of spelling, for example, the goal for teaching standard/non-standard variations may be simply a heightened, more informed awareness of differences, whereas the spelling demons may be taught for mastery. Or again, the goal of teaching regular standard inflections may be improvement (a significant reduction in inflectional errors) whereas the goal for sentence completeness may be

mastery (the elimination of all structures in an essay that have too little or too much in them to be sentences).

2. What is the best *method* of instruction? What cognitive strategy, that is, will work best in teaching a particular skill? Some skills cannot be effectively taught head-on. They need to be blended into the intuitions of the learner over time and in relatively natural settings. The idioms of academic prose are best acquired in this way. Other skills can be acquired more directly, through memorization (the forms of the irregular verbs), rules (basic punctuation), or examples that accelerate the discovery of important patterns (the structure of paragraphs).

3. What is the best *mode* of instruction—the most effective social organization and the best technology? Some skills can be introduced efficiently to large audiences (key linguistic concepts such as inflection or agreement, rhetorical principles, research techniques, etc.); the ability to revise or proofread is probably most effectively developed when students in small groups become one another's audiences; and the conference between teacher and student remains the best way to discover how students have perceived their instructions and to create the bonds of concern and encouragement that energize both teacher and student. As for technologies, books and blackboards and the marked manuscript remain the most flexible and comfortable inventions for teachers of writing, but no teacher should ignore the advantages of audio-tapes in working with students whose spoken English diverges widely from standard written English; of videotapes for the animation of words or sentences to illustrate such phenomena as inflections, sentence transformations, or the structure of words and paragraphs; or of computers in taking the tedium out of practice and individualizing those features of study that would otherwise take up classroom time.

4. How do the individual items of instruction relate to one another? Where do they come in a *sequence* of instruction and how much time can be allowed for each? Our analytic view of basic writing has left us with the pieces of a course but not with the course itself. Yet writing is not simply the sum of a number of discrete skills but an expanding world of competencies that interact and collide and finally merge into something we can more easily identify than explain as good writing. It is in the nature of a course to take up one thing at a time in an order that makes pedagogical sense. Unfortunately, it is difficult to prescribe such an order for teachers whose strengths and preferences are unknown and whose local situations may demand one concentration

rather than another. But let us venture one model for the first semester that will place, roughly and tentatively, most of the pieces we have discussed in a course framework.

Ideally, the students in this course should meet in a workshop setting five days a week for at least one class period a day, preferably for two. The class sessions are used for three purposes: for introducing writing assignments (one class session every two or three weeks); for lessons on the sentence and on words (one day a week); and for supervised writing practice (three to four days a week). In a class of fifteen, at least one teacher and two student tutors should be in attendance during the writing sessions. The social organization of the class should vary according to the work being done. The formal lessons on the sentence and on words should be supplemented by practice sessions in a writing center under the guidance of tutors who have access to various types of instructional materials.[5]

Writing assignments for this first semester should aim at developing the students' perceptions of rhetorical structure and at introducing the first three thought patterns mentioned in Chapter 7. Two papers should be written for each pattern, the first one drawing upon models already familiar to the student (the story narrative for pattern 1, for example) and the second drawing upon less familiar models that are nonetheless common to academic writing (a narration of an historical event, for example, or an account of a laboratory experiment). A full session should be given to introducing each assignment, and the assignments themselves should be highly specific in such matters as length, structure, and possible difficulties. All assignments should be accompanied by at least two examples, one by a student.

The work on these assignments, particularly in the early stages of the course, should be regulated so as to provide class time for generating and selecting ideas, for composing first drafts, for revision and proofreading. Suggestions and criticisms should keep pace with the students' daily work, and students should be free to request editorial help while they are writing. In addition, their work should be reviewed by tutor and teacher at the end of each writing day and comments or suggestions attached to students' individual folders. On weekends before a paper is due, students should be free to prepare their final

5. The most efficient method for selecting and training tutors is to admit qualified upperclassmen and graduate students to a seminar on the teaching of English which requires them to meet once a week in seminar and the rest of the week in class or tutoring sessions.

drafts outside class, preferably on ditto mats. An anthology of each completed assignment should be distributed to the entire class and discussed among them. Before the next assignment is due, the teacher should meet with each student to discuss the student's gains and decide what needs to happen next.

Lessons on the sentence and on words should be aimed at developing in students a conceptual grasp of their difficulties with syntax, inflections, and punctuation. Mastery tests that indicate their ability to control isolated sentences for specific features (mainly subject-verb agreement, terminal punctuation, and verb tenses) should be given throughout the semester, but it cannot be assumed that a student who has demonstrated by an objective test that he *understands* a grammatical convention will habitually observe it. For this, he needs more practice. Nonetheless, by the time he leaves his first semester, he should have the understanding he needs to become, within two semesters, a self-sufficient proofreader.

The class lessons themselves should of course relate to the common difficulties of the students in that class. Difficulties peculiar to a few students or common problems that hang on for some students after most of their peers have successfully dealt with them should be worked on individually or in small groups. While a concern for correct form should carry over to the students' regular writing assignments, particularly where they have received instructions on specific forms, the process of getting things right should be a central concern of the writer only during the proofreading stage of each composition.

Assuming a class that has the typical problems of the basic writers we have been discussing here, the sequence and periods of instruction might go as follows:

Weeks 1-5   Combined work on syntax and punctuation, following recommendations in Chapters 2 and 3.

Weeks 6-7   Spelling—principles of word formation, diagnostic techniques. (After this, spelling instruction should be individualized.)

Weeks 8-12   Common errors—verb inflections for number, noun inflections for number, verb tenses, agreement.

Weeks 13-15   Vocabulary—prefixes, suffixes, roots, abstract-concrete words, precision.

Having been *introduced* during the first semester to those basic conventions of written English that are unfamiliar and troublesome to him, the student is ready by the second semester to take up assignments that will increase his power to sustain commentary over longer and longer units of discourse without losing his or his readers' bearings. At the same time, he must continue to reduce errors through the discipline of proofreading and, where necessary, further individual instruction. Work on the basic thought patterns can be continued into the second semester. Reading now becomes a major source of data for the development of ideas, and the structures of essays should become more elaborate and fulfilled as students increase their staying power and accept new criteria for thoroughness.

At the beginning of the third semester, the student should be ready to begin work on the research paper, which introduces him to rigorous procedures for directing and sustaining a line of inquiry that will meet academic criteria for thoroughness and correct form. This is usually the point of confluence for basic and regular students, and while it would be unreasonable to expect students who started out with twelve years of disadvantage to overtake their academically advantaged peers in the space of two semesters, the gaps that separate the two types of students begin now to appear manageable.

Conclusion

Most of what has been written in this book has been intended for teachers, particularly for teachers who are only beginning, or are about to begin, their work with BW students. But BW teachers are far from autonomous beings in their departments and divisions and colleges. It is not usually they who set limits on class size or teaching load or the number of semesters granted to writing instruction. They do not control the extent to which writing permeates a college curriculum and therefore reinforces their work, nor can they rearrange the reward system in such a way as to encourage teachers to concentrate their scholarly energies in the sorts of questions that arise in basic writing. Such matters are in the hands of administrators, whose perceptions of the so-called remedial problem largely determine whether basic writing is to be viewed as a college contagion ward staffed by teachers who are brought in for the emergency and expected to perform miracles (even though they are at the same time restricted from having a professional future there) or whether it is to be viewed as a frontier in higher education which, while it may send some hurrying back to the safety and familiarity of the past, ought to draw many others of talent into its challenge.

To say this is not by any means to consent to an educational system that has failed in countless ways and for countless reasons to educate all its youth. Now that we have begun openly to admit to this failure, we can hope for reforms which over the next decade may close the shocking gaps in training between the poor and the affluent, the minority and the majority. Open admissions colleges, by having exposed the academic deficiencies of students who supposedly went to school for twelve years and by having developed fresh ways of coping with these deficiencies, have already begun to contribute to the improvement of elementary and secondary-school teaching.

But there is another sense in which the students we have been describing ought not to be viewed as transitional—as students, that is, whom colleges must sustain in a kind of holding action until the lower schools begin doing their jobs. They are, in some respects, a unique group from whom we have already learned much and from whom we can learn much more in the years ahead.

From them we have begun to discover how critical and creative a juncture late adolescence can be. Far from being eleventh-hour learners, these students appear in many ways to be beginning their lives anew. And while the skills and priorities of studenthood are not easily acquired at the age of eighteen or over, students are demonstrating that competency *can* be acquired at that age. And much of the energy they mobilize for the effort seems to come from the opportunity college gives them to redefine themselves as young adults who might accomplish something in the world. To encourage this emerging view they have of themselves while at the same time representing honestly to them the amount of work that lies ahead is the teacher's most delicate and essential task.

From these students we have also begun to learn much about learning and teaching. Capable because of their maturity of observing the processes they are going through as learners, they can alert us easily and swiftly to the effects of instruction. They work, in this sense, collaboratively with teachers in ways that are impossible with child learners. In a hurry, also, to learn what we have to teach them, they press us to discover the most efficient ways of presenting what we would have them understand. The result will be, in time, not so much a simplified view of written English as a more profound grasp of what lies below the prescriptive bits and pieces of instruction we once called English composition. They are urging us, in short, through their needs and their capabilities, to become better teachers.

Finally, from these students we are learning to look at ourselves and at the academic culture we are helping them to assimilate with more critical eyes. Neglected by the dominant society, they have nonetheless had their own worlds to grow up in and they arrive on our campuses as young adults, with opinions and languages and plans already in their minds. College both beckons and threatens them, offering to teach them useful ways of thinking and talking about the world, promising even to improve the quality of their lives, but threatening at the same time to take from them their distinctive ways of interpreting the world, to assimilate them into the culture of academia without acknowledging their experience as outsiders.

At no point is the task of representing both claims upon the student —the claims of his past and of his future—more nervously poised than at the point where he must be taught to write. Here the teacher, confronted by what at first appears to be a hopeless tangle of errors and inadequacies, must learn to see below the surface of these failures the intelligence and linguistic aptitudes of his students. And in doing so, he will himself become a critic of his profession and begin to search for wiser, more efficient ways of teaching young men and women to write.

For unless he can assume that his students are capable of learning what *he* has learned, and what he now teaches, the teacher is not likely to turn to himself as a possible source of his students' failures. He will slip, rather, into the facile explanations of student failure that have long protected teachers from their own mistakes and inadequacies. But once he grants students the intelligence and will they need to master what is being taught, the teacher begins to look at his students' difficulties in a more fruitful way: he begins to search in what students write and say for clues to their reasoning and their purposes, and in what *he* does for gaps and misjudgments. He begins teaching anew and must be prepared to be taxed beyond the limits he may have originally set for himself as a teacher of writing. He will need to give not simply more time but more imaginative and informed attention to what his students write than he may have given in the days when freshmen had learned most of what they needed to know about writing *before* they got to college. He will need to question and even abandon styles and methods of teaching that seemed to work before. He will need to cultivate patience for the slow pace of progress in this most complex of crafts and find ways of refreshing his own belief that writing is not only a necessary skill in college and an advantageous skill in work but the most accessible way people have of exploring and perfecting their thoughts.

And having done all this, he will then have to admit that it is not enough, that he does not know enough about how people learn to write or about what writing is to be content with himself as a basic writing teacher. He will want to venture into fields where he is not a scholar— into psycholinguistics, perhaps, or learning theory, or discourse analysis —in search of fresh insights and new data. He will wish for more precise descriptions of the behavior called writing, for models of the ways in which learners of different ages acquire the sub-skills of writing. He will begin to see the difficulties of so-called remedial students as the difficulties of all writers, writ large. For the problems of getting an idea and beginning to write, of remembering where one is going as sentence generates sentence, of sustaining the tension between being right and readable and being oneself—these are problems few writers escape. The BW student merely comes to them later than most and must therefore work harder and faster to solve them.

Colleges must be prepared to make more than a graceless and begrudging accommodation to this unpreparedness, opening their doors with one hand and then leading students into an endless corridor of remedial anterooms with the other. We already begin to see that the remedial model, which isolates the student and the skill from real college contexts, imposes a "fix-it station" tempo and mentality upon both teachers and students. And despite the fine quality of many of the programs that have evolved from this model, it now appears that they have been stretched more tautly than is necessary between the need to make haste and the need to teach the ABC's of writing in adult ways. We cannot know how many students of talent have left our programs not for want of ability but for the sense they had of being done in by short-cuts and misperceptions of educational efficiency.

Just how we are finally going to reconcile the entitlements and capacities of these new students with our traditional ways of doing things in higher education is still not clear. As we move closer to this goal, however, we will be improving the quality of college education for all students and moving deeper into the realizations of a democracy.

Meanwhile we must hope that our enterprising new students will somehow weather *our* deficiencies and transcend our yet cautious expectations of what they can accomplish in college.

Appendix
Placement essay topics

1

Write an essay in which you discuss the way or ways in which you expect your life to differ from your parents' lives.

2

The U.S. Labor Department expects about 2.8 million jobs to open up each year during the mid-1970's. The highest number of openings will occur in fields such as the following:

Stenographers	237,000 openings per year
Salespeople (retail)	150,000
Hospital Attendants	110,000
Engineers	97,000
Mechanics/Repairmen	89,000

Among the jobs *least* in demand will be the following:

Physicists	3,200
Psychologists	3,100
Architects	2,300
Historians	800
Sociologists	600

In the field of teaching, openings are expected to occur as follows:

Kindergarten and Elementary School   56,300
Secondary School   40,000
College and University   17,000

As you have perhaps observed, the jobs that are going to be in most demand are not, for the most part, the jobs that colleges train people for. In the light of this information about what colleges produce and what the labor market demands, does it make sense for a young person getting out of high school today to go on for a college degree?

Write an essay in answer to this question, giving as full a defense of your position as possible.

3

Write an essay in response to the passage below. In your essay, state briefly what you consider to be the main point of the passage. Then go on to discuss it in terms of your own experience. That is, do you believe at this point that the education you have received has prepared you for the society you live in?

The world that college graduates will be entering requires writing and reading skills of a high order. I refer not to the "gift of gab" but to those forms of communication that have been developed for the academic, political, and scientific professions. There will be more reading and writing for college students to do than ever before, because the jobs available will be predominantly the jobs of a service rather than of a manufacturing economy. (It is estimated that by 1980 a majority of the American labor force will be working in "service" activities. They will have to carry on the counseling, conferring, interviewing, proposing, reporting, reading, interpreting, and writing that most jobs are already requiring.)

Although the economy will be demanding increasingly a level and kind of language skill that was once expected of a small part of the population, our schools are failing on a massive scale to teach young people to read and write at the levels that will be required of them in the job world. A recent report on educational progress tells us that Americans from nine through the twenties are at best mediocre writers. College teachers complain that students can neither read textbooks adequately nor write coherently about what they have learned. The recent Fleischmann report illustrates what we already know—that most children in New York's public schools are performing below national standards. Even a superficial look at the world that students must one day enter reveals that many are not likely to be prepared to succeed in that world.

Suggested readings

Little has as yet been written about the problems and progress of basic writing students. Only recently admitted in large numbers to post-secondary schools and still viewed by many educators as eleventh-hour learners with dim prospects for improvement in writing, they have attracted little scholarly interest among teachers and researchers. This short list of suggested books is therefore a list of "borrowings" from other areas of language study. Some may provide insights into the nature of writing; others may illuminate the situation of the language learner or point to a style or object of inquiry that promises fresh insights for the basic writing teacher. Each of them offers a place to begin in a field where almost everything remains to be done.

Writing and the writing process

Abercrombie, M. L. J. *Anatomy of Judgment.* New York: Basic Books, 1960. An account of a course developed to improve the diagnostic judgment of medical students in England. Reviews research on the use of group learning in teaching judgment. Useful to the writing teacher in pointing up the social aspects of thinking, the conditions under which people are most likely to get ideas.

Baker, Sheridan, Barzun, Jacques, and Richards, I. A. *The Written*

Word. Rowley, Mass.: Newbury House, 1971. Four stimulating essays on the written language, its nature and its future.

Barzun, Jacques. *On Writing, Editing, and Publishing.* Chicago: University of Chicago Press, 1971. A collection of essays about writing at its various stages. Especially useful for its insights into the pre-writing stage.

Bloom, Benjamin S., Hastings, Thomas, and Madaus, George F. *Handbook on Formative and Summative Evaluations of Student Learning.* New York: McGraw-Hill, 1971. A major reference work on learning, valuable to the writing teacher for its table of specifications for writing (see Joseph J. Foley's Chapter 21, "Evaluation of Learning in Writing").

Braddock, Richard, Lloyd-Jones, Richard, and Schoer, Lowell. *Research in Written Composition.* Champaign, Ill.: National Council of Teachers of English, 1963. A useful review of research up to the early sixties with suggestions for future research that have, for the most part, not yet been acted upon.

Burgess, Tony, ed. *Understanding Children Writing.* Harmondsworth, Eng.: Penguin, 1972. Analyses of students of various ages writing both expressive and formal papers on a range of subjects. Valuable for its discussion of the writing process and for its insights into the nature of academic discourse.

Diederich, Paul B. *Measuring Growth in English.* Urbana, Ill.: National Council of Teachers of English, 1974. A guide for teachers in the evaluation of student writing but useful as well for its statement of criteria for judging maturity in written English.

Elbow, Peter. *Writing without Teachers.* New York: Oxford University Press, 1973. A challenging presentation of an approach to writing that is intended to release the writer from the inhibitions that ordinarily cut him off from his best ideas and words.

Emig, Janet. *The Composing Processes of Twelfth Graders.* Urbana, Ill.: National Council of Teachers of English, 1971. An exploration, using the case-study approach, of the ways students compose. Valuable for the contrast it offers between the ways students behave as writers and the ways textbooks and teachers often have assumed they ought to behave. Full bibliography of works on writing.

Macrorie, Ken. *Uptaught.* New York: Hayden, 1970. The book that introduced most teachers, through its lively account of the inhibitions and restraints traditionally imposed upon students in composition classes, to the activity called free writing.

Miller, Susan. *Writing: Process and Product*. Cambridge, Mass.: Winthrop, 1976. A guide for the novice writer which takes him through the steps of composing and answers questions about the process that traditional texts too often ignore.

Murray, Donald M. *A Writer Teaches Writing: A Practical Method of Teaching Composition*. Boston: Houghton Mifflin, 1968. A practical and lively demonstration of a way to teach writing. Concentrates on the craft of writing, with close attention to each of the stages of composition. Many samples of student writing, with excellent marginal comments that show the reader what rewriting and revising are about. A wide-ranging and alluring bibliography of works on writing.

Vygotsky, Lev. *Thought and Language*. Translated by E. Hanfman and G. Vakar. Cambridge, Mass.: MIT Press, 1962. One of the few theoretical works on language that comments upon writing as a special form of language involving different intellective strategies than speech.

The learner's situation

Abrahams, Roger D., and Troike, Rudolph C., eds. *Language and Cultural Diversity in American Education*. Englewood Cliffs, N.J.: Prentice-Hall, 1972. A text, not formidably complex, with a wide selection of positions on the sources and implications of language diversity.

Barnes, Douglas, Britton, James, and Rosen, Harold. *Language, the Learner and the School*. Baltimore: Penguin, 1971. Report on the role of teacher and student talk in the classroom, with many insights into the ways teachers use and misuse language in their presentations of information and in their dialogues with students.

Britton, James. *Language and Learning*. Harmondsworth, Eng.: Penguin, 1970. A description of the process whereby children acquire and develop their skill with language. Synthesizes much current knowledge on language learning in a way that meets the needs of teachers.

Bruner, Jerome S. *The Process of Education*. New York: Random House, 1963. A short and influential statement on the will and capacity of students to learn.

Cazden, Courtney B., John, Vera P., and Hymes, Dell. *Functions of Language in the Classroom*. New York: Teachers College Press, 1972.

A collection of essays viewing the problems that arise in the classroom from an anthropological perspective. Directed toward elementary-school situations, the essays nonetheless shed light on some of the misunderstandings that arise in the college classroom as well.

Cosin, B., et al. *School and Society: A Sociological Reader*. Cambridge, Mass.: MIT Press, 1972. Essays that point up the ways in which language differences affect teachers and learners.

Cross, K. Patricia. *Beyond the Open Door*. San Francisco: Jossey-Bass, 1974. A study of the interests, abilities, and expectations of open admissions students, with recommendations for the reform of college teaching methods and goals.

Ginsburg, Herbert, and Opper, Sylvia. *Piaget's Theory of Intellectual Development: An Introduction*. Englewood Cliffs, N.J.: Prentice-Hall, 1969. A good place to begin a study of Piaget, whose theories of development are considered by many teachers to have relevance for basic writing instruction.

Schoolboys of Barbiana, *Letter to a Teacher*. New York: Random House, 1971. The report of eight Italian working-class and peasant boys on their educations, both in the formal state classrooms of Italy and in a special program created for them by a parish priest. A moving expression of the disadvantaged student's mistrust of the educator and his respect for an education.

Sennett, Richard, and Cobb, Jonathan. *The Hidden Injuries of Class*. New York: Random House, 1972. An analysis of the effects of class prejudice upon blue-collar workers. Includes comments upon language attitudes that help explain the reluctance of some basic writing students to put their thoughts on paper.

Williams, Frederick, ed. *Language and Poverty*. Institute for Research on Poverty Monograph Series. Chicago: Markham Publishing Co., 1970. Valuable for the variety of views and issues it explores through the papers of linguists, sociolinguists, and educators who disagree among themselves about the ways in which poverty affects language. See particularly the essays by William Labov, Siegfried Engelmann, and Basil Bernstein.

Grammar and vocabulary

Allen, Robert L. *English Grammars and English Grammar*. New York:

Scribner's, 1974. An introduction to sector analysis, a linguistic system based on tagmemics and widely used among second-language and second-dialect teachers. See especially Section Four.

Cattell, N. R. *The New English Grammar: A Descriptive Introduction.* Cambridge, Mass.: MIT Press, 1969. A lucid, short introduction to the fundamentals of structural and transformational grammar, with examples and methods of analysis easily adapted to classroom explanations.

Cook, Walter A. *Introduction to Tagmemic Analysis.* New York: Holt, Rinehart and Winston, 1969. A full description of a major system of analysis that introduces the grammatical unit called a *tagmeme*, a concept introduced by Kenneth L. Pike in the fifties.

Emig, Janet A., Fleming, James T., and Popp, Helen M. *Language and Learning.* New York: Harcourt, Brace and World, 1966. An expansion of a special issue of the *Harvard Educational Review*, in which major figures in linguistics examine the implications for teaching of research in language. One of the best of such anthologies.

Fries, Charles Carpenter. *The Structure of English: An Introduction to Construction of English Sentences.* New York: Harcourt, Brace and World, 1952. An important work in the development of structural grammar. Useful to the teacher in providing a way (other than abstract definitions of the parts of speech) of observing the differences among words in sentences.

Jespersen, Otto. *Essentials of English Grammar.* University: University of Alabama Press, 1969. A description of English by a great philologist and pioneer linguist. Originally published in 1933 but still useful in mapping out the territory called grammar and in providing insights into the patterns and peculiarities of English.

Joos, Martin. *The English Verb: Form and Meanings.* Madison, Wis.: University of Wisconsin Press, 1968. Certainly one of the few truly entertaining works on the English verb. Invaluable for the teacher who has never had to take up the intricacies of the verb system in the classroom.

————. *The Five Clocks.* New York: Harcourt, Brace and World, 1961. A memorable and delightful explanation of levels of English usage, a classic attempt to temper harsh prescriptive attitudes toward language use.

Keyser, Samuel Jay, and Postal, Paul M. *Beginning English Grammar.* New York: Harper and Row, 1976. A demanding work, despite its innocent title, but a worthy introduction to transformational grammar.

Lyons, John. *Introduction to Theoretical Linguistics.* Cambridge: At the University Press, 1968. Probably the best place for a teacher to begin reading about linguistics.

Mellon, John C. *Transformational Sentence-Combining: A Method for Enhancing the Development of Syntactic Fluency in English Composition.* Urbana, Ill.: National Council of Teachers of English, 1969. Description of an experiment in which seventh-grade students were given instruction and practice in combining sentence kernels to produce complex, mature sentences. Valuable as a guide in the teaching of nominal and relative embedding and as a key work in the search for criteria for maturity in written English.

O'Hare, Frank. *Sentence Combining: Improving Student Writing without Formal Grammar Instruction.* Urbana, Ill.: National Council of Teachers of English, 1971. Description of an experiment with seventh-grade students who were given practice in sentence-combining without formal instruction in grammar. Useful for the combining problems it describes and for the promise it holds of getting at the dynamics of sentence production without getting into deep grammatical waters.

Petty, Walter T., Herold, Curtis P., and Stoll, Earline. *Vocabulary: The State of Knowledge about the Teaching of Vocabulary.* Urbana, Ill.: National Council of Teachers of English, 1968. A report on the state of vocabulary teaching based on a review of some 3,000 studies. Selects important studies for comment and recommends research designs.

Roberts, Paul. *English Sentences.* New York: Harcourt, Brace and World, 1962. One of the early books that applied the principles of transformational generative grammar to the teaching of English in high school. Valuable for its classification of sentence patterns and for its evocation of the student reader's linguistic intuitions.

Ullmann, Stephen. *Semantics: An Introduction to the Science of Meaning.* Oxford: Basil Blackwell, 1970. A survey of the field, especially useful for its early chapters on the nature of words.

Spelling

Hanna, Paul R., Hodges, Richard E., and Hanna, Jean S. *Spelling: Struc-*

ture and Strategies. Boston: Houghton Mifflin, 1971. The best single-volume introduction to the subject of spelling. Presents the theoretical foundations of spelling and suggests a sequence of spelling strategies for levels K-8.

Hanna, Paul R., et al. *Phoneme-Grapheme Correspondences as Cues to Spelling Improvement.* OE-32008. Washington, D.C.: U.S. Department of Health, Education, and Welfare, 1966. A key work of research which establishes a wider range of predictability between phoneme-grapheme correspondences than was previously thought to exist. Includes charts of correspondences which are useful in classifying the patterns of misspellings of individual students.

Horn, Thomas D., ed. *Research on Handwriting and Spelling.* Champaign, Ill.: National Council of Teachers of English, 1966. Collection of research reports by specialists in handwriting and spelling.

Second-language and second-dialect methods of instruction

Davis, A. L., ed. *Culture, Class, and Language Variety.* Urbana, Ill.: National Council of Teachers of English, 1972. A collection of essays on a variety of dialects. Includes a classification of problem areas (Chapter 6), a checklist of significant features for discriminating social dialects (Chapter 7), and a tape of dialect samples.

George, H. V. *Common Errors in Language Learning.* Rowley, Mass.: Newbury House, 1972. Impressive for its use of communication theory and statistical and theoretical linguistics to illuminate the errors of second-language learners.

Labov, William. *Language in the Inner City: Studies in the Black English Vernacular.* Philadelphia: University of Pennsylvania Press, 1972. A classic study of black vernacular which documents, through an analysis of the speech of black inner-city youth, the existence of a black dialect with its own inner logic, grammar, and ritual forms of expression.

Mencken, Henry L. *The American Language: An Inquiry into the Development of English in the United States.* Abridged. Fourth edition. Edited by Raven I. McDavid. New York: Alfred A. Knopf, 1963. Mencken's classic study brought up to date. Valuable for a broad yet intriguing view of language variety in the United States.

Moulton, William G. *A Linguistic Guide to Language Learning.* New York: Modern Language Association of America, 1966. A short introduction to foreign-language learning which identifies those features of language in general and of English in particular that are central to the task of learning another language.

Wolfram, Walt, and Fasold, Ralph W. *The Study of Social Dialects in American English.* Englewood Cliffs, N.J.: Prentice-Hall, 1974. Probably the best single introduction to dialect study, its methods and applications. See especially chapters on the socially diagnostic phonological and grammatical features of various dialects of American English.

Academic discourse

Christensen, Francis. *Notes Toward a New Rhetoric: Six Essays for Teachers.* New York: Harper and Row, 1967. Proposes a way of analyzing sentences and paragraphs that illuminates the role of modification in the creation of structure. Especially useful in introducing students to the concepts of coordination and subordination in writing.

Kinneavy, James L. *A Theory of Discourse.* Englewood Cliffs, N.J.: Prentice-Hall, 1971. An attempt to explore the fundamental purposes of language and to bring the various theories of rhetoric into one theoretical frame. Valuable for its comments on academic styles of discourse and for pointing the teacher in a number of promising directions for future reading and research. Full bibliographies on all types of discourse.

Lawrence, Mary S. *Writing as a Thinking Process.* Ann Arbor: University of Michigan Press, 1974. A text for students, with exercises and explanations that highlight the semantic and rhetorical features of academic writing.

Moffett, James. *Teaching the Universe of Discourse.* Boston: Houghton Mifflin, 1968. Presents the theoretical base upon which the author developed an English curriculum from K through 13. Proposes a sequence of concentrations that begins with dramatic discourse and moves toward analytical. Not directed toward the timetables of compensatory courses but valuable for its insights into the forms of discourse and the readiness of students at different ages to produce and enjoy them.

National Council of Teachers of English. *The Sentence and the Paragraph.* Urbana, Ill.: National Council of Teachers of English, n.d. A collection of articles that appeared in *Composition and Communication* and *College English* in the sixties. Offers an excellent introduction to recent thinking on the two units of rhetoric. Articles by Francis Christensen, A. L. Becker, Paul C. Rodgers, Jr., and Josephine Miles.

Wilson, John. *Thinking with Concepts*. Cambridge: At the University Press, 1971. A small book designed to prepare English students for entrance/scholarship examinations. Focuses on the style and analytical methods expected in academic discourse.

Index

p 29 -30 Teaching sentence structure
35 Connectives

134 Common errors Chapter
↓
Thinking things
problem as
they arise

274 — Can't do
"intellect" in
a semester